Queer Communism and The Ministry of Love

For my family

Queer Communism and The Ministry of Love

Sexual Revolution in British Writing of the 1930s

Glyn Salton-Cox

EDINBURGH
University Press

Edinburgh University Press is one of the leading university presses in the UK. We publish academic books and journals in our selected subject areas across the humanities and social sciences, combining cutting-edge scholarship with high editorial and production values to produce academic works of lasting importance. For more information visit our website: edinburghuniversitypress.com

© Glyn Salton-Cox, 2018

Edinburgh University Press Ltd
The Tun – Holyrood Road
12(2f) Jackson's Entry
Edinburgh EH8 8PJ

Typeset in 10.5/13 Adobe Sabon by
Servis Filmsetting Ltd, Stockport, Cheshire

A CIP record for this book is available from the British Library

ISBN 978 1 4744 2331 1 (hardback)
ISBN 978 1 4744 2332 8 (webready PDF)
ISBN 978 1 4744 2333 5 (epub)

The right of Glyn Salton-Cox to be identified as the author of this work has been asserted in accordance with the Copyright, Designs and Patents Act 1988, and the Copyright and Related Rights Regulations 2003 (SI No. 2498).

Contents

Acknowledgments	vi
Introduction: The Perverts of Modernity	1
1 Boy Meets Camera: Christopher Isherwood and Sergei Tretiakov	44
2 Sylvia Townsend Warner's Queer Vanguardism	77
3 The Hymning of Heterosexuality: Katharine Burdekin and the Popular Front	113
4 Orwell's Hope in the Proles	140
Coda: A Little Window for the Bourgeoisie	174
Notes	191
Index	227

Acknowledgments

This book would have been impossible without the intellectual stimulation and scholarly support of a great number of people. It would have been similarly impracticable without the conviviality and companionship of many others; there is of course some considerable overlap between the two groups, and it goes without saying that the patience of my friends has at times been frankly astounding.

I would like to thank first of all my PhD dissertation committee, Katie Trumpener, Katerina Clark, and Joe Cleary, who oversaw the beginnings of this book with great intellectual energy and much kindness. Katie was involved with this project from its inception, and her brilliant, encouraging presence has been absolutely central to my scholarly development. At graduate school I was intellectually, socially, and politically sustained by a wide cast of mentors and peers, and I would like to thank Grey Anderson, Ryan Carr, Jonathan Cayer, John Cooper, Ian Cornelius, Paul Fry, Colin Gillis, David Kastan, Ed King, James Knabe, Tom Koenigs, Anne-Marie McManus, Erica Mias, Lina Moe, Tessie Prakas, Anthony Reed, Erica Sayers, Justin Sider, Josh Stanley, Michael Warner, and Emily Yao.

At UCSB I have a fantastic group of colleagues and friends, and I would like to thank Paul Amar, Felice Blake, Heather Blurton, Eileen Boris, Maurizia Boscagli, Brian Donnelly, Enda Duffy, Jeremy Douglass, Bishnupryia Ghosh, Andrew Griffin, Melody Jue, Ross Melnick, Rita Raley, Swati Rana, Russell Samolsky, Bhaskar Sakar, Rachael Scarborough King, Tess Shewry, Tyler Shoemaker, MR Staton, Jennifer Tyburczy, Meg Wilson, Naoki Yamamoto, and Xiaowei Zheng. Graduate students in my class on Marxism and queer theory and my advisees have made me think about a lot of different problems in fresh ways. The New Sexualities Research Group provided a vital intellectual forum, as did the English Department's Center for Modernism, Materialism, and Aesthetics (COMMA).

My thanks to The Hellman Family Foundation, the Interdisciplinary Humanities Center, and the Academic Senate at UCSB for their generous funding of this project. The staff at the British Library, the Beinecke Library at Yale, the Huntington Library, and the Dorset County Museum were welcoming, knowledgeable, and helpful. At EUP, the support and professionalism of James Dale, Ersev Ersoy, Jackie Jones, Geraldine Lyons, Rebecca Mackenzie, and Adela Rauchova has been invaluable.

Leo Mellor first propelled me in the direction of the 1930s, and has been a constant intellectual companion for over fifteen years. Other important '30s comrades include Ben Harker, Benjamin Kohlmann, James Smith, Matt Taunton, and my chosen cousin Cathryn Setz. A special mention to Len Gutkin and Stuart Smith for reading large parts of the manuscript and for their close friendship over the years; to Edgar Garcia for his vital contribution to our joint survival of graduate school; and to the always astute Tiffany Nichols. Dan Mayer and Hassan Akram continue to teach me about politics, and many turns in this book would have been unthinkable without them. The cover is the work of two loyal friends and brilliant artists: Genevieve Stawski provided the central image, and Foad Torshizi the design. John Wright's superb conversation and friendship has been long-lived and sustaining. My family has been encouraging throughout, including when I have been rather difficult. And finally, my thanks to Beth Sadler for many things, including motivating me as this book neared completion.

An earlier version of Chapter 1 was published as "Boy Meets Camera: Christopher Isherwood, Sergei Tretiakov, and the Queer Potential of the First Five-Year Plan," *MLQ* 76/4 (2015), pp. 465–90.

Can a homosexual be a member of the Communist Party?
                    Harry Whyte to Joseph Stalin, May 1934

Introduction: The Perverts of Modernity

Communists are queer creatures. Emerging around the middle of the nineteenth century, they are at times shunned by polite society, at others increasingly incorporated and appropriated. They make loud, proud speeches scandalously proclaiming their identity; they hold secretive and cliquey meetings; they are bohemians and misguided moralists; they rant, they rave, they demand attention. Theirs is not only a politics of the factory floor, but of the street, the smoke-filled room, the bar – and, we might add, the bedroom. "Tearing away the decent drapery" of capital to parade its freakish constitution of human interiority, and driven by a solemn madness to endlessly diagnose, correct, and abjectly celebrate their own deviations, Communists must surely rank among the foremost perverts of modernity.[1]

Many have, of course, tried to put the record straight. While the performative power of *The Communist Manifesto* (1848) has been rightly celebrated, there is also a certain defensiveness at work from the very start, an anxious desire to "counterpose to the horror stories of communism a manifesto of the party itself."[2] Marx and Engels go on to counter claims of Communist sexual immorality with a little sexual panicking of their own: "Our bourgeois, not content with having the wives and daughters of the proletariat at their disposal, not to mention legally sanctioned prostitution, take the greatest pleasure in reciprocal seduction of married women."[3] This indictment of bourgeois family life and its traffic in women is a powerful heuristic for radical sexual politics – to be further developed by Engels in *The Origin of the Family, Private Property and the State* (1884) and by various strains of Marxist feminism – and also serves a tactical purpose in allaying fears and recruiting new adherents.

However, this counter-moralizing movement also instantiates a foundational tension for Communist, and more broadly Marxist politics; a tension always overdetermined by questions of sexuality, whether or not explicitly raised, because it operates within and against a paradigm of moral scandal.

The question is: how can one answer accusations of moral turpitude without replicating the terms of such condemnation and thus upholding elements of bourgeois life? The signature maneuvers of Communist politics can be re-charted along the lines of this reverse discourse. Communist history has typically been seen as a series of negotiations between revolutionary and reformist strains, between statist and anti-statist impulses, intellectual and plebeian identities, peasant and proletarian radicalisms, and so on. Yet a persistent, underexplored dialectic underlies these strategic shifts, deeply marked but not entirely exhausted by the infamously sticky question of normativity. How to practice politics both within and against a moral order, and make legible new ethical claims within social forms one wishes to dismantle? How might this question be imbricated with sexual desires and practices, or to be less coy, as Wilhelm Reich and others pondered with lesser and greater degrees of success: how, when, and where is a Communist to fuck? What are the artistic forms best suited to promote Communist identity and yet problematize the terms in which identity itself emerges in bourgeois society? And how might the embodied styles of the politics of everyday life be a crucial site for these questions? What does it mean, for instance, to don a boiler suit or partisan's beret as opposed to a jacket and tie or intellectual's threadbare tweed, to meet in a bar, the street, or at a private residence? Put this way, the history of the Marxist left begins to appear a lot more like that of gay, lesbian, and queer politics than has usually been assumed – a convergence that has troubled Communists and queers alike, not least because these modalities of radical life have often been seen by the liberal left as mere pretensions, distractions from the properly political business of working-class representation or the articulation of gay rights to the state.

This uneasy identity is particularly evident in the interwar period. As Foucault points out in his final lecture series *The Courage of Truth*, European Communist parties between the wars were in a strange position. Still committed to an outlaw ethos of the "revolutionary life as scandal of an unacceptable truth" and yet increasingly prescriptive of bourgeois standards of conduct, they sought to preserve a sense of radical élan in the everyday life of their members, and yet to rein in the excesses of cultural revolution in their social and sexual practices.[4] Foucault's remarks should be placed in the context of his career-length polemic against the French Communist Party (PCF), motivated by his experience of the PCF's marked homophobia during his brief membership.[5] But in this aside from the late lectures, Foucault is not merely dismissing Communism out of hand, but rather explicitly adumbrating a new line of historical inquiry:

> It would be interesting to see how the problem of the style of life was raised in the Communist Party, how it was posed in the 1920s, how it was gradually transformed, elaborated, modified, and finally reversed, since we end with that paradoxical result, but which in a sense only confirms the importance of style of life and the manifestation of truth in the militant life.[6]

What, in other words, are the forms of life, modes of embodied polemic, and praxes of truth of interwar Communist culture? The Bolshevik decriminalization of homosexuality gave this question particular urgency. From 1917 to 1932-4, Soviet Russia stood at the forefront of homosexual reform, giving left-leaning queers a powerful motivation to support the Soviet cause, and hopes only to become cruelly disappointed with recriminalization in 1934.

This book addresses an intersection in literary, cultural, and intellectual history where Foucault's problematic becomes intensified and its implications explicit. *Queer Communism* reconstructs the British left's contradictory sexual politics in the 1930s through analyses of two overlapping moments. First, the reception and transformation of Soviet Marxism by queer British writers in the early to mid-1930s; and, second, the broader left's mounting rejection of sexual dissidence from the mid-1930s onwards, precisely as these queer writers gained prominence and their major works appeared in print. Before laying out some of the stakes, sources, and arguments of this project, I would like to begin *in medias res*. In November 1937 the lesbian Communist writer Sylvia Townsend Warner wrote to fellow Communist Edgell Rickword to voice her concerns about the newly-recruited Party member Stephen Spender.[7] Noting that his poetry has "definitely fallen off" since he joined the Communist Party of Great

Britain (CPGB), and displaying alarm at his "violent displays of individualism," Townsend Warner cautions that:

> If SS has lost in poetry while he is with us he has gained largely in newspaper prestige; and this will make him a considerable danger if he chooses to write a Backwards from Communism or to air his grievances [...] Having brandished him so much in the beginning it will be a great mistake not to brandish quite as much the fact that he has not proved up to our standards. In fact, let us be sure that it looks like a purge.[8]

It's hard to fault Townsend Warner's main point here, which acutely foresees Spender's active service in the anti-Communist cultural politics of the Cold War, calling for the CPGB to publicly disown him before he can make a "nuisance" of himself.[9] The interest of this letter, however, is surely not limited to Townsend Warner's prediction of Spender's anti-Communism. To focus on the passage's most prominent phrase (bearing in mind that the term primarily means expulsion from the Party rather than execution), what does it mean for one queer writer to call for a public disavowal of another that "looks like a purge"? I pose this question not to add to the endless lamentations of the dangerous naïvety of 1930s intellectuals' support of the Soviet Union, but rather to question the governing assumptions underlying usual accounts of queer writers' commitments to Communism. Despite the fact that many queer and gender-dissident British writers were affiliated and aligned with Communism during the 1930s – as Party members (including Townsend Warner, Valentine Ackland, and, very briefly, Spender) or affiliates and sympathisers (such as John Lehmann, T. C. Worsley, Christopher Isherwood, W. H. Auden, and Katharine Burdekin) – this particular intersection of radical identities has yet to be explored. Focusing heavily on the later retractions and evasions of Auden, Spender, and Isherwood, queer writers' engagement with Communism has largely been dismissed as mere fashion, a "collective fever," as Perry Anderson once described the political commitment of the period's writers in general.[10]

The juxtaposition of Spender and Townsend Warner is a salient point from which to approach this problem, for Spender's queasy liberalism and abrupt "Backwards from Communism" have become paradigmatic for the standard position: queers and Communism do not mix. The thoroughgoing antinormativity of queer life, so the argument goes, is completely incompatible with the po-faced puritanism of Communist discipline, particularly in the increasingly sexually conservative atmosphere of the 1930s left. But why can't queers be stern and Communists playful? Isherwood, for instance, was well known for a fierce insistence on queer life and, in his younger days, an ironic yet committed stance toward Communism. The case of Townsend Warner and her partner Valentine Ackland offer an even starker rejoinder to such bifurcated accounts: a committed lesbian couple who were prominent activists, witty contributors to Communist publications such as *Left Review*, *Daily Worker*, and *Our Time*, and leading members of the CPGB in the west of England.[11] While Townsend Warner and Ackland make imperative an investigation of queer Communism in what might be called its strong sense, the figure of the less hardcore "fellow traveler" also urges reconsideration, as a designation deeply and lastingly inflected by queer sexuality in Britain, particularly with reference to the Auden group. Tellingly, T. C. Worsley's 1971 memoir of the 1930s, reprinted by Gay Modern Classics, is entitled *Fellow Travellers: A Memoir of the Thirties*, the book cover itself expressive of a sense of mutual intelligibility between the terms "gay," "fellow traveller" and "thirties."

Before beginning to tease out the implications of queer Communism in the 1930s, it is important at the outset to clarify this study's position on the relationship between the British left and Soviet Communism during the period. There have been two major waves of scholarship on this relationship. The first reading, prevalent during the Cold War and most influentially proposed by George Orwell, holds that the British left in the 1930s was in thrall to a virulent Soviet Communism directing its every move.[12] This apparent control operated right across the cultural field. From the literary forms prescribed at the 1934 Soviet Writers' Congress, the networks of institutional affiliation between leftists developed during the period, to the support of the Republican forces during the Spanish Civil War, a culpably blind left supposedly followed Moscow's every command. More recently, combating this Cold War orthodoxy of monolithic, totalitarian Soviet influence, cultural and literary historians such as Michael Denning, Janet Montefiore, Rod Mengham and others have stressed that the formation of leftist writers and intellectuals of the period was not primarily a product of Communism, both in the sense that the cultural institutions in which these figures were imbedded were not predominantly Communist-controlled, and the aesthetic-ideological landscape of the 1930s was not solely dominated by the approved form of socialist realism.[13]

This body of scholarship undoubtedly provides a much-needed corrective. But the picture is still incomplete, missing the vital importance of Communist-run organizations and publications for the period's artistic production, and western leftists' engagements with Soviet intellectual life and cultural forms. Drawing on archival research and revisionist social histories of the British left, this book argues for a more nuanced view.[14] *Queer Communism* reframes British leftist culture as crucially shaped but not overwhelmingly controlled by Communist institutions, publishing networks, and aesthetic ideologies. Despite low membership figures, the CPGB, the Comintern (Communist International), and the Soviet Union exercised a powerful but often indirect influence over British cultural life during the 1930s and 1940s. Indeed, as E. P. Thompson pointed out some time ago, Communism enjoyed the most sustained prestige during the period in the field of culture, and, moreover, that to write the history of the British labor movement without Communism would be "to write *Wuthering Heights* without Heathcliff."[15]

The central argument of *Queer Communism* is that to tell the story of the British left in the 1930s without queer writers would be equally nonsensical, as would be any account of queer literary history without Communism. And yet there has been no attempt to address this intersection, accounts of the decade always sidestepping and evading what any student of the period might very well suspect from a mere roll call of canonical figures. Why, then, this blockage in literary history? A series of obvious answers can be sought in the anti-Communism and heterosexism of literary historians, with canonical scholarship on the 1930s exhibiting at times a genteel near-silence, at others an outright homophobia.[16] An ongoing suspicion of what Judith Butler diagnosed as the left's perception of gender and sexuality as "merely cultural" has also played a role – to say nothing of leftist homophobia itself, which is the focus of the second half of this book.[17] During the Popular Front period, leftists in Britain, Europe, and the US increasingly sought to purge homosexuality and other forms of gender and sexual dissidence from their ranks as they aimed to broaden the appeal of the left amongst the middle class.[18] This process of heteronormalization was carried out under the sign of antifascism, ironically mirroring Nazi homophobia as what the fascists called "sexual Bolshevism" was now seen by many on the left as "fascist perversion."[19]

As has been often pointed out, sexuality is no guarantee of political radicalism, and queers are of course often far from insusceptible to anti-Communism. This is partly for the obvious reason of leftist homophobia, but also because, however sympathetic, many have been deeply uneasy with the association of Communism with queerness and culture under the sign of pathological treachery – a pervasive triangulation brutally posited by the McCarthyist state and always lurking in the Anglo-American political unconscious.[20] In Britain, the case of the culturally-minded and mostly queer "Cambridge Spies" continues to exercise a fascination in the popular imaginary, with these agents' Communist commitments and treachery seen as pathologically intertwined with their sexuality and interest in art. John Banville's novel *The Untouchable* (1997) is perhaps the most striking literary document of this assumption, detailing an Anthony Blunt figure's utter snobbery, self-absorption, and self-deception as he is pathetically flattered into becoming a Soviet agent.[21] This series of assumptions has had a direct effect on the reception of queer leftist writers of the 1930s, because Auden, Isherwood, and Spender all knew one of the spies, Guy Burgess. Harassed by a McCarthyist group in the 1950s Isherwood denied his former commitments and activities in Weimar Berlin, and taken out of this context his disavowals might lead one to presume his rather lukewarm commitment.

Naturally, I do not deny these fundamental reasons for the occlusion of our understanding of queer Communism, but there is also a more recent, perhaps more theoretically interesting disciplinary movement in operation. As has been pointed out by Kevin Floyd, Elisa Glick, and others, queer theory and Marxism have proved uneasy bedfellows from queer theory's inception in the 1990s.[22] If from the beginning Communists have attempted to straighten out their scandalously queer edges, an obverse maneuver is also observable. One of the signal interventions of the field, the collection of essays edited by Michael Warner, *Fear of a Queer Planet* (1993), insistently positions itself against a Marxist left (surely uncoincidentally in disarray following the fall of the Soviet bloc).[23] As Floyd has pointed out, in this now-canonical volume, queer theory centrally defined itself against Marxism's evasions of questions of sexuality and heterosexist assumptions. The audacious intent of the volume's title simultaneously seeks to sublate minoritizing, rights-based paradigms of gay and lesbian politics and make a play for Marxism's now-tattered claims of world-historical heuristic power and political sway (as Chapter 2 argues in more detail, this vanguardist impulse is an overlooked commitment shared by early Soviet Communism and queer theory, both concerned with the imparting of radical consciousness to the massed proto-subjects of revolution). In Warner's introduction he boldly yet provisionally states that "core elements of the Marxist paradigm may have to be seen as properly ideological moments in the history of reproductivist heterosexuality."[24] *Queer Communism* takes up the challenge of this polemical subjunctive, arguing that a series of major concepts in Soviet Marxism not only vitally shaped the evolution of queer literary history in Britain but also provide important intellectual resources for antiheteronormative critique.

In what follows I also contend that queer leftist writing of the 1930s has been fundamentally misunderstood because we lack a robust morphology of its specific social forms. Since the work of Samuel Hynes, it is a commonplace to observe that the period brought the relationship between public and private spheres into stark relief, a particularly marked negotiation for queer leftist writers, but also for Communist cultural producers more generally. Both Raphael Samuel and Isherwood's friend Edward Upward have written extensively on the ways that Communist commitment involved an intricate relationship between intimate life and public activism, to the extent that the two can never be separated; both these heterosexual intellectuals, for instance, have stressed the extent to which a Party member's choice of partner was always seen as a directly political act (to borrow Orwell's much-cited phrase).[25] And yet, work on the 1930s has not convincingly articulated how these imbrications worked – a particularly glaring gap when supple accounts of the public/private problematic have emerged from scholars focusing on other sites, most notably perhaps Nancy Frazer, Warner, Davina Cooper, and Lauren Berlant. Meanwhile, overturning to a degree the earlier mutual mistrust, a number of theorists and cultural historians have offered new syntheses of Marxism and queer theory, and begun to recognize the role of Communism in the emergence of late-twentieth-century identity politics.²⁶ *Queer Communism* draws on these two bodies of work, arguing that the scene of reception and transformation of Soviet Marxism by queer British writers emerges through an overlooked set of social forms, and offers a series of generative syntheses between Marxist and queer literary modes.

It would be impossible to capture anything like a comprehensive picture of queer British Marxist writing of the 1930s in a single monograph, and a number of omissions necessarily mark this study. Most obvious of all, apart from some fairly brief references in this Introduction and in the Coda, I do not discuss poetry. This is partly for reasons of space, but also because the Soviet-Anglophone transmission of Marxist aesthetics in the period was largely routed through discussions of prose narrative and cinematic technique rather than poetic form. The reception of Brechtian dramatic technique by Auden and Isherwood is another omission, but the debate around this question has to my mind already been largely played out.²⁷ For better or worse, *Queer Communism* is a study of prose narrative.

Forms of queer Marxism

This study may be seen to contribute to modernist studies, adding to the ever-broadening canon of writers, literary institutions, and print cultures today defined as modernist. Here I build on the important work of Tyrus Miller, Leo Mellor, Gill Plain, Jessica Berman, Jed Esty, Benjamin Kohlmann, Marina MacKay, Cathryn Setz, and others who have tirelessly argued for the importance of 1930s and 1940s writing to any robust understanding of modernism.²⁸ From this body of work, I am particularly indebted to Jed Esty's *A Shrinking Island* (2004) and Benjamin Kohlmann's *Committed Styles* (2014). Esty's study argues that mid-century modernist English culture was marked by what he calls "redemptive Anglocentrisms," as British expansiveness made way for a Herderian conception of English national culture. In the second half of this book, I explore a different archive of redemptive Anglocentrism – English writing of the Popular Front – and Esty's formulation has proved invaluable in tracing this genealogy, as has the work of Ben Harker on the British left's progressive patriotism.²⁹ Kohlmann's study is one of the most sophisticated recent explorations of 1930s leftist writing in Britain, arguing that writers such as Edward Upward were not mindless followers of socialist realist doctrine, nor thoroughgoing modernists, but rather drew on a concept of literature as social action derived in part from I. A. Richards and catalyzed by urgent political concerns. Rather like Berman in *Modernist Commitments* (2012), but with less insistence on the reach of modernism as such, Kohlmann thus argues that experimentalism should not be divorced from political commitment but rather that these terms can operate symbiotically. In differing ways, these scholars have all enriched the study of 1930s literature, which has increasingly become not an embarrassing minor note in the history of modernism, but rather a vital part of our understanding of the broader period.

However, *Queer Communism* is not situated squarely in the field of modernism. Under the aegis of the New Modernist Studies, such has been the further expansion of the term that a very broad definition of modernism indeed seems to be in operation, stretching back at least to the nineteenth century and reaching forward into the present as the concept of postmodernity wanes in critical purchase. As stressed in a recent special edition of *MLQ* edited by Coleen Lye and Jed Esty, "Peripheral Realisms Now," this expansion has also been territorial, as ever more global sites of cultural production are unevenly drawn into the ambit of modernism.[30] If, as the title of the major field journal *Modernism/Modernity* more or less explicitly designates, modernism is defined as any experimental cultural expression or instantiation of modernity as such, then in the case of Europe literary modernism would have to go back as far as *Tristram Shandy* (1759–76), or possibly even *Don Quixote* (1605/15). This broad historical vantage necessarily posits nineteenth-century realism as an aberration, a strange interregnum running between, say, Walter Scott and the *Futurist Manifesto*, albeit persisting in some less exciting genres such as the middlebrow novel.[31] One begins to suspect, then, that the most ambitious versions of New Modernist Studies rely on a direct inversion of Georg Lukács's infamously dogmatic location of normative literary history exclusively within the realm of realism; an over correction to and ironic recapitulation of a position that has been subjected to robust critiques from its very inception.

Queer Communism does not directly tackle this process, not least because in a certain iteration it is unassailable without a thoroughgoing critique of global modernity itself – a crucial project but outside the scope of this present study.[32] For similar reasons nor do I grapple with the most sophisticated dialectical version of this thinking to be found in Frederic Jameson's declaration that "realism is in fact itself a kind of modernism, if not the latter's first form," and explored in his recent work through a series of wide-ranging investigations of cultural modernity at large.[33] I do, however, want to briefly note that, to borrow Esty's terms for the British Empire between the wars, the motors of Modernist Studies' imperial expansion appear to be starting to sputter.[34] We might then see a return to modernism as an object of study rather than the heroic world-historical subject of cultural modernity (of course, I may be proved wrong in this).

Queer Communism makes a relatively particularist argument about the styles and modes of 1930s leftist writing. Drawing on extensive archival research and close readings of literary texts, this study re-centers realism in 1930s literary production. Closely intertwined with the recent denial of Communist influence discussed above is a rejection of the old critique of 1930s writing, which held that that committed literatures of the period attempted to overwhelm modernism in a sort of stylistic revanchism, vainly groping back to Balzac's Paris via Moscow in search of the political. This is a much-needed corrective; again, however, the picture is incomplete, for a broad sense of realism *was* the politically dominant mode of leftist aesthetics in the period in Britain. This is not to say that writers of the period were all suddenly brought to heel, zombie-like, by the 1934 Soviet Writers' Congress's proscription of modernism. Rather, working within a literary culture that insistently proclaimed committed literature as inherently realist, yet producing manifestly experimental texts, 1930s leftist writers include modernism in realism. This argument may be applied to a wide variety of leftist and left-liberal writers of the period in Britain and the US, including Olivia Manning, Edward Upward, George Orwell, Muriel Rukeyser, and Patrick Hamilton. But it is particularly salient for queer novelists such as Townsend Warner and Isherwood. Rather than directly participating in the realism debates on the Marxist left in the period, Townsend Warner and Isherwood mediate the terms of these debates through a pressing need to catalyze queer literary history. More specifically, they include modernism in realism insofar as realism is the politically privileged problematic from within which the modernity of their queer literary forms emerge. Neither overweening prescription nor outmoded style, realism is instead the terrain of their engagements, the hotly contested ground upon which they boldly stake out new territory for queer literary production.

Jameson's acute observation that we always find ourselves "talking about the emergence or the breakdown of realism and not the thing itself" is pertinent here, particularly in the case of Isherwood, whose *Berlin Stories* (1935–9) tease realist narrative just up to the point of no return.[35] In Chapter 1, "Boy Meets Camera," I explore Isherwood's renegotiation of an overlooked iteration of the realism debates in German and Soviet aesthetics, arguing that his transformation of this debate opened up new prospects for antiheteronormative critique. While Lukács's polemical exchanges with Brecht and Adorno are well known, and Brecht's influence on Isherwood has already been debated, I turn instead to Isherwood's mediation of another of Lukács's key adversaries, the Soviet writer and polymath Sergei Tretiakov.[36] A major figure in the Soviet cultural scene in the late 1920s and early 1930s, Tretiakov proposed a mode of avant-garde reportage he called "factography." Explicitly positioned against proletarian realism's tendency to "smuggle in the contraband of idealism" and thus uphold bourgeois humanism, factography aimed to overthrow the human subject and instead offer a "biography of the object," a form of collectivist literary praxis in which the processes of production and socialist construction would take center stage.[37] Tretiakov outlined these precepts in a famous 1931 lecture in Berlin, "The Writer and the Socialist Village," when Isherwood was living in the city and mixing in Communist circles. Also living in Berlin at the time, Lukács mercilessly attacked Tretiakov's ideas as "crassly fetishistic" in a number of Germanophone Communist periodicals (as well as the multi-lingual Soviet journal *International Literature*, much read in Britain in the 1930s).[38]

Drawing on Kevin Floyd's and Eric O. Clark's concept of "sexual humanism," Chapter 1 argues that Tretiakov's elevation of the object simultaneously refuses property ownership and legitimizes queer instrumentalizations of the body. I read Isherwood's narrative as picking up and developing this queer possibility in Tretiakov's antihumanism, contending that his famous declaration "I am a camera" does not evince a detached narrative perspective but rather an active self-instrumentalization, a queer Marxist transformation of the old cliché of "boy meets tractor." Meanwhile, the other half of the collection, *The Last of Mr. Norris*, empties out realist typicality through the bizarre machinations of its anti-hero, Arthur Norris. While Isherwood is undoubtedly more committed to the radical implications of Tretiakov's antihumanism than to Lukácsian realism, this commitment is nevertheless carried out in a prose style far removed from Western modernist experiment; in a style recognizably realist, in fact. In this way, Isherwood demonstrates how realism remained fertile soil for queer writing of the 1930s, even as realist narrative buckles under the strain of his objectivist intervention.

In Chapter 2, "Sylvia Townsend Warner's Queer Vanguardism," I argue that realism functions in a very different way for her 1936 novel *Summer Will Show*. Drawing on José Esteban Muñoz's stark observation that "queerness is not yet here," I contend that Townsend Warner's historical novel demonstrates the queer possibilities of a more classically Lukácsian mode.[39] While Lukácsian typicality might be seen to necessarily insist upon a rigidly normative characterological scheme, in a number of 1930s essays Lukács pursued a polemic against the concept of the scientistic "average" he argued was prominent in the naturalist novel. The typical character must not express a static concept of the sociological norm, but rather a dynamic mediation of past and present, the creation of the "men of the future," as Engels famously declared.[40] In *Summer Will Show*'s account of two queer women's involvement in the 1848 revolution in Paris, Townsend Warner explores the ways in which new radical subjectivities can be depicted through the mediations of realist typicality. At the same time, the novel's clear partisanship and serpentine structure resist the realist inheritance, as do its fantastic, oneiric plotting and picaresque turns. *Summer Will Show* is the obverse to *The Berlin Stories*, operating very differently yet navigating an overlapping realist topography.

Drawing on research in Townsend Warner and Valentine Ackland's archive, Chapter 2 also develops the concept of queer vanguardism. Counterintuitively perhaps, it was the two women's situation in the backwaters of the English countryside that made their Communist vanguardism so urgent. In *What Is To Be Done?* (1902) and elsewhere, Lenin reformulated classical Marxism for the needs of a largely rural country.[41] In order to catalyze the spontaneous but untutored radicalism of the Russian peasantry, the vanguard emerges as a fundamental formation in Leninism, a group of highly-dedicated activists and theorists imbued with high levels of revolutionary consciousness.[42] Townsend Warner and Ackland pick up Lenin's concept of the vanguard, taking up the pressing needs of the rural poor through a series of consciousness-raising schemes. Crucially, Ackland's female masculinity was central to this process, as she shaped a complex embodied critique of rural injustice through a queering performance of a series of rural identities that enabled her to pursue her activism with a particular purchase among young farm workers. This queer vanguardism might initially appear to have some affinities with the artistic avant garde. But this would be to misread their politics and Ackland's "sartorial semiotic," to use Jack Halberstam's useful term.[43] There was indeed some shock of the new going on in their queer vision of a Soviet future for Dorset, but it was not articulated in terms of a self-conscious stress on aesthetic form. Rather, Ackland stressed the instrumental practicality of her trousers, while Townsend Warner's arguments about consciousness-raising literature were firmly located outside of the realm of the experimental aesthetic (even as her own literary praxes belied such a position to a certain degree).

Another way in which this book seeks to obliquely intervene in modernist studies is through a reconfiguration of the relationship between the writers who became known as the "Auden Gang" and their queer modernist forebears. It might be tempting to presume that Auden, Spender, and Isherwood recapitulated the queer coterie social forms of the Bloomsbury Group. Prominent figures such as E. M. Forster and Virginia Woolf privately advocated great frankness in discussions of their non-normative sexual practices and desires, and yet were also (very understandably) hesitant to extend such outspokenness to their modes of public address. For a younger generation of queer writers, some of the same caution obviously still applied, given that homosexuality was illegal in Britain until 1967. Moreover, Auden, Spender, and Isherwood not only associated closely with Lytton Strachey, Forster, Woolf, and others, but also themselves displayed certain features of the coterie – circulating manuscripts with one another, writing private jokes into their works, sharing an intimate sense of themselves as a self-contained group, and so on. For all its apparent plausibility, this argument occludes our understanding of the social forms of queer literary production of the

1930s, supporting a view of an apparent split between private and public, which necessarily renders "public" an increasingly confident leftist public sphere and "private" a closeted nascent gay and lesbian culture. This is not to say that such a complete split was at work in Bloomsbury, for no overwhelming stress on the closet or binary conception of public and private can ever convincingly account for queer formations (nor for cultural production at large, for that matter), but rather to suggest that there was a genuine break between Auden and his contemporaries and Woolf et al. Whether or not entirely accurate for Bloomsbury, the model of the coterie is manifestly inadequate to describe Auden, Spender, and Isherwood, who were crucially formed by a pressing need for intimately public political engagement, in part due to their experiences in Weimar Berlin, and then increasingly motivated by the rise of fascism that blew apart the incipient social fabric that enabled such experiences.

A more robust understanding of queer leftist writing is suggested by the concept of the counterpublic, which received its most powerful exposition to date in Michael Warner's *Publics and Counterpublics* (2002). Warner argues for a recalibration of our understanding of the supposedly stark opposition between private and public discourses and embodied practices that provides vital ways of understanding queer leftist writing. But Warner's model cannot exhaustively account for queer leftist culture of the period, which was deeply marked by the Leninist organizational unit of the cell, an oppositional social formation that has received less attention than the coterie and the counterpublic in literary and cultural history. The cell is a vital mediating term in the 1930s – simultaneously turned inwards and out, paranoid yet confident, a crucial, overlooked formation operating somewhere between coterie and counterpublic modes of association, yet with its own distinct social texture. The next part of this introduction will explore these modes of oppositional sociality that undergird my readings of Isherwood and Townsend Warner in Chapters 1 and 2, before turning to a discussion of how the normalizations of the Popular Front increasingly overturned their radical élan, as Chapters 3 and 4 will go on to argue in more depth.

Coterie, counterpublic, cell

The famous group of Spender, Auden, Isherwood, and their publisher John Lehmann might at first appear to be almost entirely an offshoot of Bloomsbury, given their overlapping publishing networks and personal contacts. However, it didn't seem quite that way at the time, not least to Virginia Woolf, who repeatedly complained that the younger generation had deserted the properly intimate scene of writing for an ill-advised engagement with politics.[44] Woolf's criticism might initially appear to rely on a naïvely bifurcated conception of the politics of literature belied by her own literary praxis, long recognized by feminist scholarship as intimately political, but she was articulating a real difference in literary aims and methods. Despite the shadow of the censor and the exigencies of the closet, writers such as Isherwood, Auden, and Spender did not just attempt to reach out from a privatized intimacy toward a broader public (which would merely continue and extend Bloomsbury's project), but rather to dialectically produce new forms of intimate public address. This break can be partly attributed to the 1928 trials of *The Well of Loneliness* and *Lady Chatterley's Lover*, which occurred when Auden and his group were just beginning their careers. While established figures such as Woolf and Forster offered cautious support for Hall, their younger colleagues were more radically energized by these trials, which they took to lay down the gauntlet to a new generation. Accordingly, as Auden famously declared in 1932, they were now searching for ways to embody "Private faces in public places" – a public intimacy – as opposed to "Public faces in private places" – a guarded intimacy shielded from intruding eyes.[45] However, certain influential critical accounts have assumed that these attempts to reconfigure public and private were largely occluded by coterie tendencies inherited from Bloomsbury.

For instance, Valentine Cunningham's *British Writers of the Thirties* (1988) characterizes queer leftist literary production as an exclusively coterie form. With undisguised homophobia, Cunningham argues that the "clique-puffery" of upper-middle-class left-wing male homosexuals unfairly dominated the literary scene, and that "Auden and Isherwood's long-standing sexual liaison [. . .] is the best example of this perverse variant on the Comintern."[46] Underlying Cunningham's disgust is a circular argument. The writers of the period best known at the time were indeed well connected; it is hard to see quite how this could not be the case. But Cunningham's remarks also raise a more serious question of canonicity and working-class writing. As is well known, upper- and upper-middle-class white men have dominated most of English literary history, and the 1930s continued to exhibit this tendency. However, the decade should also be seen as the start of a long process of contestation over the class formation of the canon – a precursor to what have become known more recently as the "canon wars," as a number of bourgeois writers became invested in getting their working-class (and, to a lesser degree, colonized) colleagues into print, while proletarian and anti-colonial writers themselves clamored for recognition in an increasingly prominent leftist publishing scene. While bourgeois interest in proletarian writing was admittedly inflected at times with a patronizing tone, it also bore some fruitful results. As Christopher Hilliard has recently argued, the energetic queer publisher John Lehmann was particularly important in this regard. Lehmann used his elite contacts (an Old Etonian, he was the Woolfs' protégé at the Hogarth Press) to publish proletarian writers in his influential international magazine *New Writing*, which had one of the most diverse class compositions of any publication of the period.[47]

For all Lehmann's patrician bearing, this was no instance of mere patronage but rather goes to the heart of queer leftist literary production. Cunningham has protested that "much of the period's writing about the proletariat is vitiated by the bourgeois bugger's specialist regard" – but rather than dismissing this remark we might revalorize it.[48] Many working-class men of course invited and returned such regard with interest, and the class-crossing sexual practices inherent in interwar homosexual life became closely intertwined with leftist politics in a powerful way.[49] Lehmann's semi-autobiographical novel *Evil Was Abroad* (1938) narrates this mutual constitution through its protagonist's involvement with an unemployed youth, a relationship that becomes synecdochal for the revolutionary upheavals of Viennese politics. In an unpublished letter discussing the manuscript, Isherwood makes explicit what he calls Lehmann's "semi-erotic interest in the working-classes." Urging Lehmann not to shy away from homosexual themes, Isherwood insists that "this kind of homosexuality is so profoundly significant. It needn't in the least be sneered at [. . .] It provides a valuable impulse."⁵⁰ From a certain perspective Lehmann's novel could seem rather closeted – as might Isherwood's own *Berlin Stories* (1935–9) – but it is important not merely to historicize these texts as products of a more repressed age, but rather to underline the radical potential of their insistent cross-coding of homosexual desire and Marxist political engagement.

This mode of queer leftist association was also particularly marked in the case of Auden, Isherwood, and Spender's trips to Weimar Berlin. As is well known, all three visited the city in the late 1920s and early 1930s in search of working-class male sexual partners, a quest for sexual fulfillment that brought them into contact with both the city's Marxist cultures, and the prominent homosexual emancipation movement centered around Magnus Hirschfeld, who was himself in alliance with the German Communist Party in the early 1930s.⁵¹ The three writers' stance toward their time in the city synthesized coterie and counterpublic modes of association. They were engaged in a process of inward-looking group self-fashioning, which was sublated through their exposure to the most radical sexual and political cultures in contemporary Europe, opening up their work beyond the confines of the Bloomsbury coterie.

In Warner's influential account, several key features define a public, which I here briefly summarize. "Self-organized" (i.e. not organized by the state), a public is the "social space created by the reflexive circulation of discourse." It is, however, distinguished from a coterie in that it is "a relation among strangers" with a mode of address "both personal and impersonal." Publics cannot be known in advance, for they are constituted by what Warner calls "mere attention": a discourse may aim to address a public, but if no one listens, reads, or picks up its embodied style, it has failed, a test which is determined by how it circulates across time. Schematizing somewhat, we could put this very broadly in Marxist terms – publics make their own history but not in circumstances of their own making. Finally, Warner argues that a public is a form of "poetic world-making."⁵² This perhaps initially quixotic-sounding designation arises from the self-generative character of a public, which creates its own social world through a series of feedback loops. A counterpublic bears many features of the public, but is distinguished by a self-awareness that its discourse could quite probably be received with repulsion, especially by those to whom it is not putatively addressed. To take two counterpublics flourishing in Weimar Berlin: a Communist pamphlet and its readership would be aware on some level that a political reactionary would be shocked and repelled should they glance over someone's shoulder at the publication; a queer magazine would produce perhaps an even more visceral reaction from the gaze of a sexually conservative reader.

Following Warner's emphasis, today the term counterpublic is most often used to describe forms of queer sociality and discursive circulation. But it has also been applied to Marxist political cultures. For instance, in his 1990 essay "A Culture in Counter-Flow," Perry Anderson moves away from his previous condemnation of British leftist culture of the 1930s to a more appreciative position, arguing that a counterpublic can be defined as a "politically organized, class readership, such as had once existed in Weimar Germany or Britain in the thirties."[53] The clearest example of this type of left-wing counterpublic was the Left Book Club (LBC). Founded in 1936 by the radical publisher Victor Gollancz, the leftist politician Stafford Cripps, and the Communist writer John Strachey, the Club operated through subscription, each member receiving a series of books at a discounted price. Initially the founders had aimed to break even with a membership of 2,500, but by 1939 it had achieved 57,000 members, and the popularity of the club has often been seen as a signal event in the leftward drift of British politics during the period, culminating in Labour's landslide victory in the 1945 election. While the LBC was not a specifically Communist-run organization, it pursued a fairly consistent pro-Communist stance during its first phase of existence (1936–9), which coincided with the Popular Front policy of alliance with other left-leaning groups.[54]

The LBC presents an intriguing case study in the evolution of a counterpublic. It was not at all obvious from the outset that it would find a mass readership, as can be seen in its rather modest hopes for membership, but then it grew to be a major force in British publishing. Yet this very success was intertwined with a compromise position with regard to a broader public, and the LBC's purported role in the Labour election victory might then be seen as the limit and overturning of its counterpublic radicalism, as its claims are articulated with the state, and thus any scandalous élan cancelled out in the moment of broader public success – somewhat like the state's later acceptance of some limited sense of gay rights. But caution must be exercised here in terms of differing national attitude toward the state; Warner's model works less well for twentieth-century Britain than the US. Davina Cooper has argued for a rather different conception of radical counterpublics, as often mediated by and instantiated through the state, and in terms of the LBC's milder aspirations this articulation was successful.[55] But, as I shall explore in Chapter 4, it remains the case that the after-effects of much of Popular Front public culture on postwar Britain were deeply heteronormalizing, precisely as they played a role in the formation of the welfare state.

Although the LBC promoted the work of a number queer writers – most notably Stephen Spender's *Forward from Liberalism* (1937), and Katharine Burdekin's *Swastika Night* (1937; reprinted by the LBC in 1941) – it was at best not particularly interested in questions of non-normative sexuality (indeed, Burdekin's novel itself displays a marked strain of antihomosexual polemic). The case of the Group Theatre is rather different. Founded in 1932 by the queer dancer Rupert Doone and his partner Robert Medley, this experimental theater company operated through membership subscriptions and artistic collaborations. It drew on various British and European models in its dramatic aims and methods, including Communist agit-prop associated with Bertolt Brecht and first popularized in Britain by the Workers' Theatre Movement, and the school of acting associated with the queer writer, filmmaker and dramaturge Jean Cocteau. The company was best known for its leftist productions – including Auden's *Dance of Death* in 1934, and the series of Auden-Isherwood collaborations starting with *The Dog Beneath the Skin* (1935) – but it also put on works by more conservative playwrights such as T. S. Eliot's *Sweeney Agonistes* in 1934, a performance attended by the exiled Brecht. In his study of the Group Theatre, Michael Sidnell notes that many key members were queer and/or Communist aligned, and that figures such as Auden, Isherwood, and Benjamin Britten "probably fused (and confused) homosexual love, artistic collaboration and Communism."[56] Sidnell also argues that the theater's queer composition was largely illegible to a broader public, while its leftist credentials were widely overemphasized. Both assertions are fine as far as they go, but they are surely complicated by Sidnell's own acknowledgement of the fusion of homosexuality and Communism. For if such fusion (even if "confused") was indeed a part of the theater's collaborative project, then to isolate its leftist and queer aspects would be to deny its distinctive modes of address. Rather than a scene of double misrecognition, the Group Theatre might rather be an example of the creative synergy of queer and Communist cultural producers, speaking to multiple publics and counterpublics in their differing yet entwined valences of sexual dissidence and Communist commitment.

From its inception in the late 1920s, Auden's poetry had also been reaching out to a counterpublic, which it did begin to form in the 1930s, as an eager readership took up his exhortation to "Look stranger, on this island now" – a line usually read as a patriotic moment, but which is equally an invitation to heed an intimate public address.[57] To take some more of his most iconic lines, Auden calls for "new styles of architecture, a change of heart," a mode of literary production and dissemination that would synthesize intimate literary experiment with a more public form of artistic address.[58] It is no accident that Auden chose architecture as his metonym for artistic form: the architect designs spaces of public circulation, which concretize the associations implicit in the heart as the organ of circulation as well as the center of affective life. In these lines Auden's chain of associations produces a tight chiasmic identity between intimate life and the rhythms of dissemination. Auden, however, grew to distrust such expansive impulses, deleting these texts from his *Collected Poems*. Even at the time he was somewhat uneasy with his growing public presence – for instance, he changed the title of his 1936 collection *Look Stranger!* to the second part of the line, "On This Island," the original title having been chosen by his publisher because, somewhat ironically perhaps, he was unreachable in Iceland when the volume went to print.

This unease with the public role of the writer has often been seen as a moment of limiting self-awareness, in which the bourgeois leftist realizes how far from a proletarian audience he is situated – in Warner's terms, a realization that not enough "mere attention" had arisen to constitute the kind of counterpublic implied and invited by the literary objects themselves. However, while such unease is indeed a symptom of the complexly articulated claims of leftist and queer politics, it need not index failure, but rather a sense of differing identity claims that operate symbiotically in their opposition to bourgeois society. This becomes clearer when we consider the organizational concept of the cell.

Following the Second Congress of the Russian Social Democratic Labour Party (RSDRP) the term cell was instituted in 1903 to describe the smallest unit of Party organization.[59] At the time, the RSDRP was an illegal organization, which necessitated a degree of secrecy in its organizational methods, but the concept of the cell continued to hold a sense of underground urgency in the decades that followed, even when it described a unit of Communist organization in a context where the Party was not illegal. While the degree of direct Moscow influence over the formation and development of the CPGB has typically been overestimated, one aspect that was adopted more or less wholesale was the Marxist-Leninist terminology – particularly from 1922–4, when the "Bolshevization" of the Party was in full swing.[60] The CPGB adopted the term to describe a group typically consisting of around ten members, divided into "factory" and "street" cells according to their primary sites of activism.[61] With the institution of the Popular Front policy of the mid- to late 1930s as much of the left attempted to reach out to a broader set of bourgeois publics, the term was dropped in 1936 and replaced with the less-confrontational-sounding "group."[62] This shift in terminology is symptomatic of the paradox of radical life pointed out by Foucault. In the mid-1930s the Party attempted to negotiate between the need for a continuing sense of revolutionary urgency, and an increasingly normalizing policy of co-operation. The precise extent to which the Popular Front vitiated the revolutionary edge of the CPGB in terms of its own specific goals is a matter of some controversy, but is not our main concern here.[63] Rather, the question is: how did these differing models of Party organization, terminology, and ethos shape queer writers' engagements with Communism and leftist politics more broadly? More specifically, did the austere concept of the cell fundamentally exclude queer antinormativity, or was the more inclusive-sounding Popular Front actually more exclusionary?

Queer Communism argues the latter. It is by no means certain that all the normative aspects of Communist culture themselves constitute a specifically heteronormative regime. All cultural formations and social spaces necessarily entail a form of normativity – this could involve, for instance, the assumption of same-sex desire in a gay social space as much as the presumptive heterosexuality of a sports bar, or equally the radicalism of a demonstration compared to the formal hierarchy of a corporate office. Normativity is imbued with widely varying levels of hegemonic sway and appears in distinctly different styles, but this does not mean that dissident sociality is exhaustively antinormative, except in relation to certain dominant aspects of society. The cell is founded upon a fiercely anti-bourgeois normativity: sworn to a commitment to revolution, the members are bound by a shared sense of rejection of the capitalist world that is the governing norm of the cell. The cell's underground, illegal connotations resonate with queer sociality in the interwar period and beyond, not just in the sense of the confined, imprisoning space of the closet, but also in a more oppositional register as the modes of illegal and semi-legal political organization which arise to counter antihomosexual repression in the early to mid-twentieth century. In other words, what Foucault called "revolutionary life as scandal of an unacceptable truth" tessellates and can even mutually constitute queer and Communist social worlds.

At this point I would like to emphasize that it is far from my intention to de-privilege antinormativity, as a recent special edition of *differences*, "Queer Theory without Antinormativity" (2016), signals and advocates in its more polemical moments.[64] As I hope has already become clear, antiheteronormativity is a major commitment of *Queer Communism*. However, I do take seriously this special issue's call to rethink with precision how normativity operates – its twists and turns, counterhegemonic as well as hegemonic functions, its uneven and contradictory fields of operation. Although he does not frame the question in quite this way, Dan Healey's recent scholarship on Soviet attitudes toward homosexuality opens up this more finely-grained account. Healey argues that there was a general "tolerance" and even positive reception of non-normative gender performance and homosexual desire in the 1920s and early 1930s.[65] This attitude developed throughout the culturally radical 1920s, reaching its climax during the first half (1928–30) of the period of the First Five-Year Plan and the "Class Against Class" hardline Communist policy (1928–32) – precisely the moment when proletarian normativity was at its height. This crossroads is vividly illustrated in Fyodor Gladkov's socialist realist classic *Cement* (1925; English trans. 1929), much read in English translation during the 1930s. In *Cement* a very queer character appears in a factory scene, sporting "an artificial mustache drawn onto his shaven lips," a bonnet and corset, he asserts that "I'm a respectable proletarian girl." This performance of gender-bending working-class identity is greeted with "admiring laughter" by an assembled crowd of hard-bitten workers, who respect this figure's gender and sexual identity as resistant to the repressive aims of religious and governmental intervention, and, by extension, related to the forms of defiant good sense of the proletariat itself. As one of the working men remarks with approval, "nothing can stop him – neither the devil nor the priest nor the Soviet!"[66]

In this remark the Soviet is placed in opposition to queer self-expression, but in the period it was by no means a given that Soviet officials would seek to reform, correct, or cure homosexuality. Rather, they sought to assimilate a fairly wide spectrum of Russian men and women into the Bolshevik polity; this involved, for instance, psychiatrists working with queer men and women with an aim to get them to accept their orientation as natural and thus remove their (sometimes presumed) gender and sexual dysphoria, seen as obstacles to a fully productive Soviet life.[67] This practice strikingly foreshadows the 1957 recommendations of the Wolfenden Report, set up in Britain to investigate male homosexuality and female prostitution and which eventually led to the decriminalization of sex in private between men over twenty-one years of age. As Richard Hornsey has pointed out, "no attempt need be made to alter the direction of the homosexual's proclivities providing that he was sufficiently well adjusted to the norms and values of society"; in the words of the report itself, "it will be a matter of guiding the patient to help himself, not only by personal influence but also by helping to manipulate environmental factors."[68] *The Ministry of Love* in my title thus refers not only to Orwell's horrified vision of state power, but also to sexual liberalization of the Soviet state in the late 1920s and early 1930s and its anticipation of the recommendations of the Wolfenden Report.

Healey notes, moreover, that "behind closed doors the country's top medical experts in 1929 argued seriously that they should be the gatekeepers to the 'right' of female 'transvestites' (women passing as men) to marry their women partners officially in Soviet registry offices," pointing to a view of a particular form of queer female masculinity as particularly amenable to the disciplined life of Communist activism.[69] This remarkable foreshadowing of gay marriage and its relation to emergent styles of lesbian identity in Britain and Western

Europe is a chapter in the history of sexuality yet to be written. The point here is that, contrary to general belief, a hardline proletarianism can coexist with and even encourage forms of queer antinormativity, as the rejection of bourgeois standards of conduct intensifies and develops other forms of social and sexual non-conformity, which themselves shape aspects of proletarian politics.

This relationship is particularly marked for the two queer Communists I address in Chapter 2. In the 1930s, Townsend Warner and Ackland were as notoriously uncompromising in their Communist engagement as they were committed to their lesbian relationship, repeatedly conceiving of their partnership in terms of a shared commitment to proletarian revolution. In other words, they were self-consciously simultaneously a unit of Communist organization and a queer couple – a formation of queer vanguardism that has resonances in radical movements to this day, and that found its most trenchant literary expression in Townsend Warner's *Summer Will Show*. Like Ackland and Townsend Warner, the two central characters' partnership grows in strength and commitment precisely as they become more and more involved with the Communist movement and its demanding, disciplined forms of political praxis. Queer Communism was not a misfiring of the energies of queer life, still less a monstrous denial of gay and lesbian community, but rather an intricate play of proletarian normativity and queer antinormativity. In differing ways, the first two chapters of this book take up the queer possibilities inherent in this play of norms, arguing that Bolshevik discipline and equally stern aesthetic precepts provide vital, counterintuitive resources for antiheteronormative critique.

It is important, however, not to gloss over the limits of Soviet sexual progressivism, nor to elide male and female homosexuality and non-normative gender performance. While certain forms of queer female masculinity were indeed prized by some Bolshevik officials, non-gender-conforming male homosexuality was generally viewed with a degree of official suspicion, at best tolerated in a good worker.[70] Moreover, as the utopianism of the first two years of the First Five-Year Plan gave way to a more hard-nosed, oppressive political culture in 1930–2, proletarian normativity began to assert itself in directly repressive ways. In these years a harsher regime of policing prostitution and public sexuality in general set in; along with lurid fears of homosexual fascists, this anti-lumpenproletarian ethos fed into to what Healey has called the Soviet Union's "homophobic turn" of 1932–4, culminating in the recriminalization of male homosexuality, proposed in 1933 and enacted into law in 1934. The most famous international result of this homophobic turn was the antihomosexual discourse mobilized against André Gide following his criticism of the Soviet Union in 1936, but, as is well known, it had wide repercussions for many more both within and outside the Soviet Union.[71]

As I explore in the second half of this book through readings of Katharine Burdekin and George Orwell, the cruel irony of the late 1930s was that as Communism appeared to open up from the confines of a sectarian proletarianism, and even as more queer writers were drawn into its ambit, it moved further away from the ideological possibilities of a queer Marxism. The Soviet Union's explicitly homophobic turn was undoubtedly at work here, but I focus more closely on the sway of bourgeois normalization motivated by Popular Front antifascism. During this period, Communists and other leftists in Britain and across Europe and the US increasingly recruited a fetishized ideal of the heterosexual family as a key weapon in the antifascist fight, deployed against a fascism insistently coded as queer. In other words, as leftist culture became less vanguardist, it simultaneously became more heteronormative.

The cruel optimism of the Popular Front

In *Cruel Optimism* (2011) Lauren Berlant argues that neoliberal modes of intimate public consciousness are underpinned by and give rise to what she calls "a relation of cruel optimism" that "exists when something you desire is actually an obstacle to your flourishing [. . .] when the object that draws your attachment actively impedes the aim that brought you to it initially." Berlant's influential thesis posits the breakdown of the "social democratic promise" of the postwar American and European state in the last three decades as the political texture through which this affective register emerges. For Berlant, false but pervasive mid-century fantasies of the "good life" are abrogated yet cruelly persist in the reigns of Reagan and Thatcher that completed the dissolution of the Fordist settlement, a process during which the "desire for the political itself" is radically reconfigured as an ever more desperate search for conventional forms of success and intimacy.[72] While specifically ranged against neoliberalism, Berlant's supple account of this structure of feeling might be applied to earlier twentieth-century political formations and other geographic sites – with varying degrees of success.

From the standard anti-Communist position one might schematically transpose Berlant's formulation to Soviet Communism, contending that the system in which so many people placed their hopes was immanently constructed in such a way to frustrate those hopes and in turn reconstitute bourgeois fantasies of the good life in mid- to late twentieth-century Russia and the Soviet Bloc (to the anti-Communist a return to the natural state of affairs). The classic New Left line, however, would hold that the Stalinist state created this relation of false optimism that was not necessarily already present in an earlier revolutionary period.[73] From an antiheteronormative standpoint, this interpretation appears attractive, given the Soviet Union's homophobic turn of 1932–4, when the Stalinist state was brutally consolidating itself. However, this historiography tends to place too much emphasis on the transition from Lenin to Stalin, when in fact the radical egalitarianism of the First Five-Year Plan under Stalin actually opened up vitally antiheteronormative possibilities; it also attributes too much agency to internal Soviet politics in a period when the left was assiduously broadening its appeal, albeit with the uneven blessing of the Comintern. The homophobic repression of the Stalinist state is undeniable but it is therefore not my primary concern here, which is rather with the Popular Front, a wide-ranging and influential political formation promoted and unevenly guided by but not reducible to Stalinist Russia.

It is a cliché of cultural history to assert that the Popular Front period (1934–9) was a time of frustrated hopes, particularly with reference to intellectuals' support of the doomed Republican cause in the Spanish Civil War, their blindness to the purges, and the final insult of the German-Soviet Nonaggression Pact of 1939. It is more accurate to say that this left-liberal coalition succeeded in a certain sense, for it paved the way for the development of the welfare state in Britain via the necessary leveling of the "People's War" and the postwar political consensus. Leftist institutions such as the LBC wove themselves sinuously through public life in World War II, going on to influence the postwar consensus around the welfare state.

Meanwhile, key intellectual personnel of the Popular Front period including Spender, Tom Winteringham, and George Orwell enthusiastically threw themselves into signature activities of the "People's War," whether the class diversity of the Fire Service, propaganda at the BBC, or the Home Guard. However, recognizing the generative aspects of the Popular Front should not lead to an erasure of postwar Britain's economic coercion of women and mounting repression of queers. Precisely as this study stresses the role of this period's coalitional politics in the formation of welfare institutions such as the National Health Service, I argue that the normalizations of the Popular Front must also be held accountable for the sexualized and gendered oppressions of postwar Britain, encoding the limitations of postwar institutions as much as their possibilities. As has often been pointed out, it is impossible to account for the welfare state and the settlement of labor and capital without a powerful regime of normative national community in place, and I argue that in Britain this formation was ideologically dependent on a series of organicist tropes that do not ultimately derive from but were vitally transmitted by Popular Front antifascism.

In other words, in Chapters 3 and 4 I am interested in thinking through what cruel optimism might mean for queer leftists in the genesis rather than the dissolution of the postwar political consensus. The central concept for this genesis is *Gemeinschaft*. Without wading too deeply into late nineteenth- and early twentieth-century sociological debates, I use this term locally to denote a vision of organic community constructed against the inhumanity of fascism and yet attempting to meet it on its own ground. Popular Front *Gemeinschaft* is not primarily ranged against technological modernity, as in some classic accounts of the concept, but rather mobilized to counter fascist claims to monopolize normative national community. In an essentially defensive tactical move, the antifascist left aimed to recuperate a naturalized conception of the nation through "radical patriotism." This strategy was announced by Georgi Dimitrov at the Seventh Congress of the Comintern in 1934, in which the Comintern chief called for a new emphasis on national tradition in the fight against fascism, exhorting Communists and fellow travelers to *"link up their present struggle with its revolutionary traditions and past of our own peoples."*[74] This new stress on the nation immediately began to accrue organicist heft, as Communists and other leftists deployed a Herderian conception of national culture in their ideological struggles against fascism.

Given revolutionary Communism's long disdain for British reformism, British Communists and fellow travelers were particularly susceptible to the lure of this recuperative process, and eagerly set about reconstructing an autochthonous radical history beginning with Saxon resistance to the Norman yoke, running through the Peasant's Revolt, the Levellers and the Diggers, and on to Chartism and modern socialism.[75] This narrative was powerfully generative for British radical historiography via the work of Christopher Hill (particularly his *The English Revolution* [1940]), resulting in important works of mid-century cultural and social history such as Raymond Williams's *Culture and Society* (1958) and E. P. Thompson's *The Making of the English Working Class* (1963). In the 1930s, leftists such as Jack Lindsay, Ralph Fox, and Rex Warner were often rather less subtle in their progressive patriotism, as can be observed in Lindsay's somewhat over-confident declaration that "in England, as nowhere else, we can find a solidly persisting communist tradition."[76] Within this body of work, there was a pervasive recuperation of insular Englishness against expansionist Britishness, and this movement was undoubtedly part of a broader shift in late empire, the leftist iteration of what Esty has called the "redemptive Anglocentrisms" that surfaced as Britain waned in world-historical importance.[77]

Indeed, Popular Front progressive patriotism explicitly presented itself as symbiotic with decolonization. As Dimitrov put it, "the road to victory for the proletarian revolution in the imperialist countries lies *only* through the revolutionary alliance of the working class of the imperialist countries with the national liberation movements in the colonies and dependent countries."[78] In the English context, Ralph Fox's much-read study *The Novel and the People* (1937) folded in the reclamation of English national tradition with a call for the dissolution of the British Empire. Closely echoing Dimitrov, Fox argues that:

> The interest of our people, the true national interest, is in supporting the freedom of the great movements for democracy and national liberty which are revitalizing the Arabian, African, and Indian peoples. An alliance of free peoples will prove a stronger guard for the liberties of all.[79]

Here it is clear that progressive patriotism was centrally constitutive for the Popular Front's claims to anti-imperialism. It is, however, unclear precisely how this articulation would have worked (despite Fox's best efforts on the subject), and indeed Paul Gilroy has pointed out the racist aspects of progressive patriotism as it resurfaced on the later twentieth-century British left, now in the Gramscian guise of the "national-popular" and positioned against Thatcherite nationalism.[80] Gilroy's critique is vital, for it seems impossible to mobilize a defensive concept of a faded imperial power against the right without necessarily replicating some elements of the chauvinism the national-popular is intended to counter. In the case of the 1930s, the problem appears to be even more marked; for all the stated anti-imperialism of progressive patriotism, Anglocentric recuperation rings particularly hollow in a British nation still in control of vast areas of the globe, smacking of a compensatory mechanism rather than a genuinely decolonial position.

Nevertheless, the Popular Front was of course undoubtedly an internationalist formation, marked by what I have elsewhere called a "transnational provincialism": a transnational network of cultural affiliations relying on a Westphalian conception of national integrity.[81] Again, this is a defensive formation, deployed against fascism's abrogation of national sovereignty. While its model of national sovereignty was Westphalian, Popular Front internationalism was at least as invested in mystical conception of national community as in the statecraft of formal treaties, as leftists paradoxically sought to both resolutely counter fascism and yet meet it on its own terms. Civil War Spain was the most pervasive location for this national *Gemeinschaft*; as I shall discuss in more depth shortly, leftist internationalists insistently fetishized an unevenly industrialized Spain as an earthy site of autochthonous radicalism.

From an antiheteronormative position, the dangers of organicist nationalism are clear, for not only does national *Gemeinschaft* require a series of constitutive exclusions, with queers often at or near the top of the list, but the organic itself is necessarily implicated in – if not entirely reducible to – a rejection of non-reproductive life (indeed, Miranda Joseph has underlined the potential normalizations of any concept of community).[82] During the Popular Front period, these exclusions were intensified by a lurid antihomosexual discourse explicitly designating Nazism as queer. The key event in the development of this discourse was the discovery of letters from the SA leader Ernst Röhm that revealed not only his homosexuality, but also that this was known and even (he claimed) accepted within the Nazi Party. The German social democratic press quickly began a homophobic campaign against Röhm that posited his apparent plans for the widespread corruption of German youth as a cornerstone of Nazi politics, rather than the more plausible conjecture that Hitler tolerated Röhm as an effective street fighter and old comrade – or, indeed, that Hitler didn't have a particularly deeply-held position on sexuality at this point. Despite continuing to support the abolition of the sodomy statute, the German Communist Party (KPD) joined in this campaign, given further impetus by antifascist claims that the Reichstag arsonist Marinus van der Lubbe was corrupted by "homosexual storm troopers" rather than acting on orders from the Comintern as the Nazis maintained.[83] In spite of Hitler's purge of Röhm and his SA in 1934, a series of associations between homosexuality, sadomasochism, and fascism became entrenched on the antifascist left, compounding and intensifying the heteronormalizing effects of the Popular Front national *Gemeinschaft* – an organic national community not only under threat from fascist abrogation of its sovereignty, but also imperiled by Nazi perversion. Faced with such threats, reproductive heterosexuality and cultural nationalism become revolutionary postulates for the Popular Front, a formulation I call *transformative normalcy*.

Chapter 3, "The Hymning of Heterosexuality: Katharine Burdekin and the Popular Front" interrogates this formulation through a reading of Katharine Burdekin's dystopian novel *Swastika Night* (1937) alongside an unpublished manuscript from her archive. Burdekin (1896–1963) was a prolific but neglected queer feminist recuperated in the 1980s and 1990s as an important dystopian writer. Her most famous novel, *Swastika Night*, is set 700 years after total Axis victory, when Jews have been wiped out, and women have become reproductive chattel. Burdekin's novel has been praised for offering a feminist critique of the phallic masculinity of fascism, but I focus instead on *Swastika Night*'s vigilant homophobia and cultural nationalism. Throughout the text, male homoeroticism is cast as the cornerstone of Nazi ideological praxis, while the novel's very English hero, Alfred, emerges as a revolutionary leader precisely because of his "normality" – a word that recurs throughout the text, always with heavy valorization. In contrast to his macho, psychologically sickly queer German friend Hermann, the stoutly heterosexual Englishman is a paragon of transformative normalcy, and holds the key not only to English emancipation from the Nazi yoke, but also to a world revolution predicated upon respect for national tradition and loving heterosexuality. Chapter 3 argues that *Swastika Night*'s hymning of heterosexuality deeply troubles the novel's feminism, as Burdekin mobilizes gender against sexuality while participating in the strategic entrenchment of the Popular Front's homophobic nationalism. Burdekin's deployment is part of a much broader historical chiasmus between paradigms of gender presentation and models of object choice as the fundamental markers of sexual identity – an overlap that is well known, but which has been hitherto unexplored in conjunction with the Popular Front.

Burdekin's unpublished novel *No Compromise* (c. 1935) is a prequel to *Swastika Night* and a leftist rewrite of *Lady Chatterley's Lover*. Set in 1940, the novel features a great-souled Communist revolutionary named Adam, who has a passionate companionate marriage with a weak upper-class woman, Romona. This pairing becomes metonymic for Popular Front coalitional politics through the recuperative power of heterosexual union between bourgeois and proletarian, and yet also paradoxically participates in Burdekin's proto-radical-feminist project of the dissolution of gender, as can be seen in her 1934 novel *Proud Man*. Burdekin's novels of the mid-1930s reveal the fraught demands of queer writers' participation in Popular Front cultural politics, the cruel optimism of an apparently inclusive formation that fundamentally excludes and demonizes sexual and gender dissidents. This problematic was intensified and gained in prominence during the Spanish Civil War, as autochthonous national community increasingly came to define leftist internationalism, and more and more queer writers were drawn into the movement.

From the Spanish earth to Deep England

John Sutherland has called Stephen Spender's relationship with the ex-Guardsman Tony Hyndman the most famous homosexual coupling since Wilde and Bosie.[84] Whether or not this is quite true, the travails of Hyndman and Spender in the Spanish Civil War have certainly become paradigmatic for usual interpretations of the relationship between queer writers and Communism during the period. The two men having split with Spender's marriage to Inez Holden, Hyndman joined the CPGB and then the International Brigades, going out to fight in Spain in 1936; Spender also joined the Party and was sent by Harry Pollitt on a fact-finding mission the same year. Hyndman quickly became ill and disillusioned with harsh brigade discipline, and Spender spent great energies in rescuing him from prison, encountering brutal homophobia from Communist soldiers and officials. Whether sympathetically or in more hostile fashion, this story is generally interpreted as demonstrating the complete incompatibility of queer life with Communist discipline as the flighty (or bracingly antinormative) Hyndman is unable to live the disciplined life of the Communist soldier, while the myopically infatuated (or brave, principled) Spender gives up his Communist commitment to save his boyfriend from the rigors of military life.

Although the basic outline of this narrative is undeniable, it has been accorded too much heuristic power for an exclusive focus on two queer men. Its overarching assumptions are belied by, for instance, the queer Communist officer whom Spender met in his search for Hyndman, who both maintained his role within the Brigade and also helped Spender to locate his boyfriend, or the continuing commitment of Townsend Warner and Ackland during their (admittedly less taxing) trips to Spain. But Civil War Spain was the site of further entrenchment of leftist homophobia, and not only for the obvious reason of the conventional heterosexism of militarized masculinity. More important, in fact, was leftist writers' elevation of national *Gemeinschaft* and heterosexual union to pride of place in the Popular Front's ideological armory.

Perhaps the most famous example of all these heteronormalizing trends can be found in Hemingway's Pulitzer Prize-nominated novel *For Whom the Bell Tolls* (1941). Hemingway's narrative focuses on an all-American Hispanophile internationalist, Robert Jordan, who is sent on a dangerous mission to blow up a bridge behind enemy lines. He is aided (and sometimes hindered) by a group of Spanish peasant partisans, including the earthy, politically-committed virago Pilar, and her weak-willed, shell-shocked husband, Pablo. Most important however is the young, beautiful victim of fascist atrocities

Maria, with whom Jordan has a passionate, short-lived affair. Their coupling in an open-air setting is repeatedly couched in terms that foreshadow Jordan's mission: he makes the earth move in more ways than one. Hemingway's novel pervasively articulates heterosexual sex, the Spanish *Gemeinschaft* as object of internationalist intervention, and heroic masculinity in the characteristic ideological formation of Popular Front engagement in the Spanish Civil War; the gender non-conforming Pilar also explicitly repudiates lesbian desire ("I am no *tortillera* but a woman made for men"), and repeatedly stresses her sexual love for men in a fairly transparent purging of the specter of queer sexuality from Hemingway's text.[85]

The characteristic trope of the "Spanish earth" was also the title of a much-celebrated documentary film, *The Spanish Earth* (1937).[86] The film's title immediately and explicitly proclaims its autochthonous conception of the Spanish nation, as does the central narrative thread concerning the plans for the irrigation of farm lands reclaimed from absentee landlords, which unfurls alongside footage of the front and to the sound of Spanish folk music. As Thomas Waugh has argued, *The Spanish Earth* is a paradigmatic product of the Popular Front, in which "the signals of tradition, exoticism, and patience, conventionally attached to the peasant icon in western culture, overshadow the signal of revolution."[87] Another important document of transnational provincialism, this was a peasant icon brought to the screen through transnational collaboration, featuring Ernest Hemingway, who narrated and wrote the script, Dutch director Joris Ivens, and editor Helen Van Dongen, with Jean Renoir narrating the French-language version. Apart from some conventional shots of soldiers leaving their wives and lovers for the front, *The Spanish Earth* is not particularly concerned with heterosexuality, but rather heroic masculinity. Most important for our purposes is the film's insistent and explicit proclamation of an organic community under threat – a formulation deeply complicit with if not entirely reducible to reproductivist heterosexuality.

Centrally featuring a similar irrigation project, Townsend Warner's 1938 novel *After the Death of Don Juan* is a feminist rewrite of *The Spanish Earth*. As the title indicates, it is also a retelling of the Don Juan narrative best known through Molière's play *Don Juan, or The Feast With the Statue* (1665) and Mozart's opera *Don Giovanni* (1787). Townsend Warner's variant sees the legendary seducer survive his supposed descent into hellfire, reconfigured as a story cooked up by Don Juan in an attempt to escape the attentions of his nymphomaniac admirers and the embarrassment of a disfiguring skin disease. One of the women in his pursuit is Doña Ana, in Townsend Warner's retelling a sexually voracious hypocrite who pursues Juan beyond the grave, persuading her foolish husband Ottavio to travel to Juan's ancestral home to break the news of his death to his family. Here they meet Juan's father Don Saturno, an ineffectual liberal-minded scholar and landowner, forever dreaming up schemes for the improvement of his peasants that never come to pass. When Juan does inevitably return to the village of his birth, predictably seeking funds from his father, mayhem breaks out, culminating in an abortive peasant's revolt brutally crushed by a detachment of troops headed by the proto-fascist Juan. At the heart of this abortive rebellion was one of Don Saturno's failed schemes. For years he had been planning the irrigation of his lands, which are almost barren from poor agricultural decisions and drought; the peasants naturally were very excited to hear of this plan, and disappointed that it had never come to pass. Apart from Saturno's aristocratic bumbling and failure to understand the plight of the poor, one of the main reasons for the plan's stalling was Juan's incessant spending, which put a drain on the estate's funds. Upon learning that the libertine was apparently dead, the prospect of the irrigation scheme again looked like a possibility. In an elegantly constructed allegory of fascist economic policy, Juan actually turns out to be in favor of the scheme, for he then intends to reintroduce serfdom and turn a profit from the rationalized land.

The novel's satire of Don Juan's brittle proto-fascist masculinity does not preclude a repudiation of queer desire. Although not as glaringly homophobic as *Swastika Night*, Townsend Warner's novel similarly mobilizes gender against sexuality, revealing how a critique of heroic masculinity can go hand in hand with the Popular Front's organicist heteronormalizations (indeed, as Ian Patterson has pointed out, particularly following the fascist attack on Guernica, notions of the family and femininity were increasingly mobilized by some anti-fascists against violent masculinism).[88] Like *The Spanish Earth*, the novel ultimately dissolves into a hymn for peasant values, effacing queer desire in the process; foreshadowing Hemingway's novel, *After the Death* sees homosexuality as incompatible with earthy peasant life. The novel features a few glancing references to male homosexuality – seen as the ulterior motive for the Commander's promotion of the handsome, preening Ottavio's suit for his daughter's hand, and by peasant women as the exclusive preserve of a decayed aristocracy. In a comic episode when Ottavio foolishly mistakes Ana's sleeping moans of desire for Juan as a ghostly presence, the hapless nobleman invites the chaplain to perform an exorcism of the bedchamber. A slapstick scene ensues, which is falsely rumored to be a passionate fuck:

> It seems that all yesterday morning the two were bawling for a bed. My cousin Antonita told me. Locked up in the bedroom they were, the blood bounding in their veins, their faces red as fire, the chaplain simpering, the gentleman panting like a tiger.[89]

The peasant woman's younger companion asks naïvely, "but surely it is a great sin," to which her knowing friend replies, "but the gentleman is an officer in the army [. . .] the gentlemen in the army are good Catholics, so they love their priests." Here male homosexuality is figured as a hypocritical coupling between the aristocracy and the church, emblematic for the ills of the Spanish polity. The younger woman goes on to remark that common soldiers do not engage in such practices, which elicits the response, "No. They have to drudge along with womankind. Black beans and long families for them."[90] Although this comment is made with a certain irony, the force of this exchange is to intertwine aristocratic decadence and homoeroticism as blockages to the flourishing of peasant life, even as it slyly suggests that smaller families might also be the answer to some of Spain's woes. Here the point is not to castigate *After the Death* for its exclusions, but rather to stress the way in which some Spanish Civil War literature participates in a process of heteronormalization under the sign of a *Gemeinschaft* under threat from fascism. Like Burdekin's homo-fascism, Townsend Warner's participation in this process reveals the cruel optimism of the Popular Front for queer writers, the demonization of non-normative desire under the sign of an apparently capacious populist formation.

A few caveats are in order here. The sexual politics of the Spanish Civil War requires book-length treatment, and for this reason Spain is not a major feature of the chapters that follow. Some readers might see this as a major omission, but it is a necessary limitation as I would not be able to do this transnational topic justice from within the confines of my study of queer Communism in Britain. However, I do hope to have very roughly sketched some possible new directions for the study of the Spanish Civil War, in particular in terms of the problematic relationship between heterosexuality and organic national community deployed by some Republican cultural producers. Work on Spain might also further explore the ways in which varying notions of femininity are mobilized against queer male sexuality in an especially powerful and troubling way by the liberal left during the period.

The complex and variegated constitution of the Popular Front itself – its iterations across Europe and beyond, its differing social formations, artistic affiliations, and so on – might also be seen to have been somewhat glossed over in my account (particularly when compared to Denning's capacious and nuanced account of the US Popular Front in *The Cultural Front*). But my concern here is with a particular, powerfully heteronormalizing effect of Popular Front culture, particularly in Britain. I am not exhaustively equating Popular Front cultural production with either homophobia or nationalism, but rather examining the ways in which certain emergent structures of feeling call forth these dominating effects. Finally, I would also like to point out that I do not seek to entirely reduce organicist tropes or rural life to reproductive heterosexuality – an assumption implicated in what has recently become known as "metronormativity."[91] Townsend Warner's queer vanguardism in the heart of rural Dorset should give pause to this complete foreclosure; it's not as though she and Ackland would somehow have been queerer if they lived in London and eschewed gardening. My intention is not to assert an exhaustive identification of queer life with urban modernity, but rather to reconstruct the genealogy of the Popular Front's particular mobilizations of organic community and their heteronormalizing effects for the British left and the formation of the postwar welfare state.

Chapter 4, "Orwell's Hope in the Proles," turns to a major conduit for this genealogy. One of the most unashamedly homophobic and antifeminist writers of the British left, Orwell's troubling sexual politics have often been pointed out.[92] Rather than focusing on his antihomosexual or misogynistic polemics, in this chapter I examine instead his obsessive desire to maintain the British birth rate. From his early novels *Keep the Aspidistra Flying* (1936) and *A Clergyman's Daughter* (1934), through his patriotic wartime writings such as *The Lion and the Unicorn* (1941) right up to his final dystopia *Nineteen Eighty-Four* (1949), Orwell anxiously dwells on the need to maintain the reproductive capabilities of the nation, apparently under desperate threat from a decayed masculinity and a frigid femininity. Focusing on a series of book-length works Orwell did not want reprinted alongside a series of salient moments from his *Complete Works*, I argue that this pervasive philoprogenitivism is the culmination of the transformative normalcy of the Popular Front. Orwell's famous declaration that "if there was hope, it lay in the proles!" comes into clearer focus, then, when we consider the original Latin use of the term to mean offspring – the only property owned by the poor and thus their only contribution to society. Orwell of course knew this usage, and I argue that pronatalism rather than socialism is the guiding force of his life's work.

To categorize the ardently anti-Communist Orwell as Popular Frontist is somewhat counterintuitive, given his many well-known polemics explicitly ranged against this Soviet-influenced formation. But recently a number of scholars have begun to unearth the marked similarities between his authorship and the characteristic ideological maneuvers of the Popular Front. Nick Hubble, for instance, has argued that Orwell pursues the dual project of both satirizing and participating in Popular Front cultural politics, and Philip Bounds has stressed the ways in which the "revolutionary patriotism" that is often seen as entirely, eccentrically Orwell's was in fact a marked feature of British Communist cultural discourse picked up by and modulated by Orwell throughout the 1930s and 1940s.[93] Drawing on this work and on my formulations of transnational provincialism and transformative normalcy, I contend that Orwell's ongoing obsession with national reproduction emerges through his engagement with the construction of Popular Front internationalism through organic national community. The usual narrative holds that Orwell's movement toward patriotism in 1940 was an abrupt about-turn, apparently a conversion that happened to him following a dream, as he claimed at the time.[94] However, the final pages from *Homage to Catalonia* (1938) tell a different story. By the end of the text, Orwell's Spain has become the site of a nationalism by proxy, as the precarious internationalist imaginary of the Spanish Civil War collapses and Orwell expresses a curious desire for the Spanish to "drive all the foreigners out of Spain."[95] In the concluding passage, Orwell then turns to the English countryside, which, in the signature move of nationalist rhetoric, is rendered vulnerable from a "roar of bombs" and thus desperately in need of protection, a valorization that in turn necessitates a national awakening.[96] In this passage and in his famous wartime essays Orwell mobilizes a vision of what Patrick Wright and Angus Caldor have identified as "Deep England," the softened southern English landscape that became an iconic image in World War II propaganda.

Chapter 4 closes with a reading of *Nineteen Eighty-Four* (1949) as the final foreclosure of non-normative desire implied by the Popular Front's national *Gemeinschaft* and the normalizations of the postwar British nation state. In the novel's depiction of Winston's and Julia's defiant affair, Orwell deploys a particularly desperate version of transformative normalcy in a dystopian vision where heterosexuality and organic community are rendered as all but impossible. In *Nineteen Eighty-Four*'s infamous torture scene, the antifascist injunction against Nazi homoeroticism is recapitulated in an anti-Communist register as statist perversion; erotically disciplined by O'Brien, Winston admits his love of Big Brother. For all Orwell's polemics against the Popular Front, I argue that his authorship was a major node of transmission between the normalizations of the Popular Front and the homely national imaginary of postwar Britain.

The sexual and gender oppressions of this imaginary are well known, but it is worth pausing over one particularly pronatalist cultural product, Humphrey Jennings's *A Diary for Timothy* (1945). Produced by Basil Wright for the Crown Film Unit with a narration by E. M. Forster read by Michael Redgrave, the film follows the first months in the life of a baby born on the fifth anniversary of the outbreak of war. Filming started in 1944, and much to the annoyance of Wright, Jennings followed the events of the end of the war as they happened, which has led some commentators to remark on the film's "ambiguity."[97] Yet the message is obvious. The narration is addressed to the baby throughout: "you're in danger, Tim, you're in danger!" the narrator exclaims – somewhat improbably given Tim is in a comfortable home in rural Oxfordshire at a time when V2 attacks were becoming less and less common (the narrator does, however, also cursorily acknowledge how "lucky" Tim is). A signature product of the "People's War," *A Diary for Timothy* also features a cast of working-class characters fighting on the home front who express hope for a better postwar world; a Welsh miner points out that the institutions for the welfare state are already in place, and that there's "nothing to stop us at all" from building a more egalitarian society after the end of the war. Yet this astute proletarian is overshadowed by the middle-class Tim, the film's incessant focus. There are some very uncomfortable cuts indeed, from a plane bombing Germany to Tim suckling a bottle shaped very similarly to the bombs, and then, in a hideously overblown climax, a close-up of Tim drooling at a Christmas party is accompanied by the words of the carol "Oh come let us adore him." Tim is a kind of inverted Christ here, held apart from the suffering carried out on his behalf and yet talismanic for totalizing cultural claims. But Tim is also the future, as he is constantly reminded of the task of postwar reconstruction; a hopeful future, to be sure, for in a characteristically Forsterian line, Tim is told that "part of your bother, Tim, will be growing up free." The narrator explains, somewhat superfluously, that "we had a feeling deep down inside us that we were fighting for you – for you and all the other babies," an assertion that is repeated almost verbatim later in the film.[98] Tim is the future.

In *No Future: Queer Theory and the Death Drive* (2004), Lee Edelman launched a ferocious polemic against the cult of the child, arguing that political futurity is so complicit with reproductivist heterosexuality that the political itself must be combated in the name of queer antinormativity.[99] Quite obviously, I don't entirely endorse Edelman's thesis, for a major argument of *Queer Communism* is that vital forms of non-reproductivist futurity emerge from a creative synergy between queer cultural producers and Soviet Marxism. But, as much as Edelman's starting point, the Clintonian US, postwar Britain was saturated with the politics of protecting the child, perhaps more than any other time in British history. Indeed, watching Tim from the perspective of contemporary queer theory, one is left with the uncanny sense that Edelman somehow traveled back in time to produce a perfect illustration of his thesis. Reading Orwell on the British birth rate creates a similar impression, illustrating the importance of Edelman's argument for any reading of the sexual politics of postwar Britain; again, however, a complete foreclosure might be too neat, for it goes without saying that queer life continued, even in the inauspicious circumstances of 1950s Britain.

Respectful conclusions

The coda to *Queer Communism* takes up an underexplored conjecture of social and literary history: the later careers of the Auden group and the figure of the "respectable homosexual." As Matt Houlbrook and others have documented, the late 1940s and early 1950s saw a marked rise in antihomosexual repression in Britain's capital, with arrests for indecent acts in London peaking in 1947, and lurid tabloid exposés mounting during the period.[100] The local reasons for the arrest figures are complex, but on a longer view, they are clearly part of a broader heteronormalizing movement in postwar British society, which Chapter 4 argues was inflected by the legacy of the Popular Front transmitted through Orwell via the "People's War." Arising in part to counter this alarming trend, the Wolfenden Report was commissioned in 1954 to investigate male homosexuality and female prostitution. In the course of the report, a number of bourgeois homosexuals provided testimony in which they maintained their normality, social productivity, and argued that their desires should not be criminalized. Accordingly, the Report recommended in 1957 that consenting acts between adults over the age of twenty-one carried out in private should be decriminalized, a recommendation that was enacted into law in 1967, signaling the full arrival of the respectable homosexual in mid-century Britain.

As prominent, upper-middle-class queer men entering middle age during this period, Auden, Spender, Isherwood, and Lehmann might on first glance appear to be quintessential examples of this relatively new personage. But none of them individually quite fits the monogamous mold. The discourse of respectability entailed a complete rejection of bisexuality, public sex (and "indiscretion" more broadly), and transactional sex – a series of exclusions that go back to Weimar Berlin homosexual advocacy, encapsulated in Magnus Hirschfeld's assertion that the male hustler was "bisexual at best."[101] None of the Auden group was entirely innocent of these transgressive forms of queer sexuality (nor, indeed, were the men who testified for Wolfenden). The Coda to *Queer Communism* examines how some of their memoirs registered and resisted this process of normalization in complexly mediated ways, as does a short story by Sylvia Townsend Warner that probes the question of respectability and the couple form.

I examine two queer memoirs of 1976, Isherwood's *Christopher and His Kind*, and Lehmann's fictionalized *In the Purely Pagan Sense*, alongside Sylvia Townsend Warner's 1964 short story, "A Love Match." Exploring these three texts' remediations of queer life of the 1930s, I argue that Isherwood and Lehmann simultaneously articulate bourgeois homosexuality and a queer resistance to that paradigm. Neither arguing that Lehmann's and Isherwood's memoirs are entirely harnessed to the forces of normalization, nor that they always resist such forces, I contend that these queer memoirs of the 1930s also exhibit the push-pull of gay rights and queer antinormativity, a constitutive paradox of later twentieth-century and twenty-first-century sexual politics in both Britain and the US. In a very different register but to some similar effects, Townsend Warner's wry allegory interrogates the limitations of domestic respectability and the concept of the closet through a tale of consensual incest between a very bourgeois brother and sister between the wars.

To deploy Sedgwick's much-cited dichotomy, it might be observed that my argument in Chapters 3 and 4 is somewhat "paranoid," Chapters 1 and 2 are earnestly "reparative," and the Coda a synthesis between the tendencies.[102] Broadly, this is perhaps true. But instead of these categories, I would rather position *Queer Communism* in terms of genealogical history and polemical critique. These strains are intertwined throughout, whether I am seeking to recapture the utopian aspects of queer writers' engagements with Soviet Marxism, interrogating the Popular Front's homophobic nationalism, or mediating gay memoir and queer antinormativity. It is inevitable that certain irritants will crop up with this type of work, and I ask for the reader's patience as these arise. Put another way, while I have aimed to practice responsible literary history, my account is patently partisan. For this I make no apology.

Alongside the reparative impulse catalyzed by Sedgwick, another prominent development in queer theory has been a movement away from progressivist and/or triumphalist narratives of gay and lesbian history. As is well known, a trenchant critique of Whiggish sexual politics was part of queer theory's self-constitution right from the start. What has become known (perhaps inaccurately) as the "anti-relational thesis" in the work of Leo Bersani and Edelman unmoors social-political virtue from queer – particularly gay male – sexuality.[103] In a different but related vein, recent work by Heather Love, Halberstam, and others has stressed a politics of loss and failure as central to queer experience and cultural history, and Elizabeth Freeman has also developed the concept of "chrononormativity" in opposition to linear conceptions of history instantiated by liberal narratives of progress.[104] I do not deny the vital importance of this work, but *Queer Communism* takes a rather different approach. Drawing on Muñoz's subtle model of revolutionary hope in *Cruising Utopia*, but exploring a very different archive, I argue that too many promisingly queer kids have been thrown out with the bathwater of liberal triumphalism. Specifically, the nascent but quickly foreclosed possibilities of queer Communism reveal how one does not have to hold to a progressivist chrononormative history in order to locate radical potential in leftist formations of the 1930s. Quite the contrary. The genealogy of queer Communism operates in a series of complex dialectical relays, anticipations and retractions, deferred actions, flickering utopias, and uncomfortable byways. There could be few formations less assimilable to mainstream gay and lesbian politics than gender-dissident Leninism or proletarianizing self-instrumentalization; yet rather than failure or loss here we might see some decidedly revolutionary possibilities.

Chapter 1

Boy Meets Camera: Christopher Isherwood and Sergei Tretiakov

Ned Beauman's novel *The Teleportation Accident* (2013) features a queer Englishman named Rupert Rackenham, a bisexual ex-public schoolboy, hanger-on to the Weimar Berlin cultural scene, and clearly a composite for the "Auden gang." Always toting a Leica camera (the favored make of the group), Rackenham stalks Berlin for material, ruthlessly exploiting the cultural scenes he encounters for journalistic and novelistic copy. But Rackenham's claim to any form of photographic record is false: his camera case is empty, hollowed out to stash the cocaine he sells to make cash. Beauman's recent depiction is perhaps the most satirically biting in a series of representations of the Auden group's supposedly parasitic relationship to Weimar culture, and more specifically Christopher Isherwood's apparently apolitical camera-eye gaze, a mere alibi for unbridled hedonism. Indeed, Isherwood's long stay in the city has become paradigmatic for an opposition between the frivolous pleasures of Weimar sexual freedom – "Isherwood's Berlin," as it has come to be known – and the serious business of interwar German politics, at which, so the story goes, the hedonistic Isherwood gazes either passively or exploitatively.

Indeed, Isherwood's famous statement of self-instrumentalization, "I am a camera," is at once the most cited and the most misread phrase in his authorship.[1] It has commonly been seen as a trope for Isherwood's detached, "passive" documentary method, often involving a crude conflation of Isherwood's narrator with his authorial position.[2] Labeling the queer writer a passive observer, this interpretation insists upon the superficiality of Isherwood's leftist commitment in the 1930s, bolstering the view of his "parlour socialism" advanced by Isherwood himself in later life.[3] On one level this is rather surprising, given the solidly Marxist credentials of the two other best-known contemporary exponents of the camera-eye trope: John Dos Passos and Dziga Vertov are hardly generally considered to be "dazzled spectator[s] of commodity culture," as one reading of *The Berlin Stories* (1935–9) remarks of Isherwood's authorial perspective.[4] Even sophisticated discussions rearticulate a sense of Isherwood's wavering political commitment. Michael North rightly points out that Isherwood's camera-eye does not reveal a belief in the camera as "dispassionate and disengaged," and yet he still argues that, for Isherwood, "observation was almost essentially distinct from action," separating Isherwood from more "confident" practitioners of the documentary style.[5] And in the most extreme, most glaringly heteronormative version of this position, the supposed passivity of Isherwood's camera-eye obviates the possibility of observation itself. Simultaneously evacuating Isherwood of any radical leftist potential and rehearsing a cliché about queer consciousness, Lara Feigel argues that in his camera-eye mode "Isherwood is more victim than witness of his world."[6] Whether as the gaze of exploiter or victim, Isherwood's camera-eye is rendered thoroughly apolitical in these accounts.

This erasure of leftist commitment from *The Berlin Stories* is shared by other work keen to emphasize Isherwood's contribution to an emergent queer politics, set in opposition to a dogmatic and sexually conservative Stalinist Marxism. In Jamie Carr's recent study, Communism merely figures as "a regime that persecuted homosexuals," and Marxist artistic production is reduced to "Socialist Realism."[7] Carr reads Isherwood's career as a progression toward an anti-identitarian queer politics engaged with a critique of the tyranny of the subject as it appears in Marxism and other oppressive structures, and consequently disregards Isherwood's works of the 1930s as written under the sway of such regimes. Yet it seems impossible to account for Isherwood's development of a queer critique of the subject without examining the camera-I trope in *The Berlin Stories*, clearly a statement of antihumanism; nor can it be ignored that Weimar Berlin was the site of intense debate among Marxists around the questions of antihumanist aesthetics and revolutionary subjectivity, precisely at the time when Isherwood was living in the city and mixing in such circles.

Archival research suggests, moreover, that Isherwood was far more engaged with Marxism in Berlin than he later claimed. Of particular interest is his correspondence with his friend and publisher John Lehmann, as Isherwood vehemently opposed the publication of their letters, ostensibly on the grounds that it would be "dull" – but also for fear of their political content (and, needless to say, their sexual content).[8] For instance, in an undated letter to Lehmann – given the topical political references, presumably written in November 1932 – Isherwood exclaims "Hurrah! Berlin is Red. We're leading."[9] Isherwood's triumphant declaration that "Berlin is Red" has been cited sneeringly by a number of critics.[10] However, what is often overlooked and generally left unsaid is what follows: Isherwood goes on to remark in the same letter that he has "just got a fat letter from Gibarti to translate into English." This would appear to be Louis Gibarti, a key figure in the Comintern and a major presence in the Communist-run international aid and propaganda organization, *Internationale Arbeiterhilfe* (IAH). The certainty with which we might make this identification is bolstered by considering one of Isherwood's neighbors in Berlin. As Isherwood recounts in *Christopher and His Kind*, for a period he lived next door to the queer sexologist Magnus Hirschfeld's Institute for Sexual Research, in an apartment building owned by Hirschfeld's sister. Isherwood's friendship with Hirschfeld and his stay next to the Institute is well known, but it has not been noted that one of Isherwood's fellow-tenants was Gibarti's boss and head of IAH, Willi Münzenberg, a central figure in the Comintern and the German Communist Party (KPD), who played a key role in recruiting western intellectuals to the Communist Party.[11] During his time in Berlin Isherwood directly resided at an intersection between queer and Marxist fields of activism and engagement. I take this triangulation between Isherwood, Hirschfeld, and Münzenberg as paradigmatic for Isherwood's formation in Berlin, and for his narrative method in *The Berlin Stories*, which emerges from a dual commitment to both queer and Marxist literary praxes.

To maintain that Isherwood drew on Marxist literary models is not new; Martin Esslin, for instance, has argued that he was influenced by Bertolt Brecht, particularly in the plays he produced in collaboration with W. H. Auden.[12] However, in what follows I instead re-examine *The Berlin Stories* through an important dispute in the period's Marxist aesthetics, between Brecht's friend and collaborator Sergei Tretiakov and Georg Lukács, a frame that enables a new reading of Isherwood's authorship as deeply politically engaged. Indeed, far from being a lukewarm socialist in his youth who later became a somewhat middlebrow bourgeois figure in gay literature, Isherwood offers a queer Marxist contribution to radical literary history, revealing a striking cultural-historical possibility: the queer potential of the First Five-Year Plan (1928–32).

In what follows I first outline the contours of the debate between Tretiakov and Lukács, before reading Isherwood's queer antihumanist literary praxis in *Goodbye to Berlin* (1939) through this debate. I examine how *The Last of Mr. Norris* (1935) embodies and critiques the problematic of Lukácsian realism, also contending that this text revalues the queer cross-class intimacies for which bourgeois leftist writers of the period were famous and which have been generally disparaged as an exploitative taste for "rough trade." However, turning to his collaborative travel volume about the Second Sino-Japanese War, *Journey to a War* (1939), I argue that Isherwood's capacious vision of radical queer life contracts in the face of racial difference, as he swaps a queer red front for the imperial gaze of the "homoerotics of Orientalism."[13] In conclusion, I then turn to Isherwood's memoir, *Christopher and His Kind* (1976). Drawing on Isherwood's unpublished correspondence with his friend Edward Upward, I argue that Marxist aesthetics continues to inform Isherwood's later writing, even as he explicitly repudiates his Marxist past.

Crass fetishism

Sergei Tretiakov (1892–1937) confounds many of the usual narratives about Soviet culture in the interwar period. Simultaneously a committed internationalist and a Soviet patriot, Tretiakov was, in Katerina Clark's words, a "cosmopolitan patriot" who functioned as an "intermediary" between Soviet culture and the international scene.[14] Tretiakov's most important international connections were China, where he lived in 1924–5, and about which he wrote the celebrated play *Roar, China!* (1926), and Weimar Germany, where his friends included Bertolt Brecht, the photomontage artist John Heartfield, and the composer Hanns Eisler.[15] Tretiakov was deeply committed both to the Soviet project and to avant-garde aesthetics. Strikingly, given Karl Radek's infamous denunciation of James Joyce at the 1934

Soviet Writers' Congress, in 1935–6 Tretiakov oversaw a Russian translation of episodes 1–10 of *Ulysses* as the editor of the Russian edition of the Soviet multi-lingual journal *International Literature*, a post he held until he was purged in 1937. Although he promoted western modernists such as Joyce, Tretiakov's anti-subjectivist literary mode was far removed from Joycean modernism. Marked by austere political commitment, Tretiakov's engagements also included the new configurations of gender politics in post-revolutionary Russia, as seen in his 1926 play *I Want a Baby*. Working as a photographer, prose author, dramatist, reporter, film scenarist, radio commentator, and lyrical poet, and collaborating with many figures including Brecht and Sergei Eisenstein, Tretiakov came to be convinced that the old genres of bourgeois art must be blown apart in a new collective cultural praxis that he called "factography."

Taking the newspaper as its privileged form and the inscription of facts as its organizing principle, factography re-evaluated artistic genre as a fluid category open to the shifting demands of revolutionary social transformation and rapidly rising literacy rates. In essays including "The Biography of the Object," "The New Leo Tolstoy," and "The Writer and the Socialist Village," Tretiakov argued for the complete deletion of the sovereign human subject from the new literature: the author-function would be dissolved in a newly collectivized and de-professionalized army of worker-writers, and the hero would be dethroned by an object biography in which material production would take precedence over psychological development.[16] As Clark argues, with its stress on collectivization, proletarianizing zeal, and manic productivity, factography was presented as the cultural form *par excellence* of the First Five-Year Plan. Tretiakov's two-year stay at a *kolkhoz* (collective farm) was crucial for this identification, as he played an active role in the collective and used his experiences as the centerpiece of key essays and addresses including "The Writer and the Socialist Village." The importance of Tretiakov's stay at this model site of the First Five-Year Plan should not be underestimated, for the processes of collectivization he encountered there became paradigmatic for his militantly anti-individualistic conception of factographic cultural work.[17] At first glance factography shares many features with the related Western European movement of documentary; however, as Devin Fore points out, it offers a far more radical epistemological frame in which literary production sets out not only to describe the world, but to actively change it.[18] Associated with the journal *Novyi LEF* (which Tretiakov edited for a time), and opposed both to the pervasive humanism of proletarian realism and to the abstractions of Constructivism, factography formed an important part of the Soviet avant-garde in the late 1920s and early 1930s.

Tretiakov also made a huge impact on the Berlin literary scene during his extended visit to the city in 1930–1, with his famous lecture on January 21, 1931, "The Writer and the Socialist Village," attracting particular attention.[19] Tretiakov's lecture laid out bold proposals for his new art of collectivized and committed fact-inscribing, designed "not simply to capture reality, but also to change it in the course of class struggle," which met with mixed reactions from the German intelligentsia.[20] In particular, Tretiakov's factography was completely opposed to Lukácsian realism, and Tretiakov came in for stern rebuke from Lukács, an important voice on aesthetics in the KPD who was also living in Berlin in the early 1930s. According to Lukács, any literature of fact would always fail to penetrate to the objective social and economic realities undergirding everyday phenomena, attending to only one side of the dialectic between the concrete and the abstract, and remaining mired in the particular at the expense of the totality. Accordingly, in "Reportage or Portrayal" (1932) Lukács attacked the "pseudo-science and a pseudo-art" involved in factography's cross-fertilization of journalism and literature, and described Tretiakov as "part of a worrying trend" toward reportage in fiction; indeed Tretiakov is "even more crass" than the main target of Lukács's critique, Ernst Ottwalt.[21] Generally unbeknownst to contemporary Anglophone readers, Lukács continued his polemic in an essay today known in Arthur Khan's translation as "Narrate or Describe." In this translation Lukács's closing polemic against Tretiakov is omitted, but it is included in a little-known early translation in *International Literature*. In "Narration vs. Description" (1937), Tretiakov again appears as "an extreme case of a universally existing tendency." As in his earlier essay, Lukács is scathing of Tretiakov's new model for literary production: "of course, the theory of such 'biography of objects' is seldom proclaimed so openly nor is it so crassly fetishistic in its practical application as in Tretiakov's declaration."[22] The antagonism between Tretiakov and Lukács presents a series of stark contraries, opposing a virtuosic objectivism to a mediated sense of typicality, a crusading transformative conception of literary production to a soberly classical reflection theory, and a radical antihumanism to an earnest humanism.

Camera-I

Isherwood's comments on the genesis of *The Berlin Stories* reveal some clues to his engagement with the Tretiakov/Lukács debate. In March 1932, Isherwood wrote to Lehmann about the novel he was starting, which became the two volumes collected as *The Berlin Stories*: "it is written entirely in the form of a diary, without any breaks in the narrative. It will have lots of characters and be full of 'news' about Berlin. I think the climax will be during the elections. Frank journalism, in fact."[23] While the last phrase could be read as a qualifier, it can also be seen as a statement of method: facts were to be the medium of this novel of frank journalism, as of Tretiakov's factography. Opposing this plan, in a note to the New Directions edition of *The Berlin Stories*, Isherwood writes that he had also initially planned "to transform this material into one huge tightly constructed novel, in the manner of Balzac" bearing the title *The Lost*. Producing, however, only "an absurd jumble," Isherwood deserted this scheme with relief, "thank goodness I never did write *The Lost*!" (xiii).[24] Two competing plans for his Berlin material emerge in these remarks, with Tretiakov's journalistic model winning out – a decision that might be seen as a failure of grand novelistic form.[25] However, Isherwood's narrative ambition, like Tretiakov's factography, expresses a commitment to a mode of literary praxis that would actively change reality in the process of recording it.

The most persuasive evidence for Isherwood's engagement with Tretiakov appears when we read the opening of *The Berlin Stories* alongside Tretiakov's 1931 Berlin lecture. "The Writer and the Socialist Village" outlined a three-stage process:

> First: the choice of object. Investigating the facts in their specificity and in their concrete manifestations.
> Second: the journalistic processing of found factual material. Enhancing its characteristic moments. Extracting the dialectical chain from the process in which the fact is the essential, determining link. Dressing the fact in an effective agitational form. Testing the fact's

public, social interest and significance. The fact therefore becomes an argument, a signal, a concrete proposal.

Third: the practical conclusions. Operationalizing the literary contribution within the reorganization of reality in accordance with socialism.[26]

Here Tretiakov's transformative model of journalistic praxis points toward a fuller understanding of the narrative method of *Goodbye to Berlin*, as seen in the famous opening passage from the first sketch, "A Berlin Diary":

> From my window, the deep solemn massive street. Cellar-shops where the lamps burn all day, under the shadow of top-heavy balconied façades, dirty plaster frontages embossed with scroll-work and heraldic devices. The whole district is like this: street leading into street of houses like shabby monumental safes crammed with the tarnished valuables and second-hand furniture of a bankrupt middle class. I am a camera with its shutter open, quite passive, recording, not thinking. Recording the man shaving at the window opposite and the woman in the kimono washing her hair. Some day, all this will have to be developed, carefully printed, fixed. (1)

When read through Tretiakov's recommendations, it becomes clear that the gaze of Isherwood's famous passage is not that of detached observer or passive spectator. The facts are isolated and noted – "top-heavy balconied façades, dirty plaster frontages" – followed by a moment of diagnosis, "the second-hand furniture of a bankrupt middle class," which undercuts the comment that the narrator is "merely recording": he is already initiating a class analysis. Finally, there is the statement that "some day, all this will have to be developed, carefully printed, fixed." The details must not only be described, but also inscribed, mirroring Tretiakov's "operationalizing" of facts in the service of socialism. This intricate, engaged dissection of the process of reportage belies accounts of Isherwood's camera-eye as dazzled by commodity culture; on the contrary, here the political itinerancies of the commodity are subjected to close, sober scrutiny.

Isherwood's explicit statements of narrative distance can also be reimagined in relation to Tretiakov's antihumanism. The first page of "A Berlin Diary" continues:

> But soon a call is sure to sound, so piercing, so insistent, so despairingly human, that at last I have to get up and peep through the slats of the venetian blind to make quite sure that it is not – as I know very well it could not possibly be – for me. (1)

Here Isherwood's prose both explicitly negates and syntactically interrupts the circuit of human identification. Rather than failing to register the call of the political, "A Berlin Diary" refuses the subject-making interpellation of the "despairingly human," a moment which also involves a queer rejection of a scene of conventional courtship. This refusal is directly followed by an object biography:

> Everything in the room is like that: unnecessarily solid, abnormally heavy and dangerously sharp. Here, at the writing-table, I am confronted by a phalanx of metal objects – a pair of candlesticks shaped like entwined serpents, an ashtray from which emerges the head of a crocodile, a paper-knife copied from a Florentine dagger, a brass dolphin holding on the end of its tail a small broken clock. What becomes of such things? How could they ever be destroyed? They will probably remain intact for thousands of years: people will treasure them in museums. Or perhaps they will merely be melted down for munitions in a war? Every morning, Frl. Schroeder arranges them very carefully in certain unvarying positions: there they stand, like an uncompromising statement of her views on Capital and Society, Religion and Sex. (2)

Strangely resistant to Frl. Schroeder's attempts to place them in "unvarying positions" (why does she have to do this every morning?), the "phalanx of objects" takes center stage in its own narrative trajectory. They trope how factographic literary praxis constantly struggles to re-inscribe the object within a heavily valorized political field, constantly rearranging and redeploying its materials in the service of the most "uncompromising statement[s]" possible. Here the distance of Isherwood's text from what might be called *mere veridicality* is particularly evident: far from a supposedly neutral "objectivity," Isherwood's camera-I offers an active, transformative conception of the object. Rather than standing free of partisan distortion, the factographic object must be recruited to active service in a political battle that will transfigure both subject and object, reordered by the processes of socialist production and revolutionary agitation.

Isherwood's method follows what Tretiakov called the "operationalizing" of facts, actively deployed in the transformation of reality; in *Goodbye to Berlin* inscription and analysis are co-extensive within a transformative process named by the camera-I. In a key essay on photography, Tretiakov argues that the psychologism of the portrait and the snapshot must be overturned; "the snapshot has its own internal flaw: the uniqueness and contingency of what it depicts." The photo-series addresses this problem, for it "delivers a momentary cross-section that cuts through the entire skein of relationships that entangle the individual."[27] Isherwood's text proceeds from the same commitment, continually cutting across the individual subject or scene to create an uneven series of relationships between characters, locales, and the political charge of both. This is evident even in what might appear to be "snapshots" or moments of scene setting, as in the following description of a slum neighborhood:

> The entrance to the Wassertorstrasse was a big stone archway, a bit of old Berlin, daubed with hammers and sickles and Nazi crosses and plastered with tattered bills which advertised auctions or crimes. It was a deep shabby cobbled street, littered with sprawling children in tears. Youths in woollen sweaters circled waveringly across it on racing bikes and whooped at girls passing with milk-jugs. The pavement was chalk-marked for the hopping game called Heaven and Earth. At the end of it, like a tall, dangerously sharp, red instrument, stood a church. (100)

This scene is set with architectural detail, "a bit of old Berlin," giving way to a focus on political symbols and on the detritus of failed economic destinies, "auctions or crimes" which provides a running political analysis. Then Isherwood selects an agitational detail to stand out from the scene, the crying children providing a plea for the reader's attention, giving way to a stark contrast between the content of the children's game and its institutional embodiment in the church. In fact, the "dangerously sharp, red, instrument" of the spire not only pierces Isherwood's cityscape but is re-inscribed through this function as an ironic trope for political art; somewhat implausibly perhaps, the spire is now red and dangerous. By the processing of these details and their inscription into a social and political process, Isherwood's method is again close to that proposed by Tretiakov: the details are disarticulated, their significance confirmed, and then they are rearticulated in a political montage. Such transformative selection, processing, and fixing of detail is similarly evident even when Isherwood appears to be providing a portrait. The depiction of Frl. Schroeder, for instance, follows this pattern of description – "Shapeless but alert, she waddles from room to room, in carpet slippers and a flowered dressing gown pinned ingeniously together" (2) – and inscription, "long ago, before the War and the Inflation, she used to be comparatively well off" (3). Here, the effect of political inscription works back to organize the individual: Frl. Schroeder is herself "pinned ingeniously together" by her class position, inscribed by the text's process of analysis and observation as a montage-like subject.

One of Tretiakov's most salient arguments held that photography was "replacing painting and becoming the active instrument of struggle in the hands of the proletariat."[28] Put in the context of these remarks, "I am a camera" surely does not reveal a passive, documentary attitude, but rather performs an active self-instrumentalization. For both Tretiakov and Isherwood, it was not only facts that were to be "operationalized," but the writer himself, simultaneously emptied out as human subject and yet active as object, operative in political struggle. Here Tretiakov's doggedly instrumentalizing collectivism calls for a complete re-valorization of the objectification of the human subject. In order to tease out the queer valences of this operation, it is useful to consider a recent study in queer Marxism. Kevin Floyd's *The Reification of Desire: Toward a Queer Marxism* (2009) re-evaluates the classic Lukácsian concepts of reification and totality, with the aim of framing the critical insights of Marxism in terms of queer theory and vice versa. Drawing on Eric O. Clarke's work on Kant's "sexual humanism," Floyd corrects the heteronormalizing tendencies of Lukács's critique of reification, arguing that *History and Class Consciousness* retains a persistent trace of bourgeois subjectivity in its upholding of the Kantian ban on the objectification of the human subject. If, Floyd persuasively argues, the human subject should never be rendered object, as in Lukács's residually Kantian ethics, then this not only upholds the fundamental structures of property ownership (people owning objects), but also has a specifically heteronormalizing force, as a foreclosure of non-reproductive uses of the body. Floyd's study thus aims to re-valorize the reified body as holding wide-ranging possibilities for queer Marxist thought and praxis, a project for which he finds uneven support in the work of Herbert Marcuse.[29] This immanent critique of Marxist humanism through the queer instrumentalization of the body is a fruitful point of departure, and yet it also appears that Floyd's argument could be broadened and strengthened from the perspective of certain branches of Marxist antihumanism. Tretiakov is particularly salient here, for there is no figure in the Marxist tradition less squeamish about the objectification of the human subject – which was, indeed, Tretiakov's explicit aim and the foundation of his conception of radical praxis. As Floyd argues contra Lukács, positively valorizing objectification not only frames the subject "in terms that refuse a definition of the human presupposing property ownership" but also potentially legitimates queer instrumentalizations of the body.[30] In other words, if a human subject becomes a camera, this not only might provide access to new – surely rather queer – pleasures, but also would prevent the camera-being from owning another camera in any recognizable sense.

Reading Isherwood's camera-I through Tretiakov reveals the queer potential of the First Five-Year Plan, a collectivization of the subject that entails the dissolution of its acquisitional agency and a reimagining of its affective and intimate functions outside of reproductive heterosexuality. However, it is also important to recognize that, particularly in its latter years from 1930–2, the First Five-Year Plan involved a particularly proscriptive sense of normative community, with collectivization giving a heavy mandate to Soviet campaigns to produce and regularize ideal proletarian subjects. This, in turn, played an important role in the genesis of what Dan Healey has called the Soviet Union's "homophobic turn," for, alongside prostitutes and other lumpen figures, male homosexuals in particular were caught up in campaigns to get deviant Soviet subjects off the streets and into properly proletarian work.[31] Proletarian normativity undoubtedly came to be implicated in the brutal repression of queers in the Soviet Union and in broader currents of leftist thought and culture, for which queer sexuality is persistently coded as "bourgeois decadence" as opposed to the healthy sexuality of the true proletarian. And yet, as we have seen, the most trenchant literary iteration of precisely such proletarianization – Tretiakov's factography – opens up a critique of humanist individualism with vitally antiheteronormative effects; as the subject is reordered outside of property ownership, it is simultaneously queered as actively self-instrumentalizing. Muñoz's recent revisiting of the period of early gay liberation through Ernst Bloch's concept of concrete utopia might be applied to Isherwood's Berlin. Muñoz seeks a radical queer futurity through "historically situated struggles, a collectivity that is actualized or potential."[32] This sense of potentiality is opened up by a study of Isherwood's queer Marxism: the flickering possibility of new collective definitions of the sexual subject glimpsed in the utopian impulses of an intense period of historical struggle. At the same time, the role of an aggressively objectivist factography in this process must surely complicate Muñoz's hostility to what he calls the "discourse of the fact" in the development of queer cultural history. For Muñoz, this discourse functions as a synecdoche for a normatively empiricist history that "cast[s] antinormative desire as the bad object."[33] But for Isherwood's Tretiakovian project, the objectifying discourse of the fact refashions the radical queer subject.

Norris or Rastignac

If the opening of *Goodbye to Berlin* activates the object in an antihumanist critique of the subject, *The Last of Mr. Norris* works obversely, foregrounding the subject to question the possibility of realist reflection. The novel's eccentric protagonist, Arthur Norris, performs this function, as a figure whose very predominance in the narrative ironically troubles the dominance of the human subject as the focal point of the text. While not homosexually aligned, Norris is persistently marked as queer, in both his gender performance ("Come in, dear boy, I'm visible now. Come and talk to me while I powder my nose" [98]), and the sexual practice of his masochism. Norris's queerness is coupled with a tendency to strange, duplicitous, and amoral behaviour – a combination that is anathema to any search for positive models for queer life. However, there remains a vital antiheteronormative force involved in Norris's bizarre activities when read as a refusal of Lukácsian typicality. For Lukács, typicality functions as a privileged access to social and political reality through the place of the character within the totality of the realist narrative, a point of legibility afforded by the mediations between part and whole, character and narrative, individual and history. This dialectical reflection of deep political movement in individual consciousness is replaced by Norris's bumbling, unsuccessful perfidy and petty meddling in Weimar politics; a bathetic reworking of the successful scheming of Eugène de Rastignac in Lukács's key example, Balzac.[34]

Moreover, following Floyd, we might see this operation as evacuating the hetero-humanist subject as focal point of the text, for Norris's opacity emerges through both his presentation as queer subject and through his dishonest scheming. The narrative opens when the somewhat naïve narrator, Bradshaw, meets Norris on the train to Berlin. Bradshaw is comically unable to interpret the shifty Norris, first reading his annoyance at border controls as a sign that Norris was "some sort of mild internationalist," then deciding that "the old boy was engaged in a little innocent private smuggling," only to find that Norris was not troubled by the customs inspection at all (3–4). And yet, their initial interaction is very obviously framed as a scene of cruising, as Bradshaw asks the "innocently naughty" Norris for a light:

> "I wonder, sir, if you could let me have a match?"
> Even now, he didn't answer at once. He appeared to be engaged in some sort of rapid mental calculation, while his fingers, nervously active, sketched a number of flurried gestures round his waistcoat. For all they conveyed, he might equally have been going to undress, to draw a revolver, or merely to make sure that I hadn't stolen his money. Then the moment of agitation passed from his gaze like a little cloud, leaving a clear blue sky. At last he had understood what it was that I wanted. (1)

Here several different levels of illegibility are at work in Isherwood's apparently innocently realist prose. On one level Bradshaw is unable to interpret Norris's flustered demeanor, which the putatively unsuspecting reader is later able to decipher as concern over one of his deceitful schemes. At the same time, the joke is on the reader who fails to recognize the language of queer intimacy coded by the passage and ironically recognized by Bradshaw himself.

The persistence of these ironic levels of opacity throughout the novel subverts realist reflection, as both the reader's and Bradshaw's apparent incomprehension of Norris become synecdoches for the breakdown of realist epistemology, which would hold that the development of characters' actions across the narrative reveals the shape of deep social and political change. By stark contrast, throughout the narrative, Norris stubbornly refuses to participate in the revelatory typicality so celebrated by Lukács. At points Norris is not even intelligible to the narrator as a human subject: "As a final test, I tried to look Arthur in the eyes. But no, this time-honoured process didn't work. Here were no windows to the soul. They were merely part of his face, light-blue jellies" (138). Here the importance of factography for this part of Isherwood's project comes into focus, for what Tretiakov called "the old idealist fairy tale about the face being the mirror of the soul" underlying literary realism is explicitly challenged by Norris's opacity. In other words, Isherwood's factographic method in *Goodbye to Berlin* and his critique of Lukácsian realism are two sides of the same coin.[35] At this possibly climactic moment, nothing is revealed to Bradshaw. Humanist identification is occluded; there is no sense of social or political change from Norris's actions, merely the petty, unsuccessful schemes of a small-time conman. Writing to Bradshaw at the end of the novel, Norris is unrepentant."'Tell me, William,'" his last letter (and the novel) concludes, "'*what* have I done to deserve all this?'" (191; emphasis Isherwood's). This ironic comment on Norris's frightful conduct throughout the narrative also involves a Tretiakovian interrogation of the status of the hero: as Tretiakov asked in essays such as "The New Leo Tolstoy" and "The Biography of the Object," how can the novelist justify the dominance of any protagonist in the light of collectivization? Although his schemes dominate the novel's action, Norris's centrality in the narrative is continually put into question, even as the plot obsessively scripts his machinations. *The Last of Mr. Norris* thus offers an antihumanist critique of the aesthetic-ideological project of Lukácsian realism by staging and subverting the problematic of reflection through its queerly incorrigible anti-hero, the bizarre, inept antipode to Rastignac.

The substitution of Norris's downward spirals, as he forever flees the consequences of his actions, for Rastignac's relentless ascension has a particular force as a critique of the political uses of high realism. The novel's major figure of political futurity, moreover, the Communist leader – and cipher for Willi Münzenberg – Ludwig Bayer, is explicitly opposed to Norris as the narrator scurries between these two figures in the climactic section of the novel. While Bradshaw is comically indulgent of Norris who endlessly seeks his approval, he in turn idealizes Bayer, desperately eager for his approval: "[Bayer's] mere attention was flattery of the most stimulating kind" (66). Bayer is not held to be typical, but rather exceptional, a rare figure of integrity in the text; by the end of the novel, Bayer is dead, killed by the Nazis, while Norris continues on the run. The respective fates of Norris and Bayer therefore refuse the easy access to political futurity implied in realist typicality, as the inept conman flees the scene of action, while the figure of historical progression meets a violent end.

Isherwood's disavowal of realist narrative praxis is not recognizable as high modernist: while Norris empties out the realist subject, his progress through the novel is narrated in a linear fashion and in deceptively simple prose. While an important organizing principle of the volume, the factographic technique at work in *Goodbye to Berlin* is similarly veiled beneath Isherwood's smooth narration and vivid description. His reception of the Tretiakov/Lukács debate offers not yet another polemic on behalf of realism or modernism, but rather a hybrid mode that mediates the debate through the need to articulate queer subjectivity. Isherwood's friend, the Communist novelist Edward Upward, was later to remark of his generation of leftist writers that, while anxious to avoid duplicating high modernist writers such as Joyce, they were also "extremely wary of taking Balzac and decanting new content into it."[36] This wry comment on the polarities of 1930s Marxist debate applies particularly to queer writers such as Isherwood, who resist the dominant categorizations of the period's literary history; and to Norris himself, who refuses to be decanted into realist typicality.

Queer red front

The figure of Norris is also central to the novel's positive presentation of queer intimacy, which offers a complex re-valorization of the usual sense of sexual "objectification" and "use" of working-class men by bourgeois queers. Matt Houlbrook's work in social history has demonstrated the limitations of these formulations for understanding queer cross-class sexual encounters in interwar London.[37] However, in the literary history of the English 1930s, there has been to date no serious attempt to rethink these intimacies as a central element of

Isherwood's, Auden's, and Spender's (to name just three well-known examples) formation as bourgeois, queer leftists. One exception is to be found in Frank Kermode's *History and Value* (1988), which offers a defense of the role of love in queer bourgeois leftists' cross-class relationships.[38] Yet his contention that the period's politicization of queer cross-class love represents a new cultural-historical formation appears somewhat misplaced; what Kermode claims as a distinctive feature of the 1930s might be more properly ascribed to an earlier period, particularly in the figure of Edward Carpenter. Any attempt, moreover, to defend Isherwood's or other leftist writers' class-crossing relationships with reference to their (often undeniable) care for their longer-term working-class partners would – while contesting directly homophobic depictions – surely serve to inscribe a heteronormative, monogamous framework which delegitimizes other potentially world-making forms of queer intimacy. In sharp contrast to this paradigm, Isherwood offers a way of thinking through queer cross-class intimacies that does not rely on humanist definitions of love, but rather suggests their politically explosive potential.

This revalorization takes place on an oblique level, not as a direct affirmation of homosexual intimacies between bourgeois and proletarian men, but rather through a reimagining of revolutionary subjectivity comprising a matrix of deviant sex and politically-charged cross-class affective bonding. In *The Last of Mr. Norris*, a few months after the narrator Bradshaw meets the dominatrix sex worker Anni and her bisexual pimp Otto at a drunken party, he attends a Communist political meeting where the opportunistic Norris gives a speech. Significantly, Anni and Otto resurface, in a crowd consisting mainly of more conventional images of revolutionary subjectivity in "the Berlin working class, pale and prematurely lined, often haggard and ascetic" (48). The following passage describes this crowd, energized not only by the speaker, but also by the presence of Otto and Anni. Bradshaw feels "a tug at my sleeve," and recognizes the pair, who "both seemed pleased to see me," while Otto "shook hands with a grip which nearly made me yell out loud" (48). The speech begins, and the crowd is transformed in a utopian moment of collective political experience:

> They had not come here to see each other or to be seen, or even to fulfill a social duty. They were attentive but not passive. They were

not spectators. They participated, with a curious, restrained passion, in the speech made by the red-haired man. He spoke for them, he made their thoughts articulate. They were listening to their own collective voice. At intervals they applauded it, with sudden, spontaneous violence. Their passion, their strength of purpose elated me. I stood outside it. One day, perhaps, I should be with it, but never of it. (48–9)

Isherwood's bourgeois narrator, like the "ascetic" working-class crowd, is energized by these queer lumpenproletarians who are exemplary bearers of revolutionary consciousness grounded in cross-class intimacy. It is worth pausing here to consider the extent to which many 1930s sexual radicals and Marxists alike were implacably opposed to viewing the lumpenproletariat as capable of genuine political commitment. Following Marx's condemnation in *The Communist Manifesto* and elsewhere, orthodox Marxists were deeply skeptical of this (non) class's ability to rise to disciplined class consciousness.[39] Alfred Döblin's 1929 novel, *Berlin Alexanderplatz* was, for instance, attacked by Marxist critics for its focus on the feckless lumpen drifter, Franz Biberkopf.[40] For Magnus Hirschfeld and other homosexual activists such as Friedrich Radzuweit, the queer lumpenproletarian was the "scourge" of the emergent figure of the "respectable homosexual" through hustlers' tendency to blackmail their clients.[41] Even the most sympathetic treatments of Berlin's hustlers of the period such as John Henry Mackay's 1928 novel *The Hustler* tended to view these queer lumpenproletarians as completely unaware and buffeted by circumstances outside their control, rather than potentially politically active agents of sexual radicalism.[42]

Here Isherwood not only inhabits an important intersection between sexual radicalism and Marxism, but goes beyond it, looking forward both to later Marxist attempts to re-conceptualize the lumpenproletariat as an explosive revolutionary force, and to modes of queer theory and activism that valorize the sex worker as an important figure in queer politics. At the same time, it is important to note that the KPD at points also valorized the lumpenproletariat as a potentially explosive political force. As Eve Rosenhaft points out, this investment was uneven and tactical, depending on whether the Party sought to gain respectability or play on its outlaw ethos.[43] In this way, the lumpenproletariat is a vital marker of the shifting terrain of Communism's praxes of embodied ethics encapsulated by Foucault's formulation as discussed in the Introduction. Foucault argues that interwar Communism was deeply marked by a vacillation between "revolutionary life as the scandal of an unacceptable truth," and a growing ethos of bourgeois respectability.[44] It is outside the scope of this present study to examine the question of the lumpenproletariat in any substantive detail, but here I would like to point out the group's role as a fulcrum between queer and Marxist politics of everyday life.

Following the rally scene, Bradshaw heads back to Norris's apartment with Anni and Otto, where he encounters a "domestic tableau," a queer transformation of the conventional family. Here George Orwell's famous, nostalgic configuration, "Father, in shirt sleeves, sits in the rocking chair at one side of the fire reading the racing finals, and Mother sits on the other with her sewing," becomes Norris, his dominatrix, and her leftist pimp:[45]

> Before I could ask any more questions, Anni and Otto returned from the kitchen. Arthur greeted them gaily and soon Anni was sitting on his knee, resisting his advances with slaps and bites, while Otto, having taken off his coat and rolled up his sleeves, was absorbed in trying to repair the gramophone. There seemed no place for myself in this domestic tableau and I soon said that I must be going.
>
> Otto came downstairs with a key to let me out of the house door. In parting, he gravely raised his clenched fist in salute:
>
> "Red Front."
>
> "Red Front," I answered. (55)

When viewed through Isherwood's camera-I, this scene offers a sophisticated revalorization of queer cross-class intimacy, a mutual instrumentalization creating the conditions for political community, a queer "Red Front." Sex work and deviant sexual practices are enfolded within a transformed domesticity, tied together by Otto's tinkering with the politically charged mechanism of the gramophone, a pervasive metonym for political communication in the period. Indeed, we might say that Otto is, like the narrator in *Goodbye to Berlin*, engaged with the mechanical remediation of revolutionary consciousness, while the scene as a whole offers a vision of self-instrumentalization, as the function of each figure is inscribed within a heavily valorized political collective. For Isherwood in *The Berlin Stories*, queer cross-class intimacies are not only legitimate forms of love, but also crucial forms of radical praxis. This transformation of the family also bears an unmistakable resemblance to the concept of the cell in Communist organization, with its own austere boundaries – as a bourgeois, the narrator has "no place" within it, and must drop away to let the radical subjects form their social world.

Otto, the leftist-pimp-father of Isherwood's scene, is also a montage-subject, constructed by Isherwood from conflicting scraps of a series of different characters and split across the two volumes of *The Berlin Stories*. While in *The Last of Mr. Norris*, Otto is a queer, politically dedicated pimp and champion boxer, in *Goodbye to Berlin*, another Otto makes an appearance, this time a naïve young amateur hustler with only a vague allegiance to Communism. *The Berlin Stories* as a whole presents a disassembled Otto, broken down into two characters and unevenly reassembled across the two volumes. This becomes clearer in Isherwood's unpublished notebooks, which reveal how the material for *Goodbye to Berlin* and *The Last of Mr. Norris* was initially completely intermingled in his creative process. These notebooks are crucial documents of Isherwood's montage at work, demonstrating how he developed Otto as a ragged composite of a number of different characters, cutting out aspects from certain figures, and unevenly pasting Otto back together from these scraps of subject-formation. In December 1933, Isherwood wrote "there's no real reason why Otto and Lothar shouldn't be fused. Is Otto credible as a Communist? No. But as a stunt-rowdy calling himself a Communist? Yes."[46] Here Isherwood ponders joining Otto's character with that of Lothar – the name of a character who was later to appear as Otto's stern Nazi brother in *Goodbye to Berlin*, although it is clear that Isherwood had initially conceived of Lothar as a Communist. Otto's political commitment is called into question – laboring under the dismissal of such subjects in leftist discourse, Isherwood struggles to invest a lumpen scoundrel with "credible" political engagement. In a note written two days later, the self-identity of this composite Otto is rent apart: "Otto isn't Otto. He's Lothar." This splintering allows Isherwood to cleave off the less traditionally masculine aspect of Otto's character for his appearance in *The Last of Mr. Norris*, revealing the split which will eventually operate across the two volumes: "I shall cut everything of the character of Otto – the soft feminine sly deceitful – out of the story. He belongs in the book of reminiscences of Berlin which I hope to write one day – not here."[47] Accordingly, in *Goodbye to Berlin*,

Isherwood's later "book of reminiscences," Otto is presented in the vein of John Mackay's young hustler Gunther: hapless, unthinkingly manipulative, and buffeted by circumstances beyond his control.

By contrast, when Otto is reconstructed in *The Last of Mr. Norris* he appears as the "father" of the alternative family; invested with various aspects of normative masculinity, he becomes the most physically active antifascist in the whole text, an assemblage of the forces of resistance. Neither the unscrupulous blackmailer of Hirschfeld's characterization – although we see Otto embracing "the Baron" early in the text (29), he does not appear to be connected to this figure's later demise at the hands of Norris's blackmailing secretary – nor a feckless drifter like his alter ego in *Goodbye to Berlin*, Döblin's Biberkopf, or Mackay's teenage hustlers, this Otto retains his commitment to Communism to the end. Otto's exhausted and battered body reappears toward the close of the narrative after the Nazi accession, fleeing persecution and intending to continue the fight further.[48] Ragged but defiant, Otto embodies the renewal of the antifascist struggle in the moment of defeat, still "astonishingly cheerful" even when "lost amidst the sauntering crowds of his enemies" (185–6). This montage of Otto-effects allows Isherwood to present a nonunitary revolutionary subject, embodying radical praxis without relying on heteronormative revolutionary consciousness.

For all the utopian potential for queer cross-class intimacy in Isherwood's distinctive domestic scene, its limitations must also be acknowledged. Although Anni's role as dominatrix carries some transgressive freight, her brutal treatment by Otto later in the narrative is related casually, which highlights the problematic role of conventional masculinity in Isherwood's vision of queer life. Indeed, questions may be raised as to the viability of the whole project of active self-instrumentalization as gendered performance, as often tied (though not exclusively) to a particular set of gay male sexual practices. A further set of shortcomings in Isherwood's revalorization of queer intimacy is to be found in his 1939 book of reportage on the Second Sino-Japanese War, *Journey to a War*, produced in collaboration with Auden, in which Isherwood narrates a nascent western gay identity, a pervasive instantiation of the bourgeois, humanist subject. In Isherwood's depiction of "wasp-waisted" Chinese men, radical queer praxis gives way to the imperial gaze of the "homoerotics of Orientalism."[49]

Isn't he to hear Beethoven?

On first glance, *Journey to a War* might appear to continue Isherwood's project of self-instrumentalization. Consider, for instance, the following passage:

> A big crowd gathered to watch us, laughing and chatting, as well they might: we certainly make an extraordinary trio. Auden, in his immense, shapeless overcoat and woolen Jaeger cap, seems dressed for the Arctic regions. Chiang, neat as ever, might be about to wait at a Hankow consular dinner-party. My own beret, sweater, and martial boots would not be out of place in Valencia or Madrid. Collectively, perhaps, we most resemble a group of characters in one of Jules Verne's stories about lunatic English explorers. (104)

Here Isherwood places himself as the object of scrutiny of a group of Chinese bystanders, offering a play of observer and observed that destabilizes the subject-object dichotomy inherent to humanist aesthetics – and, it might appear, the epistemology of imperialism itself. A similar process is at work throughout the narrative, such as in the following description of his and Auden's odd travelling habits:

> The two armed guards in the corridor – one of them surely not more than twelve years old – peered into our compartment to watch the foreign devils screaming with laughter and mysterious jokes, singing in high falsetto or mock operatic voices, swaying rhythmically backwards and forwards on their rears, reading aloud to each other from small crimson-bound books. (47)

Again Isherwood writes in himself and Auden as eccentric objects of a Chinese gaze, putting on a performance, it seems, for their puzzled observers. But this camp show, complete with falsetto voices, is not primarily for the benefit of the young Chinese guards, but rather functions as a foregrounding of Auden's and Isherwood's collaborative queer subjectivity, simultaneously scripted and "read aloud" to one another in their joint performance. This performance is rudely interrupted by the appearance of some "coolies" who "jostled blindly against us, with the averted, snot-smeared, animal faces of the very humble, the dwellers in Society's smallest crevices, the Insulted and

Injured" (49). In stark contrast to Berlin's queer lumpenproletarians, here Isherwood sees the Chinese "coolie" incapable of revolutionary consciousness in their economic and social abjection. This necessarily involves a reinscription of the bourgeois subject, not "elated" by the revolutionary consciousness of a capacious collective, but rather a liberal subject, concerned for the plight of the racialized poor from above.

This view from above is explicitly explored further on in the narrative, when Isherwood details his guilty ruminations on being carried on a litter chair for part of his journey to the front, describing how he and Auden "rehearsed every dishonest excuse for allowing ourselves to be carried by human beings" (226). The possibility of class consciousness inhering in the "coolies" carrying them is, again, entirely foreclosed: "our coolies, unaware of these qualms, seemed to bear us no ill-will, however. At the road-side halts they even brought us cups of tea" (226). In the same passage, an alteration from the original manuscript of Isherwood's diary reveals a crucial juncture at which Isherwood's conception of the humanist value of art comes into question in relation to these abjected subjects. In the original diary – which is generally very close to the finished text of *Journey to a War* – there is a striking moment during Isherwood's ventriloquism of a series of typical bourgeois excuses, part of which is excised from the finished text:

> They are used to it, it's giving them employment, they don't feel. Oh no, they don't feel – of course they don't – they haven't read Rilke or had tea with Virginia Woolf – but that lump on the back of his neck wasn't raised by drinking champagne, and his sweat remarkably resembles my own.[50]

In the text of *Journey to a War*, however, Isherwood omits the clause "they haven't read Rilke or had tea with Virginia Woolf." While Isherwood's initial impulse when writing up his diary that evening was to violently reject a conception of human worth which hinged upon the reception of high culture (even as he troublingly reveals a particular set of co-ordinates for full subjecthood at work in his mind), this explicit rejection drops away in the published text, revealing a softening in Isherwood's attitude toward the complicity of high culture in oppression. Isherwood's eventual decision against the inclusion of the miniature polemic against high art is a telling marker of his movement toward a humanist narrative mode in *Journey to a War*.

Indeed, at other points in his Chinese journey Isherwood appears to be entirely certain that European high culture is beneficial to all. During a drunken conversation with Auden and their traveling companion, Peter Fleming, which develops into "an argument on the meaning of the word Civilization," (tellingly, in the unpublished manuscript, "an argument on the meaning of civilization") Fleming had claimed that China didn't necessarily have anything to learn from the west. Isherwood contends that "you can't pretend that the coolie is well off, in his present condition? Isn't he ever to hear Beethoven? Or see your wife act?" (231). Fleming responds, "he's got them both pretty well taped," while Auden's contribution was, facetiously, "more for providing the coolies with meals from a really good French restaurant," having "decided, finally, against Chinese food" (231). None of the three British travelers comes off well in this scene, but what is most significant here is that Isherwood argues for a position based on human presence at the performance of western art. The "coolie" can't merely hear Beethoven on a gramophone or see a film or recording of a play in order to be "well off," but must be actually present at these performances. High art at this moment represents the enrichment of the human spirit, necessary for its autotelic completion as the sovereign subject of the aesthetic realm, and there could be no better demonstration of Isherwood's drift toward humanism than this unashamedly bourgeois and deeply Eurocentric position on the betterment of the "coolie."

In this passage, humanism does not only work against an abjected other, but also against technological modernity. Isherwood's proscription of the work of art mediated by mechanical reproduction signals a desire for the return of the auratic art object: a move away from the thoroughgoing valorization of radical modes of photography in *The Berlin Stories*, and perhaps a strange position to appear in a volume containing an extensive selection of photographs.[51] In fact, a close look at the photographs in *Journey to a War* reveals their immersion in the logic of portraiture as opposed to montage or other antihumanist photographic modes. Each subject is clearly framed, either as a portrait or group scene, and each photograph or page of photographs is given a descriptive caption, such as "British Sailor,"

"Japanese Prisoner," or "IN THE TRENCHES." Indeed, the photographs in *Journey to a War* provide a synoptic lens through which to view Isherwood's narrative mode in the text. Like Isherwood's prose, the photographs are at some points playfully performative (a photograph of Auden in the trenches appears to have been staged as a parody of the usual depiction of the manly war correspondent, while a photo of a train is captioned simply as "Delay"), and at other moments engaged in a more earnest project of bearing witness, such as seen in a series of photographs of a refugee camp. Taken as a whole, what the photographs tend to offer is a somewhat eccentric but recognizably humanist outlook in which the logic of the portrait is at points parodied, but never truly subverted; a mediation of authorial subjectivity, to be sure, but hardly an attempt to evacuate such subjectivity in a transformative objectivism, as in *The Berlin Stories*. As opposed to *Goodbye to Berlin*'s refusal to fully register the human subject, here the text's condescending gaze pictures the completion of the "coolie" at the concert.

Journey to a War, then, is a humanist text that operates by the occlusion of the non-western individual from full subjecthood: it is, in other words, organized by paradigmatically Orientalist modes of perception and representation. One of the most striking features of critical work on *Journey to a War* is, however, its unwillingness to see the text in this way.[52] In some readings, this positioning is implicit and carried out by blithe statements of Auden and Isherwood's "empathy," simply ignoring the possibility of the deep complicity of Auden and Isherwood's perceptions.[53] Other accounts, such as Douglas Kerr's, offer a more direct denial of the Orientalism of *Journey to a War*.[54] Kerr recuperates Isherwood's text from a putative claim of Orientalism, his argument resting on the inability of Isherwood's prose to find any stable, authoritative center from which to pursue a classic project of imperialist anthropology. In Kerr's reading, this failure of imperial epistemology is linked in a somewhat gestural manner to questions of normative masculinity, Kerr noting that Isherwood's failure to "put China into English to his own satisfaction" was a failure in "one form of the test for men from Europe."[55] This intersection of masculinity and imperialism is given greater stress in Marsha Byrant's and Maureen Moynagh's accounts of *Journey to a War*, which both hold that Auden's and Isherwood's critique of conventional masculinity proceeds symbiotically with their critique of imperialism. Their arguments rest on the same assumptions about imperialist epistemology that govern Kerr's account. For Bryant, *Journey to a War* destabilizes both "the heterosexual/homosexual binarism that defines Western constructions of masculinity, and the colonized/colonizer binarism that underpins the Griersonian model of British documentary."[56] Moynagh argues in similar vein that Auden's and Isherwood's "revolutionary drag" destabilizes a hegemonic nexus of performative masculinity and militarism, particularly apparent in their depiction of a straight, upper-class traveling companion, Peter Fleming, whose own identity performance is flagged throughout Isherwood's narrative by such remarks as "he is altogether too good to be true – and he knows it" (156).[57]

Auden and Isherwood, it seems, do not reproduce the imperialist gaze, with its veridical orientation from a stable, normative masculine center. Rather they deconstruct this gaze through their queer performance, destabilizing both their own subject position – marked as non-identical with the imperialist subject – and that of the imperialist subject himself, in the form of Peter Fleming. It is this reading of the intersection between queer sexuality and imperialism that is, in fact, far too "homogenizing and deterministic" (as Kerr dismisses Said's *Orientalism*), seeing the imperialist gaze simply in terms of normative masculine veridicality, and any deviation from such a position as *de facto* anti-imperialist. Isherwood's gaze throughout the text belies such a reading, as in the following description of western servicemen and a Cantonese crowd:

> British and American gunboats were moored alongside the outer shore. Their crews were playing football – hairy, meat-pink men with powerful buttocks, they must have seemed ferocious, uncouth giants to the slender, wasp-waisted Cantonese spectators, with their drooping, flowerlike stance and shy brilliant smiles. (31)

In this passage the imperial masculine subject is clearly unsettled, with western imperialists recast as dehumanized barbarians gazed upon by a Chinese crowd, Isherwood again turning the tables on the usual configuration of observer and observed, at least initially.[58] But this spectatorship is framed within another gaze, appreciatively taking in the elegant and androgynous Cantonese viewers, simultaneously destabilizing the masculinity of both sets of spectators – the "wasp-waisted" Cantonese, "drooping and flower-like" compared to the white servicemen, and Isherwood and the reader's own gaze, engaged in what Joseph Boone, in the title of his pioneering essay, has called "the homoerotics of Orientalism."

Boone's article is an early example of a series of interventions in queer studies which aim to reveal "how contingent and Western its [queer studies'] conception of 'homosexuality' – as an identity category, a sexual practice, and a site of theoretical speculation – often proves to be when brought into contact with the sexualities of non-Western cultures."[59] In particular, Boone's article, and the work of Joseph Massad, have demonstrated the way in which gay western subjects take part in an "appropriation of the so-called East in order to project onto it an otherness that mirrors Western psychosexual needs," which "only confirms the phenomenon that Said calls 'Orientalism' in his book of that name."[60] Such an Orientalist appropriation forms a key part of the epistemological and ontological apparatus of imperialism, particularly in the Arab and Muslim worlds. Crucially, as Boone points out, normative western masculinity is continually destabilized during this process, either in the form of a slippage in sexual identity experienced by the straight-identified traveler confronted with "polymorphous Eastern sexuality," or in the form of the emerging gay subject who defines his subversive identity through a series of sexual conquests of Arab men or boys.[61]

Boone notes two usual stereotypes upon which the homoerotic gaze alights in the Arab world: the "effeminate Asiatic," and its reverse image, the hyper-sexualized, spectacularly endowed Arab man.[62] The configuration of Chinese masculinity produced by Isherwood's text overlaps somewhat with these stereotypes, while involving some obvious differences. While the "wasp-waisted," androgynous type was one particular figure from *Journey to a War*, in keeping with widely circulating stereotypes about the sexlessness of East Asian men, this androgynous type is not accompanied by the hyper-sexualized stereotype. In fact, Isherwood also appears to see the Chinese – particularly heterosexual Chinese men – as sexless, as the following passage reveals:

> In general, the Chinese aren't very highly sexed – so people tell us. The average young man will be quite contented to spend the evening

dancing, flirting, and drinking tea with his girl friend. Sex is an affair of jokes and compliments and gaiety; a graceful minor art, harmless, pretty, and gentle as flower-painting on a fan. Most of the girls are attractive, but few are really beautiful: as a rule their faces are too broad and flat. Nearly all of them have superb figures. (158)

In this passage Isherwood erases Chinese sexual desires – which are reduced to the non-threatening status of a "minor art" – while disparaging the physical appearance of Chinese women, apparently often "attractive" with "superb figures" but rarely "really beautiful." This malfunctioning of heterosexual desire on the part of Chinese men is the counterpart to the "lively" boys who accompany Auden and Isherwood on train journeys. Consider the following description of one of these "car-boys," featuring another use of "wasp-waist":

The liveliest of them was called Chin-dung; his long floppy hair framed a charming, flat-nosed, impudent face. Chin-dung was exceedingly vain: he was eternally combing his hair or admiring his figure in the glass. He wore a thick rubber belt, like a bandage, which squeezed his pliant body into an absurdly exaggerated Victorian wasp-waist. None of the car-boys spoke English, but they made themselves perfectly at home, prying into our luggage, examining and trying on our clothes, eating nuts, splitting seeds with their teeth, and helping themselves liberally to our cigarettes. (122)

Here the "car-boys" appear as a troublesome but desirable rabble: "impudent" yet "charming" they surround Isherwood and Auden, inviting an intimacy sanctioned by their wild behavior, and the object of an amused and intrigued gaze. Isherwood's indulgent and long-suffering attitude toward these androgynous, simian figures inscribes his own mastery of the situation very precisely through the uncontrollable, polymorphous objects of his desire, and there could be no better demonstration of how his performance of non-normative masculinity serves not to undo but to continue the perceptual structures of colonialism.

Such persistence of these structures entirely forecloses the possibilities raised by the antihumanist critique of *The Berlin Stories*. Instead of self-instrumentalizing revolutionaries, Isherwood and Auden emerge as proto-subjects of the gay bourgeois couple holidaying in a poor nation, with light reading matter, attractive local boys, temporary hardships, and a certain sense of guilt characterizing their travels.[63] Through his distaste literally in the face of the "snot-smeared" "coolie," Isherwood is unable to avoid a contraction back into the bourgeois subject, and from queer revolution to a nascent gay tourism. This retrenchment is precisely the point at which Isherwood's authorship becomes involved in the creation, as Joseph Massad has put it, "not of a queer planet, in Michael Warner's apt phrase, but a straight one."[64] In the place of a capacious collective, *Journey to a War* offers an insistent series of binaries – between the "coolie" and the bourgeois individual he carries, between Peter Fleming's gendered performance and that of Auden and Isherwood, between sexless Chinese men and desirable Chinese boys, and between these lumpen boys and Isherwood himself. The master binary underlying these pairings is that of Auden's and Isherwood's collaboration, which is also a central nexus of normalization in the text. As opposed to the free-flowing mixture of their work presented by their plays of the period such as *The Dog Beneath the Skin* (1935) and *The Ascent of F6* (1936), their contributions are rigidly separated in *Journey to a War*, Auden's photographs and poetry and Isherwood's prose presented as complementary opposites. At the same time, even in moments when Isherwood sought to blend their contributions more fluidly, the logic of the couple appears. Both Auden and Isherwood wrote sections of the diary upon which the final prose narrative is based, but Isherwood wrote up their joint diary, crediting Auden's contributions to the diary in the final text by attributing them to remarks he supposedly made in speech during their travels. The continual but quiet presence of these short, irreverent remarks, often about food (Auden, for instance, reassures Madame Kai-shek that poets do indeed like cake [65], and complains about Chinese food [231]) creates a strong sense of a marital dynamic, Auden's pining for domestic comforts providing the counterpoint to Isherwood's assured prose.

Fiction to fact

Reading *Journey to a War* as instantiating the nascent bourgeois gay subject may appear to lead directly to Isherwood's later, apparently "middlebrow" authorship, itself generally seen as primarily participating in a liberal, bourgeois paradigm of gay rights. The importance of the middle-class narrative of *A Single Man* (1964) to the Violet Quill Group, for instance, is an obvious example of how Isherwood's work has been harnessed to the forces of normalization.[65] And yet, categorizations of Isherwood's contribution to the politics of sexuality as confined to a safe middle ground are surely mistaken.[66] It is not only in *The Berlin Stories* that cracks in such ground are visible, but also in Isherwood's later texts, even as his authorship becomes foundational for the emergent bourgeois gay subject. Indeed, Isherwood continued to be influenced by Marxist literary models in his later career, particularly in his landmark queer memoir, *Christopher and His Kind*.

Crucial to this contention is his friendship and correspondence with Edward Upward, which started when they were undergraduates at Cambridge in the 1920s, and continued up to Isherwood's death in 1986. As young men, the two friends jointly composed a series of surrealist stories that satirized the complacencies of British bourgeois life through grotesque imagery and characterization in a fantastic land they called Mortmere.[67] While Isherwood was in Berlin in the early 1930s, Upward became deeply invested in Communism, attending meetings from the start of the decade and joining the Communist Party of Great Britain in 1934. He was to remain an unrepentant leftist who left the Communist Party in 1948 but maintained his commitment to Marxist politics and literary praxis, as can be seen in his autobiographical trilogy *The Spiral Ascent* (1962/1969/1972). Upward's austere political commitment is often contrasted to Isherwood's apparently less committed dabbling in left-wing causes – a concern for Isherwood himself, as he wrote to Upward in August 1939 following his move to the US, "laziness, dilettantism and cowardice have prevented me from doing the only possible thing: becoming a humble rank-and-file worker, as you did."[68] This sense of Upward's apparently more forceful role in the two friends' relationship might be further supported by the fact that, alongside Auden and E. M. Forster, Upward was Isherwood's most revered literary mentor; in a letter from 1947, he writes that "you are still, and always will be, a member of that small terrible Supreme Court to which I mentally submit everything I write."[69]

But this is only part of the story. A careful reading of their correspondence – which contains a series of extended meditations on the novels both writers were working on throughout their careers – shows that their relationship was always more reciprocal, despite Upward's more certain tone. For one, Upward sent his work to Isherwood as much as the other way round, and clearly valued Isherwood's feedback. But perhaps more tellingly, the two writers constantly sent each other reading material, often by leftist writers. For instance, while Isherwood was in Berlin, Upward wrote a series of letters in which he extolled his new-found belief in the political task of literature, going so far as to proclaim that "now Proust, Gide, Shakespeare are worthless and only Barbusse and Lenin are relevant."[70] But it was Isherwood's position in Berlin that gave him access to the new texts Upward sought:

> Bring over all German translations of Russian literature and you can read them to me on the esplanade. I cannot bear to hear any book mentioned which is not frank Soviet propaganda [. . .] Have you read 'Cement' by Fyodor Gladkov? It sounds good and I'm trying to get it."[71]

This scene of intimate, politicized literary exchange is typical of their correspondence, a series of documents that stand as a unique archive of twentieth-century literary history. Here the two friends are pictured sharing the experience of Marxist texts, a process Isherwood also shared with others such as John Lehmann, who sent him a copy of Ralph Fox's work of Marxist criticism, *The Novel and the People*.[72]

Crucially, Isherwood and Upward continued to send each other "subversive literature" later in their lives, even when Isherwood's proclaimed commitment to Communism had waned.[73] Moreover, as he discussed his work, Upward continued to hold up Marxist models such as Gorky into the 1970s.[74] For his part, Isherwood wrote to Upward in 1973, bemoaning how he couldn't remember the outline of events of his life in the 1930s as he wrote *Christopher and His Kind*. He decided, however, that he shouldn't fret too much about this:

> As soon as I have arranged all the dates in order I can start to remember – or to invent, it doesn't matter which. There is a fruitful theme in all this – the relation of fiction to fact – and I hope the first chapter may turn out to be quite exciting.[75]

This project is ironically announced, in a statement echoing his 1932 letter to John Lehmann, from the opening of Isherwood's narrative: "this book I am now going to write will be as frank and factual as I can make it, especially as far as I myself am concerned."[76] In this moment of ironic distance and engaged inscription, the trace of Tretiakovian "frank journalism, in fact" is unmistakable in Isherwood's self-instrumentalization, even at such points of personalizing advocacy. As a paradigmatic coming out narrative, *Christopher and His Kind* is obviously engaged in a process of bourgeois subject construction, operating under the sign of disclosure – but it also involves a thoroughgoing distantiation, as the generic expectations of the memoir are undercut by Isherwood's defamiliarizing reference to himself in the third person. Isherwood's Tretiakovian project of self-instrumentalization is most apparent in his persistent deployment of "Christopher" rather than "I," as he operationalizes his younger self in the service of queer narrative. Throughout the memoir, Isherwood again mediates the claims of realist prose and antihumanist distance, simultaneously naturalizing his experiences as typical of his "kind" and social class, and yet flagging up their construction as self-interestedly selected. Isherwood's performance of these two modes is his enduring contribution to queer writing, for this dialectical tension between the subject-making claims of identity politics and the radically destabilizing effects of a critique of the subject forms a core dynamic of queer theory and literature.

While his later work bears the trace of interwar Marxist aesthetics, Isherwood came to explicitly repudiate his leftist past. Indeed, a sense of mutual exclusiveness is at play for the later Isherwood, whereby coming out as gay takes place in tandem with a repudiation of his former leftist commitments. Isherwood himself seemed well aware of this double movement, and wittily couched his former leftism in terms which recall the clichés of adolescent dabbling in homosexuality: it was only a phase, he was a hanger-on, "ambiguous," influenced by more hardcore friends.[77] And yet, the language of this disavowal suggests a certain imbrication – and even identity – between queer and Communist modes of sociality as forms of illicit association with distinctive discursive codes and networks of affiliation; as, in other words, similarly constituted counterpublic formations. Isherwood appears as an exemplary figure, therefore, for the constitutive paradoxes of 1930s queer leftist culture: unlike less forthrightly queer contemporaries such as Auden and Spender, Isherwood's later career very clearly invites the genealogy I have been tracing, as he self-consciously moves from celebrated fellow traveler to major gay icon. But while it may be singular, Isherwood's authorship presents just one example of the ways in which queer literary, cultural, and intellectual history must turn back to the 1930s. Indeed, looking to Isherwood's less radical friends might open up some particularly fruitful questions I address in later chapters: what might, for example, a re-examination of the queer memoirs of figures such as Spender and Lehmann reveal about how the figure of the "respectable homosexual" emerges and is resisted in mid-century Britain?[78] More broadly, queer leftists' incessant itinerancies and investments in Communist internationalism provide new ways of interrogating both the transnational turn in queer studies and the internationalist aspirations of contemporary gay rights discourse. And as I shall explore in Chapter 2, the engagement of queer writers such as Sylvia Townsend Warner and Valentine Ackland with Communist vanguardism surely demands serious attention in a longer historical perspective, particularly given the marked vanguardist tendencies of both early gay liberation and certain strains of contemporary queer theory. It may, then, be appropriate to remark in conclusion that there was surely rather more to the old cliché of "boy meets tractor" than might first meet the eye.

Chapter 2

Sylvia Townsend Warner's Queer Vanguardism

Largely neglected for many years, the past two decades have seen a resurgence of scholarly interest in Sylvia Townsend Warner from literary historians drawing on feminism and queer theory, yielding some groundbreaking readings of her work.[1] However, this recent scholarship has not taken account of her archive, instead largely relying on William Maxwell's and Claire Harman's heavily-edited published correspondence and diaries, volumes that systematically downplay Townsend Warner's commitment to and involvement in Communism.[2] For instance, the letter I cite in the Introduction remains unpublished in full, no doubt because of the clear, troubling allegiance to Communism it displays. In this 1937 letter to a prominent fellow Communist Townsend Warner calls for Stephen Spender to be ejected from the CPGB, and that they should "make it look like a purge."[3] Even though the term primarily denoted expulsion from the Party rather than execution as it is commonly taken to mean today, this is shocking language indeed; but a full consideration of Townsend Warner's life and work in the 1930s must surely take into account the extent of her commitment to Soviet Communism.

The first challenge faced by any attempt to re-evaluate Townsend Warner's politics in the 1930s is therefore archival. The problem is twofold: first, the extent to which published editions of Townsend Warner's letters and diaries paint a misleading picture of her life and work in this period, for very obviously anti-Communist reasons (Wendy Mulford's excellent critical biography is an exception to this tendency); and, second, the sheer scope and size of her archive at the Dorset County Museum. Accordingly, this chapter takes shape from the most salient letters and diary entries that have been excised from William Maxwell's and Claire Harman's published editions. Paying particular attention to those texts which bear, as Maxwell remarks, "the irritating tone of the newly converted," or, to put it more charitably, the boldest statements of Communist commitment, I reconstruct Townsend Warner's cultural politics in the 1930s from a series of redacted or excised documents of her political allegiances and affiliations.[4] I have paid particular attention to an extensive series of letters sent to two close friends and fellow CPGB members, Julius and Queenie Lipton, which barely feature at all in the published edition of the letters and which provide a particularly rich account of intimate, everyday political commitment.

Any reconsideration of Townsend Warner's cultural politics in the 1930s must involve a re-evaluation of the role of her partner Valentine Ackland. Ackland is usually seen as at best the lesser talent and something of a drain on Townsend Warner, and at worst a monstrous, talentless drunk who ruined her partner's emotional life. (At Townsend Warner's archive, one of the helpful and knowledgeable volunteers was bemused that I wanted to look at Ackland's papers at all, simply asking "but *why?*"). While Ackland's and Townsend Warner's published poetic collaboration (*Whether a Dove or a Seagull* [1933]) was admittedly unsuccessful, accounts that completely dismiss Ackland's role in their partnership are particularly mistaken when it comes to the two women's political activities. Whatever troubles their relationship would come to face, Ackland and Townsend's political, sexual, and romantic commitments functioned symbiotically in the 1930s. Equally active in the Communist movement, they worked together on local, national, and international campaigns, repeatedly and explicitly conceptualizing their relationship as a shared political engagement. Among many other publication venues, the couple were two of the most prolific contributors to the most prominent leftist periodical of the period, *Left Review*, to which Warner contributed eleven pieces, and Ackland nine.[5] In fact, Ackland's political journalism of the mid-1930s was at least as important in Communist circles as Townsend Warner's, as witnessed by the publication of her series of "Country Dealings" pieces in book form by Lawrence and Wishart in 1936, a volume that was praised extensively in the left-wing press.[6] Accordingly, I have paid equal attention to Ackland's and Townsend Warner's unpublished papers, regarding their political enterprise as a joint one throughout my reconstruction of their archive. This is not to say that the focus will be equally placed on

Townsend Warner's and Ackland's published works, for Warner's novel of queer revolution *Summer Will Show* (1936) is the major focal point of this chapter.

While archival research is the foundation for my reading of *Summer Will Show*, a reconsideration of this text as vitally shaped by Communism is overdue on internal textual evidence alone. While a number of sophisticated readings of Townsend Warner's novel have recently emerged, none has taken serious account of the novel's specifically Communist themes, quite an omission given that this is a narrative set in Paris during the 1848 Revolution, featuring a character named Inglebrecht, and which closes as the protagonist reads from the *The Communist Manifesto*. Paying close attention to the novel's representation of revolutionary theory and praxis, I argue that its central queer partnership should be read through a prominent dynamic of the Bolshevik political imaginary, the dialectic of spontaneity and consciousness. This dialectic was Soviet Russia's reconfiguration of classical Marxism's interplay between determinism and voluntarism – tightly integrated with Lenin's concept of the vanguard, a reworking of classical Marxism for the revolutionary needs of a largely rural country. In *Summer Will Show* Townsend Warner picks up and transforms this dialectic through the novel's central lesbian figures' engagements with Communism; this political drive and utopian futurity is crucially formed through the sense of queer revolutionary partnership that Warner found with Ackland. In other words, I read *Summer Will Show* as the literary development of a politics vitally informed by the organizational culture of Communist activism as experienced by the lesbian couple. I call this articulation *queer vanguardism*.

In what follows I first briefly outline Lenin's concept of the vanguard, before offering a reading of Townsend Warner's and Ackland's unpublished papers. Their queer vanguardism, I argue, is an overlooked aspect not only of the two women's careers but also of the sexual politics of Communism more broadly, and the constitution of emergent forms of lesbian identity in interwar Britain. Next, the focus will shift to *Summer Will Show* as a paradigmatic text of queer vanguardism; pushing back against Heather Love's recent reading of the novel as characterized by affects of despair, I argue that the novel is at least as much concerned with radical possibility as it is with hopelessness and loss. In conclusion this chapter considers some of the ways in which the novel might be understood in relation to Lukácsian realism, contending that, as opposed to Isherwood's critique, Townsend Warner offers ways of thinking typicality as a mode of queer, non-reproductivist futurity.

Lenin in Dorset

Responding to the revolutionary needs of a largely unindustrialized country, one of Lenin's signal interventions in Marxist thought was to recast the voluntarist/determinist debate in specifically Russian terms. In classical Marxism, there is a dialectical tension between the necessary progression of history toward proletarian revolution, and the need to catalyze such revolution by conscious revolutionary agitation; between a determinist view of class struggle and a voluntarist conception of political activism. Picking up an existing dichotomy in Russian culture, Lenin recasts this tension as a dialectic between spontaneity and consciousness. These terms had circulated for some time as an opposition between European rationalism and Russian expressive creativity, and Lenin cannily reworked them to refer both to the voluntarist/determinist problematic and the dialectic of theory and praxis. For the Bolshevik political imaginary, "consciousness" comes to stand for the disciplined, theoretically-informed activities of dedicated revolutionaries, "*a party that is guided by an advanced theory.*"[7] "Spontaneity" referred to the less tutored radicalism of the large Russian peasantry, poor on theory and revolutionary consciousness, but with a strong tendency toward powerful rebellion against the injustices of the existing order.[8] A distinct formation must guide this dialectic:

> the vanguard of the proletariat which is capable of assuming power and of *leading the whole people* to socialism, of directing and organizing the new order, of being the teacher, guide and leader of all the toiling and exploited in the task of building up their social life without the bourgeoisie and against the bourgeoisie.[9]

In this paradigmatic statement from *The State and Revolution* (1917), Lenin lays out the role of the vanguard as "teacher, guide and leader" of the people against the bourgeoisie, one of the most generative and most infamous concepts in modern political thought. For as is well known, vanguardism has gotten something of a bad name for its condescending attitude toward the peasantry in particular – in the language of contemporary queer theory, its metronormativity – and for its apparent rigidity and inapplicability outside of Russia. But it is worth pausing before condemning Lenin's formulation as inherently elitist or inflexible. Here Georg Lukács's *Lenin: A Study on the Unity of his Thought* (1924) is invaluable for two main reasons. First, Lukács points out that the criticism leveled against Lenin that his thought is inapplicable outside Russia was made earlier against Marx and Engels in a different form, i.e. that they generalized from British capitalism general laws that do not hold in other national and international contexts.[10] Whatever position one takes within Marxism even quite broadly considered, this criticism cannot be meaningfully sustained; we might immediately turn to Frantz Fanon's unorthodox yet unmistakably Marxist-Leninist theory of decolonial revolution in *The Wretched of the Earth* (1961), to take but one important example of the transnational reach of Marxism – to say nothing of the variegated praxes of decolonial revolt themselves or revolutionary movements in Europe, China, and beyond.[11]

Harder to dispel is the apparent elitism of Lenin's vanguard. As Katerina Clark points out, Lenin did place considerably more emphasis on consciousness than on spontaneity, and yet, as Clark also notes, he also asserted that spontaneity itself contains a form of "embryonic" consciousness.[12] Moreover, following Marx's famous declaration that "the educator must be educated," Lenin also argued that revolutionary thinkers must "not be afraid to learn from the great movements of the oppressed classes."[13] Lukács again elucidates the question with clarity: "In no sense is it the party's role to impose any kind of abstract, cleverly devised tactics on the masses. On the contrary, it must continuously *learn* from their struggle and their conduct of it."[14] In other words, the vanguard's role is not one of mere theoretical instruction, but rather organized preparation for the revolutionary moment that it necessarily cannot know precisely in advance. It is of course outside the scope of this present study to pursue any sort of detailed defense or evaluation of Lenin's thought, and I offer these remarks merely to correct the assumption that the vanguardist dialectic moves exclusively in one direction from the party to the masses.

In 1934, the CPGB brought out *Lenin on Britain: A Compilation*.

Featuring an introduction by the Party's general secretary Harry Pollitt (who was shortly to become closely acquainted with Townsend Warner and Ackland), this volume collected Lenin's writings on Britain from a variety of sources, including canonical texts such as *What is to be Done?* but also lesser-known sources such as Lenin's 1919 letter to Sylvia Pankhurst urging the formation of "a strong, seriously concentrated *organisation of the revolutionary vanguard*, which knows how to carry on by all possible means revolutionary work among the masses."[15] Pollitt's introduction pursues a polemic against Labour Party figures who assert that Lenin is not applicable in Britain, and exhorts every Communist to make a detailed study of the volume. It seems unlikely that avidly self-educating Communists such as Townsend Warner and Ackland failed to do so; but beyond their immersion in Lenin's thought as Party members, there is a further, counterintuitive reason why we should read them as vanguardists – their position in sleepy rural England.

Although Britain was the most "advanced" capitalist economy in the world, and had a strong trade union movement, it was famously lacking in revolutionary élan because of the reformism and self-protection of a powerful labor aristocracy created by its huge empire, particularly so in the case of England compared to the poorer Scotland and Wales. In *What is to be Done?* Lenin invokes England as the definitive example of how revolutionary class consciousness does not necessarily develop organically from capitalist development and the labor movements it calls forth; in many of the later texts collected in *Lenin on Britain* he inveighs against the compromises of the British labor movement.[16] Beset by reformists and opportunists, England was, as Pollitt repeatedly stressed, badly in need of a vanguard party. And within England, the heavily industrialized north and the radicalized East End of London were the major sites of highly-developed class consciousness compared to the south and west of the country. Rural Dorset, in other words, was one of the least auspicious sites for revolutionary action in Europe, which called for unconventional yet recognizably Leninist forms of activism. Dorset desperately needed revolutionary consciousness, and the two women set about the task with great energy and determination.

Townsend Warner was particularly drawn to Lenin, and had a marked respect for what she called the "serpentine" intellect as a virtue in the struggle. In an unpublished letter from 1935 she ponders the relationship between the workers' movement and such mental prowess:

> And though my mind must admire pure intellect, my flesh warns me against it. I would never call workers, revolutionary or otherwise, a dynasty of slow combustion, a cold-blooded crew. There is always something slightly luxurious about the snake, that icy brooding, those suave contours. The intellect is serpentine, and it always interests me to see in that portrait of Lenin which we have that the pose of his head is exactly like the snake's. Not the head itself, but the way it is carried. His great intellect put the dash of snake into him.[17]

This intricately dialectical passage unfurls Townsend Warner's commitment to Leninist political theory and praxis not only in its striking praise of Lenin himself, but through its densely-coded tropic structure, constantly turning in on itself in a distinctly Bolshevik dialectic. First, consciousness and its negation: Townsend Warner "admires pure intellect" even as she is warned against it by her embodiment, which leads to a disavowal of the proletariat as merely predetermined to build a revolution, as "a dynasty of slow combustion, a cold-blooded crew." Then this deterministic potential of the proletariat is sublated by Lenin's radical consciousness, and the cunning of revolutionary consciousness brings the workers to "combustion."

One of Townsend Warner's and Ackland's most striking attempts to catalyze rural workers was their establishment of a book-lending scheme. They lent left-wing books to local villagers which would contain slips for comments, and a spur for discussions; these books would then be circulated, and further lending and borrowing encouraged. It is worth stressing that the two women set up this scheme *before* the better-known Left Book Club was inaugurated later in 1936, so it should not be considered a derivative or imitative idea as might be assumed. In fact, when the LBC was founded some months later, Townsend Warner and Ackland were listed as founding members of its readers' and writers' group, and it is very possible that the women's Dorset activities influenced the LBC, especially as their idea was known to various figures in the CPGB.[18] Of course, Townsend Warner's and Ackland's scheme could never attain the reach of the LBC – but they were one step ahead of the Party and may even have played a vital intellectual role in the formation of the better-known organization.

Discussing one text they circulated, John Sommerfield's *May Day* (1936), Townsend Warner underlined the importance of maintaining a firm political message:

> I don't mind at all it being sectarian, myself. For lending down here (and this is not a bad literary standard of criticism, after all, though it may sound rather parochial) a certain sectarian stiffening is all to the good. There will be a danger as long as workers are under capitalism that they will read for a change of thought, a relaxation and release from their conditions. We have found that very objective books, though they enjoy them, don't remain in the memory as much more than a circus. A sectarian novel like this may stay in the mind as a circus with a message, as a relevant circus.[19]

Here Townsend Warner's desire to shape the consciousness of the rural poor is clear, who must not read for "relaxation" and for whom merely "objective" literature is not sufficient. Wendy Mulford cites a truncated version of this passage in *This Narrow Place*, omitting the austere central sentence concerning the "danger" of relaxation, perhaps motivated by a desire to airbrush the extent of Townsend Warner's vanguardism.[20] There is again a counterintuitive, serpentine quality to Townsend Warner's political thinking here, for it might be expected that "relaxation" would be associated with the circus-like texts, and political engagement with "very objective" books, but Townsend Warner's prescriptions are rather more dialectical. Like Lukács in *The Historical Novel* (1937), she aims to mediate the objective, the sectarian, and the popular according the exigencies of Communist political development, a process by which all the constitutive terms are themselves necessarily reordered.

Another initiative Townsend Warner and Ackland worked on during this period was an attempt to organize the women of the village. Unfortunately, it did not meet with much success, hobbled by the machinations of a local woman – named, somewhat improbably perhaps, Blanche Rocket – who sowed discontent and jealousy. As Townsend Warner wrote in her diary in an entry excised from Harman's published edition: "while B.R., damn her, sets every married woman at each other's throat, not much hope for organizing the Chaldon Women's March on the Estate Office."[21] Rocket was infamous in the village for her disruption of marriages, and Townsend Warner's and Ackland's failure to organize the women of the village could be read as a moment in which the brittle sociality of the heterosexual couple form occludes both gender and class solidarity. This episode as a whole might lead one to underline the vital importance of queer vanguardism within a broad political field.

Grounded in local struggles, both Townsend Warner and Ackland increasingly came to be involved in Communist politics on a national level, traveling up to London to visit friends such as Julius and Queenie Lipton, and dropping in the offices of *Left Review* and the CPGB headquarters at King Street. They viewed these visits to London as vital to their involvement with the wider movement, the necessary counterpart to their rural activism, not only in the sense that they were able to meet with important figures such as Harry Pollitt and glean the latest news from Party headquarters, but also because their work in Dorset necessarily required contact with the (perhaps presumed) higher class consciousness of the town proletariat. As Townsend Warner wrote to the London worker Julius Lipton, "it is like bathing in a tonic for us to come up to London – and I only hope you realise how much of the tonic is seeing you, and getting a good sniff at the work you are doing."[22]

The two women's engagement with Communism was also catalyzed from the start by international politics.[23] As Townsend Warner repeatedly recalled, it was the Reichstag Fire Trial and its Communist hero, Georgi Dimitrov, that had been the most important catalyst for these internationalist commitments: "whatever one might feel about Communism, whatever holes one might pick in the arguments of its adherents, Dimitrov's resolution and pugnacity and fighting cunning were fact, not theory."[24] Dimitrov was the Bulgarian Communist wrongly accused of the Reichstag arson in 1933, and whose defiant speech at the trial won him great respect on the left during the 1930s, becoming head of the Communist International after his release from Nazi custody, and spearheading the adoption of the Popular Front policy. Dimitrov was celebrated in Communist writing and culture across Europe during the period, from German artist John Heartfield's famous photomontage *Dimitroff!* to Ralph Fox's recommendation that British writers should look to Dimitrov's trial as a master-plot for writing socialist realist novels.[25] What is also telling here is Townsend Warner's use of "cunning": an attribute that might not initially appear be associated with heroic moments of speaking truth to power such as Dimitrov's trial, but a cardinal virtue of the vanguardist fighter, and as we have seen one Townsend Warner attributed to Lenin himself.

Queer vanguardism

To step back a moment from 1930s Communism, this apparently aggressively paratactic phrase is immediately legible when we turn to certain strains of canonical queer theory. At its most ambitious, queer theory has always been vanguardist in the broad sense of the term, as an epistemology and ontology of culture that seeks to fundamentally reorder governing assumptions about the human through the white heat of its intellectual interventions. To take perhaps the most famous instance of this tendency, Eve Kosofsky Sedgwick's opening to *The Epistemology of the Closet* (1990) is one of the boldest statements of this project, with its stated aim of redefining the history of twentieth-century western culture.[26] In a different way, gay and lesbian history has celebrated the figure of the pioneer who forges new forms of intimate life within a repressive climate and thus inspires other to do the same; as I hope has already become clear, I aim to situate Isherwood, Townsend Warner, and Ackland within both these tendencies.

There is a further sense in which certain queer theorists operate as vanguardists, a tendency that can be read in a more specifically Leninist sense, as a particular strategic relation between intellectuals and the proletariat, here restaged as a polemical engagement between the queer theorist and the yet-to-be-conscious LGBTQI masses. Michael Warner, for instance, is frank about his belief in false consciousness, and *The Trouble With Normal* (1999) can be read profitably alongside Lenin's *What is to be Done?*[27] Both texts are biting attacks on the reformist right wings of their respective movements; Lenin and Warner are similarly concerned with the clarification of modes of communication of (queer/revolutionary) consciousness from the theorist to the massed (gay and lesbian/worker and peasant) subjects, while also acknowledging the existence of spontaneously radical subjectivity. To take another canonical moment: the dialectic of spontaneity and consciousness is also ironically explored in the closing passages of "Sex in Public," where Warner and Lauren Berlant wryly ponder their appropriate response "as good academics" to the scene of queer erotics they have just witnessed (Berlant, it should be added, has made contemporary theory's most trenchant formulation of false consciousness in *Cruel Optimism* [2011]).²⁸ In "Sex in Public" Lenin's precept that the vanguardist theorist must learn from the masses rather than merely impose preordained theory is in particular evidence. As Berlant and Warner witness the erotic vomiting and ponder its meaning they are following the fundamental tenet that radical embodied praxis is intricately intertwined with revolutionary theory.

José Esteban Muñoz's *Cruising Utopia* (2009) further develops this dialectic. From the start of his study, Muñoz pays tribute to the example of queer performers, to which his intellectual response is a respectful reframing and re-presentation in the name of a utopian politics drawn in part from the Marxism of Ernst Bloch. He argues that a queer hermeneutic must necessarily be "humble":

> Such a hermeneutic would then be *epistemologically and ontologically humble* in that it would not claim the epistemological certitude of a queerness that we simply "know" but, instead, strain to activate the no-longer-conscious and to extend a glance toward that which is forward-dawning, anticipatory illuminations of a not-yet-conscious.[29]

Here there might appear to be a complete rejection of vanguardism as commonly understood. But we might also read this passage as a radical reformulation of the vanguard intellectual that in its humility goes beyond Lenin's and Lukács's insistence that the vanguard must teach and learn from the masses – for Muñoz the theorist never "simply knows," from whatever source – and yet retains a fundamental similarity in the concept of "activation." The no-longer-conscious and the yet-to-be-conscious must be articulated and thus an unpredictable queerness to come activated. The queer theorist helps make history, but in circumstances not of their own making, of which they are necessarily incompletely aware, and yet which others may have forgotten completely. And indeed Muñoz's main object in *Cruising Utopia* is gay culture around the time of Stonewall, that great moment of queer spontaneity, to which much queer theory may be said to have a re-vivifying theoretical relation of re-presentation. Indeed, one might profitably return to classic texts of gay liberation and radical feminism to see a marked vanguardism at work, the manifestos of a Wittman or a Solanas having more than their fair share of vanguardist élan.[30]

Muñoz's humble vanguardism might sound a stretch. But he does have another more thoroughly vanguardist figure in mind: the queer performer. Muñoz notes the prevalence of a certain macho, usually white body in mainstream gay culture, and argues that the black transgendered performer Aviance "figuratively and literally rises above this pervasive bodily mode."[31] The key term here is "above." Muñoz further elaborates:

> When he is on that stage, he performs gestures that few others can perform. His gestures are not allowed in the strict codes of masculinity followed by the habitués of most commercial queer dance spaces [. . .] As an icon, a beacon above the dance floor Aviance uses gestures that permit the dancers to see and experience the feelings they do not permit themselves to let in. He and the gestures he performs are beacons that the throng is not allowed to feel.[32]

Here a taboo embodied consciousness is imparted to the "throng" of proto-radical subjects whose interpellation by a dominant homonormative culture has prevented the expression of their collective, not-yet subversive identity. While this club scene sounds rather far from reading *Capital* in night school or leafleting on the factory floor, it is worth pointing out that interwar British Communist culture was deeply invested in bodily style – in dress, deportment, attitudes toward leisure, and choice of sexual partner, as the novels of Isherwood's friend Edward Upward document at length, and as has been explored in a number of other national contexts, particularly Weimar Germany.[33] Nevertheless, any easy mapping of proletarian consciousness onto queers or indeed any other group is necessarily a futile endeavor. But here I am concerned with strategy, not identification, with the ways that queer and Communist counterpublics and cells seek to communicate between exceptional agents of radical change and the proto-subjects of a utopian world to come. Queer vanguardism names the ways in which these strategies can illuminate one another and sometimes operate in creative syncretism to forge new, distinctive cultural forms.

An intriguing letter from Townsend Warner to Ackland exemplifies these overlaid forms of radical subjectivity. Describing a meeting with the Communist scholar and expert on Spain, Stanley Robinson, Townsend Warner enthuses about her new friend:

> His voice is like embattled mice, small and shrill, I daresay it could be loud and shrill. He looks as though you could knock him down with a feather, and obviously has the most fiery and passionate temper. And he is the velvetiest pansy I have met in years. We instantly coagulated, and had a lovely time, partly buttering each other, partly finding how simultaneously we felt about anarchists, partly deploring the vagaries of poor dear Stephen.[34]

Here Warner and Robinson instantly bond, as Communists and as queers, Warner's "coagula[tion]" with the scholar framed in terms of a personal description simultaneously stressing non-normative gender performance, "shrill as mice," and political toughness, "fiery and dedicated," indicating a valorization of queerness not so much as a cross to bear as a Communist, but rather as a positive attribute in the struggle, a particular modality of the commitment needed in a dedicated activist. This passage indicates the ways in which queer Communists' self-understanding was not necessarily informed by a tortured push-pull of Party normativity and queer self-expression, but rather could work on a symbiotic level, as the tessellation of different modes of counterpublic association and vanguardist consciousness. "Stephen" here is Spender, whom as we have seen Warner had called to be removed from the Party "like a purge" in a letter to Edgell Rickword the previous month, and his casual inclusion in the conversation reveals the way in which queer writers were embedded in different locations in the Popular Front, Warner here disparaging the "vagaries" of Spender's poster-boy affiliation within the movement in comparison with hers and Robinson's more dedicated political positions.[35]

As we have seen, Townsend Warner's and Ackland's local activism was triangulated with the national Party center in London, and broader international affiliations; as Gay Wachman has pertinently observed, "for Warner and Ackland in the thirties, their political writing, local and international activism, and 'deviant' sexuality were inextricably intertwined."[36] But it was undoubtedly the local that was their starting point – in more ways than one. As Wachman points out, the two women came together "following an evening of village activism."[37] This was in October 1930, several years before they became CPGB members; the two women had gone to interrogate a local woman suspected of abusing her foster child. Townsend Warner recalls Ackland taking a loaded pistol to the confrontation, and that she "shook her stick like a squire" at the child's abuser. Townsend Warner was clearly impressed with Ackland's assured performance of iconoclastic female masculinity, and her description of Ackland's ire in her diaries is framed in terms of sexual attraction: "righteous indignation is a beautiful thing, and lying exhausted on the rug I watched it flame in her with severe geometrical frames."[38] Later that night, the two women became lovers, the politicized tone of their relationship having clearly been set by that initial encounter. This can be seen in a series of love poems sent between the pair in 1936–8, as the convention of the anniversary functioned as an annual reminder of how their personal relationship was imbricated with political struggle and commitment to Communism. The following image comes at the end of the series.

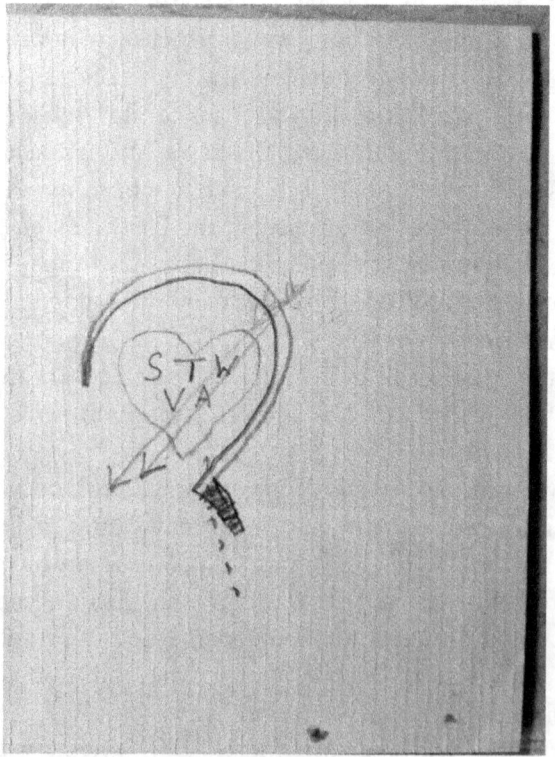

Valentine Ackland, Pencil Drawing (1938?), STW: H(R)/5/12

In this image the sickle encircles the two women's initials, starkly symbolizing a shared identity as queer Communist lovers. Several poems return to this sense of commitment, and the ways in which their love had not closed them off from the wider claims of political witness, "faced with confused alarms of struggle and fight [. . .] since then learning not to close ears, shut eyes, and not to fear more than we love."[39] It is this register of political struggle that is the crucial missing piece in debates around Townsend Warner's and Ackland's relationship to Communism as lesbians. First of all, Janet Montefiore's assertion that "the notion of lesbians finding a happy home in the Communist Party is distinctly naïve" is complicated by the archival record: for all Soviet Communism's mounting heteronormativity during the mid-1930s, Warner and Ackland were – remarkably, to contemporary ears – accepted as a couple by the CPGB, traveling together to headquarters, and on the writers' delegation to Spain in 1937. Warner and Ackland made no secret of their relationship with friends from the CPGB, inviting figures such as Julius Lipton, Edgell Rickword, and Tom Winteringham down to stay in their cottage in Dorset, where sleeping arrangements were tight.[40]

Nevertheless, Townsend Warner and Ackland never developed a wide public presence as "out" lesbians; Warner's later desire for their love letters that she carefully collected and annotated only to be published after her death being an obvious example of this. But the exigencies of the closet are far from exhaustively helpful in understanding these two women's sexual politics in the 1930s, not least because scholars have increasingly argued that the existence of a broad public awareness of a specifically lesbian identity in interwar Britain is rather doubtful, even after the famous trial of Radclyffe Hall's *The Well of Loneliness* in 1928.[41] There might rather appear to be a sense of what Terry Castle famously called the Queen Victoria principle of erasure at work here, and there seems to be no direct evidence that their relationship itself was positively valorized by leading CPGB members. However, Dan Healey has pointed out that in 1929 some Soviet experts had argued for official legal recognition of marriages involving female husbands, implying a positive attitude toward certain forms of female homosexuality for some medical and legal professionals in the Soviet Union.[42] It is of course hard to gauge to what extent such an ethos may have penetrated to the CPGB leadership or the rank and file of British Communism. Maroula Jannou's measured verdict on Townsend Warner's place in the CPGB might seem to make the most sense: that they were "recognized as a couple" and "judged, if they were judged at all, on the usefulness of the work they did in public and not for their sexuality."[43] Given the CPGB's emphasis on organizational results as a cardinal virtue and the respect Ackland and Townsend Warner received from many Party members, this reading is initially attractive.

However, in its bifurcation of private and public, Jannou's judgment assumes that the two women's sexuality was in some sense anterior to their commitment to radical politics, a given property of their subjectivity rather than a series of acts and performances indivisible from their political commitments and activities. It is also necessary to push back against this evaluation both in terms of the chronology of the two women's relationship, and the emergence of certain forms of gender and sexual dissidence in Britain in the period more broadly, to which the case of Soviet Russia makes a telling counterpoint. The Soviet experts' discussion of cross-identifying marriage coincided with the central constitutive moment for a certain type of queer identity in Britain that emerged with the prosecution of *The Well of Loneliness* in 1928 and was further shaped by the case of Valerie Barker, who had lived as the military officer Colonel Victor Barker, married a woman Elfrieda Haward, and was brought to trial upon discovery in 1929.[44] Barker's passing and subsequent trial have been viewed as the transition between a broadly appreciative public gaze upon heroic female masculinity in World War I that was then rendered increasingly problematic in peacetime Britain. Emerging from civil war in 1923, Soviet Russia is again a salient point of comparison. Healey notes that "Women who served in military formations and were known to be lesbian or were regarded as 'masculinized' (inclined to dress in a mannish fashion or indeed to assume a male identity) were viewed with an intriguing degree of indulgence during the 1920s."[45] In both Soviet Russia and Britain, the assumption of traditionally male roles by women in times of crisis was praised as a valuable contribution, with the radical ethos of Soviet Communism continuing this valorization further into the 1920s.

There is a very tightly chronologically integrated transnational history here, further shaped by the publication of the *Great Soviet Encyclopedia* in 1930, containing a famously progressive entry on homosexuality, in which the psychiatrist Mark Ia. Sereiskii trenchantly argued for tolerance and acceptance, albeit in the pathologizing sexological language of the time – a landmark intervention explicitly influenced by Magnus Hirschfeld's research and activism, in turn motivating his alliance with Communism in the early 1930s (as we have seen in Chapter 1, Isherwood also arrived in Berlin and became acquainted with Hirschfeld in 1929–30).[46] While acknowledging that fascism had a certain appeal for some cross-identifying women, Jack Halberstam has influentially stressed that female masculinities are not always overwhelmingly conservative assumptions of male privilege but "also ways for women to pioneer forms of masculinity that change the meaning of modern gender and sexual identity."[47] Ackland's defiant gender performance and Townsend Warner's queer Leninism are vital pioneering forms, which reorder sexual identity through their thoroughgoing engagement with Soviet Communism.

Some of the complex maneuverings involved in Ackland's gender-dissident Communism can be seen in the following unpublished letter to Julius Lipton. Ackland and Warner invited Lipton and his wife Queenie to stay with them in Dorset, and Ackland's letter gives a brief sketch of Ackland's life since arriving in Dorset, warning Lipton that her appearance is somewhat unconventional:

> I had little cash, and no experience of living on little. So I first of all found a practical way of saving on clothes (which I did not then know could be an inexpensive item -) and I bought a pair of corduroy trousers for ten bob, which I have still – They never wear out, you know. Then I found that flannels cost little, in comparison with the skirts I had before. So from that day to this, whenever I am in the country proper, I always wear these clothes. It makes a difference, too – I feel freer and – most important – as I made the change when I was miserable, and was determined to alter my misery to something better and less squalid I feel liberated by the change in apparel. But it is, I know, a curious difference that they make. So I warn you beforehand![48]

In this passage there is a distinct movement from what might initially be read as the excuses of the closet to a more celebratory mode, as Ackland states that she "feel[s] liberated" by this change in dress. What is striking about this movement is that it must be read back through the initial "excuse" which claims economic necessity for the declassed Ackland. The letter continues:

Now, of course, so many women wear trousers that it doesn't look odd any longer. But then I suppose it did. But no one down here minded, except one or two old labourers and their wives. The younger people all became friendly to me because, I think, it made me unlike the people who so much oppress them (as you'll find when you talk to them), the "County" grandees, and the clergy and their wives.

To borrow another of Halberstam's astute formulations, here the "sartorial semiotic" of Ackland's female masculinity turns out to be an intersectional asset in her Communist organizing, as it brackets (while not entirely erasing) her bourgeois class origins in dealing with the younger members of the rural poor, enabling her to become friendly with important targets for her organizing: she is "unlike the people who so much oppress them" in more ways than one.[49] In his study of Lenin, Lukács urged that the vanguardist fighter not only must have great "clarity of consciousness" but also an "equal ability to merge themselves totally in the lives of the struggling and suffering masses."[50] Clearly Ackland isn't merging as such with the rural poor, but her self-presentation is absolutely intertwined with her Communist activism in a reordering rather than rejection of Lukács's politics of everyday life.

To deploy Muñoz's supple term, the best way to describe Ackland's gender and class performance might be disidentification – as can be seen from pictures of her from the time, her preferred mode of dress veered between poacher and country squire, with the occasional foray into upper-class male evening dress ("Valentine had spent a queer night in a white tie and a tailcoat, falling in love with a young woman called Dorothea," Townsend Warner recorded in 1935, in yet another passage excised from published editions of her diaries, perhaps depicting a reading of *Middlemarch*).[51] This performance of rural authority and its subversion allowed her to shape a complex embodied critique of country injustice, as a shape-shifting insider-outsider to the rural ruling classes. Ackland's 1930s diaries, written in a punchy, telegraphic style, are a particularly rich source for this positioning:

Shot 3 rabbits.
Communists had good gains in French municipal elections. [. . .]
Shot 4 rabbits – one shot each and at a good 50 yards off – clean through the head.

Did 2 ½ hours gardening.
Did 5 of the *Left Review* poets.[52]

This remarkable parataxis juxtaposes delight in her shooting skills with international news and writing assignments for Communist publications, again showing how Ackland perceived her gender performance and political work as intertwined. There's a sense of target practice going on in her insistent return to the rabbits, a training in readiness for violent revolution that is simultaneously a gender-dissident praxis when undertaken by a woman; book reviewing is placed alongside such concerns in an attempt to integrate theory and practice paradigmatic of 1930s Communist thought and political organization. Here Ackland's disciplined approach (note the quantification of every activity) suggests that to assert that Townsend Warner and Ackland navigated their queer Communism with serene ease would indeed be misplaced – not for the reasons Montefiore implies, but rather because it would go against the grain of the Communist ethos of continual struggle to which they both adhered.

It is clearly very easy to disparage Townsend Warner and Ackland's commitment to the Soviet Union, as can be seen in Patrick Wright's sneering account of them as "sisters in militancy" gazing at the "reflected light of a glorious Soviet future."[53] More subtly – but I would argue, equally mistakenly – one might see their intertwined commitments as an unfortunate by-product of the energies of queer life, to be acknowledged as part of a variegated history unassimilable to a progressivist narrative of gay and lesbian history yet ultimately to be understood as a political dead end.[54] But here is neither failure nor loss, for as with Isherwood's articulation of the queer potential of the First Five-Year Plan, it is in no small part the most implacably Soviet aspects of Townsend Warner's and Ackland's cultural politics that open up a capacious sense of queer futurity, the non-reproductivist model of intimate struggle that lies at the heart of *Summer Will Show*.

Revolution retriangulated

More than any other British novel of the 1930s, *Summer Will Show* insistently intertwines queer desire and revolutionary politics. The novel features Sophia, a Tory heiress who leaves her country seat upon the death of her children to seek out her errant husband, Frederick, who is living in Paris with his mistress, a Jewish storyteller named Minna. When Sophia arrives, however, she falls in love with Minna as the February Revolution of 1848 breaks out in the city. Both women become involved in the revolution, Minna as a romantic revolutionary, whose words inspire the bohemians and revolutionaries constantly congregating at her apartment. But it is Sophia who begins to work for the Communists, whose chief theorist, Inglebrecht, is attracted by her strong-willed practicality and clear-minded thinking. The novel draws to a close as the revolutionaries are defeated in the fighting of the unsuccessful June rebellion. Both women fight on the barricades; Minna is killed in picaresque fashion by an illegitimate relation of Sophia's from the Caribbean, who Sophia kills in turn. The novel's final page pictures Sophia starting to read one of the pamphlets she had been distributing for the Communists, which turns out to be *The Communist Manifesto*.

Simultaneously and inescapably a novel of queer desire and Marxist revolution, *Summer Will Show* poses in acute fashion what might appear to be the central question of 1930s queer Communism: how can a such a supposedly rigidly normative scheme of political action and theory be reconciled with or accommodated to a set of practices, desires, and experiences so necessarily antinormative? Perhaps in response to this dilemma, critical readings of the novel have generally emerged in "extremely polarized terms," as Heather Love has pointed out.[55] Either the novel is read as concerned with "class politics," as Claire Harman would have it, or it with lesbian fantasy, as Terry Castle has argued.[56] However, Love's recent reading in *Feeling Backward* (2009) has broken new ground in an attempt to think revolutionary Marxism through queer experience in the novel. Deploying Walter Benjamin's and Raymond Williams's "tragic" reworkings of Marxism, and focusing on the novel's affects of despair, Love argues that "despair in the novel appears as a kind of resource: as much as hope, it is necessary to make change happen."[57] This allows Love to construct an intriguing synthesis, between the historical "impossibility" of both queer desire and revolution itself: "revolutionary consciousness in *Summer Will Show* is imagined as a desire for an impossible redemption – a total transformation of society that cannot and yet must take place."[58] Love directly opposes this sense of the "impossible objects" of queer desire and revolution to a "forward-looking, scientific Marxism," contending that the novel's orientation toward the past, rather than the future, and its incessant focus on despair rather than hope or utopia puts *Summer Will Show* completely at odds with the progressivist history of such a politics.

Love's is one of the most sophisticated interpretations of *Summer Will Show*, and offers a subtle model for understanding how the novel imbricates queer desire and revolutionary action. However, her exclusive focus on "dark affects," moments of despair, and on the novel's backward-looking moments seem rather strange in a novel so insistently structured around the dynamics of a specifically Communist revolutionary ethos. Crucial to Love's argument is the claim that "Minna's idiosyncratic revolutionary desires and regrets," explicitly opposed to Inglebrecht's "scientific socialism," are the novel's privileged model of politics and desire; on this reading, Sophia's path through the novel, from mistress of a country estate to Communist revolutionary, is exclusively scripted by her increasing identification with Minna, rather than Inglebrecht.[59] I want to propose a very different reading of the relationship between these three characters, one that reconstructs the novel's vanguardist élan, expressed through the distinctively Bolshevik dialectic of spontaneity and consciousness in Townsend Warner's letters. Driven by this dialectic, *Summer Will Show* constructs a sophisticated triangulation between Minna, Sophia, and Inglebrecht, a group dynamic that is fundamental not only to the novel's Communist élan, but also to its model of non-reproductivist futurity.

As the term triangulations suggests, it is worthwhile to recount Castle's classic reading of the novel. According to Castle, *Summer Will Show* is a paradigmatic lesbian novel because it overturns the male homosocial triangle diagnosed by Sedgwick and puts in its place a new configuration, in which female bonding (Minna–Sophia) is transformed into lesbian desire, and the male point of the triangle (Frederick) drops away.[60] Castle's interpretation is convincing, but incomplete: she fails to notice that a new, intimately politicized triangulation emerges at precisely the point at which Frederick is most surely ejected from the two women's erotic lives. Indeed, almost at the very moment of their erotic consummation, Inglebrecht is hovering in the background, the notes for *The Communist Manifesto* in hand: a completely desexualized and thus vitally important figure for Sophia's queer development.

Following a conversation between the two women during which sexual tension is clearly building, they experience "a flush of pleasure, a triumphant cry" capped by Minna licking an oyster shell.[61] This moment is preceded by an encounter with her husband when he cuts Sophia off from her money and she strikes him around the face. Clearly, as Castle argues, this is a moment of de-triangulation in which the male falls away – particularly as it is a sign of supposed sexual complicity from Frederick that causes Sophia's reaction, "a booncompanion's grin" that calls forth her punch (216). And yet, between the encounter with Frederick and Sophia's and Minna's consummation, Inglebrecht appears, having been by the sick Minna's bedside while Sophia was away confronting Frederick. Indeed, Sophia's most pressing thought following her encounter with Frederick was that she wished to see her new Communist acquaintance:

> Stronger than rage, astonishment, contempt, the pleasurable sense that at last she had slapped Frederick's face, the less pleasurable surmise that his slap back would be longer-lasting; stronger even than the desire to see Minna was her feeling that of all things, of all people, she most at this moment wished to see Inglebrecht, and the sturdy assurance that she would find in him everything that she expected. If she had gone up the stairs in the rue de la Carabine on her knees, she could not have ascended with a more zealotical faith that there would be healing at the top; and when he opened the door to her, enquiring politely if her errands had gone well she replied with enthusiasm, "Perfectly. My husband – it was he I went to see – has just threatened to cut me off with a penny." (218)

This long sentence moves through a series of intertwined affective moments – Sophia's new-found physical dominance of her husband, his "longer-lasting" financially brutal response, her desire to see Minna, but above all to see Inglebrecht, with whom she now zealously identifies – before finishing with a wry, succinct statement of the economic power of patriarchal control. The passage continues:

> "A lock-out," said Inglebrecht. "Very natural. It is a symptom of capitalistic anxiety. I suppose he has always been afraid of you."
> She nodded, and her lips curved in a grin of satisfaction. (218)

Here Sophia comes to stand, with grim certitude, for the proletariat itself, locked out of the means of production by Frederick's capitalist anxiety at her increasingly manifest power, an identification that subtly indicates the ways in which the growth of capitalism complicates and then supersedes a fully patriarchal sexual economy. Such an identity might seem to place her merely as the object of Inglebrecht's Marxist analysis, yet another fixing of the female subject by the male gaze. But Sophia not only grins in satisfaction, but has her own uses for Inglebrecht: "He is everything, she thought, that I expected, everything that I desired; grim and flat, positive without any flavor, a man like plain cold water" (219). Here Inglebrecht appears as a desexualized masculine subject, a socially refreshing and politically invigorating substance for Sophia's transformation. This depiction of Inglebrecht clearly echoes Lenin's famous exchange with Clara Zetkin on the subject of Soviet sexual revolution. During this conversation, Lenin railed against the supposedly glib way in which young people were conducting their sexual lives – apparently sex was seen as akin to merely drinking a glass of water, and Lenin castigated this attitude for its misreading of Marx and Engels on sexuality and for its frivolousness.[62] Lenin's comments have generally been seen to signal the foundering of Soviet sexual radicalism, but here Townsend Warner slyly repurposes them to foreground lesbian desire as opposed to heterosexual union.

Minna had been asleep during Inglebrecht and Sophia's conversation; she soon wakes, and Inglebrecht reads the two women a long passage from the pamphlet he has been writing. There is no direct quote from Marx or Engels in the passage, but it clearly draws on denunciations of romantic revolutionaries from across their writings.[63] Inglebrecht mischievously tells Minna that she is his model for this type, *"penetrated with artistic and historical feeling"* but unable to become disciplined revolutionaries (220; emphasis in original). Inglebrecht's discourse negates and yet preserves Minna's earlier storytelling that held so many romantics captivated earlier in the narrative, and it also parodies an earlier charity concert where Sophia met Frederick; in a further turn, it is then echoed in Sophia's later performance of English hymns as she and Minna scrabble for sources of income. An accomplished musicologist before she became a full-time writer, Townsend Warner's lifelong engagement with music centrally shapes major episodes and themes in the narrative. In addition to Engels and Brecht, it is worth considering another likely source for Inglebrecht's name here, the French conductor and friend of Debussy, Désiré-Émile Inghelbrecht (1880–1965). Inghelbrecht was a major figure on the French music scene in the period, and in 1934 he became the conductor of a new prestigious radio orchestra, which was to become the *Orchestre national de France*. Inglebrecht the Communist is compared to "a recording angel" (219), surely significant given Inghelbrecht's prominence as a radio conductor.

The metaphor of the conductor has clear Leninist overtones, as a figure who brings the collective to a shared rhythm by directing a script of their actions that is necessarily informed by their performance. More broadly, Inglebrecht's resonance with music – Sophia also compares her sensation when listening to him and Minna to "what I have seen painted sometimes on the faces of people listening to Beethoven" (219) – indicates the importance of not overstating the dry, cold aspects of revolutionary theory in Townsend Warner's political thought and literary praxis. It would be far too simplistic a reading to suggest that Minna simply represents embodied passion, and Inglebrecht detached reason (to say nothing of this position as a reifying anti-intellectual cliché). Inglebrecht is indeed desexualized, but he is not disembodied, his paradoxically fragile yet resilient physicality stressed throughout, reminding Sophia "of an animal" wrapped in a shawl to protect him from a permanent chill he contracted from one of his many periods of imprisonment, yet pursuing his aims "swiftly and circumspectly [. . .] true to his own laws" (222). The shawl usually associated with women, his affective labor in caring for Minna, his animality, and yet his traditionally masculine intent political purpose and self-contained certainty mark Inglebrecht as a distinctive subject of revolutionary modernity, "true to his own laws and oblivious of all else" (222). Yet Inglebrecht is not without humor, even in moments of heavily instrumental political discourse. As he entreats Sophia to fight Frederick for her money in order to donate it to the Communists, he improbably winks: "it seems unbelievable that such an eye could wink. Wink, however, it did" (222). Sophia is, however, not in the least offended and promises to "write to her man of business tomorrow" (222). This wink, entirely devoid of sexual flirtation, negates Frederick's "boon companion's grin" (222); a transposition of masculine complicity into political community, it signals the emergence of a new affective triangle.

Inglebrecht must himself drop away, at least for a while. After he leaves, Minna declares that she "appreciates" Inglebrecht, and would be ready to mend her romantic-revolutionary ways at his request (223). Yet she also declares that all the time he was with her, her thoughts were mainly of Sophia's return. Sophia then reveals how Frederick has "cut off [her] supplies," and the two women ponder their future, in perhaps the most famous exchange in the novel:

> "You will stay? You must, if only to gall him."
> "I don't think that much of a reason."
> "But you will stay?"
> "I will stay if you wish it."
> It seemed to her that the words fell cold and glum as ice-pellets. Only beneath the crust of thought did her being assent as by right to that flush of pleasure, that triumphant cry.
> "But of course," said Minna a few hours later, thoughtfully licking the last oyster shell, "we must be practical." (224)

Here sexual consummation is drawn from a rejection of the masculine side of the triangle – a thought initially "cold and glum" that is negated by the "right" of lesbian desire. The juxtaposition of erotic imagery with Minna's desire for "practicality" is, as the following lines make clear, heavily ironic, as the sybaritic Minna is anything but practical: "this remark she had already made repeatedly, speaking with the excitement of an adventurous mind contemplating a new and hazardous experience" (224). However, this sense of practicality carries several further valences, organized around the concept of commitment. It signals the cementing of the pair's consummation, the constitution of Minna and Sophia as a couple. But even as the couple form emerges, such commitment is broadened through a complete identification of Minna with revolutionary politics itself: "and though you may think you have chosen me, Sophia, or chosen happiness, it is the Revolution you have chosen" (227). Here the "practicality" of the emergent lesbian couple-form is co-constitutive with radical political praxis and a totalizing identification with revolution.

In the following scenes in the novel, Sophia continuously encounters Minna as a figure of seductive (at times problematically exoticized) difference, both in her espousal of revolutionary ideals and her infuriating impracticality, set against the Englishwoman's residual

Tory politics and clear-minded prudence. Very quickly, however, Sophia undergoes a series of transformations and within a matter of weeks "the prudence of her class had shriveled" (236); and yet this declassing is coupled with a frustration at the inept nature of the hapless would-be revolutionaries with whom she now finds herself. "They are like – the thought jumped up, exact and clinching – they are like people sickening for a fever; excited, restless, listless, blown this way and that like windlestraws in the gusts that stir before a thunderstorm" (232). Such annoyance at the febrility of the romantic revolutionaries already contains the germ of Communist praxis, and is immediately followed by a reconsideration of Minna and Inglebrecht:

> Minna, God knows, was idle; but she was completely without arrogance, and her idleness was coupled with such energy that it seemed like the flourish of a vitality too rich to be contained in any doing, a stream too impetuous to turn any mill-wheel [. . .] The one wholly untainted was Inglebrecht. Whatever the sickness, there was no taint of it on him, whatever happened he, resolute, discreet, self-contained, alert, would trot like some secret busy badger along his own path. (232–3)

We can read this passage as an articulation of the dialectic of spontaneity and consciousness: Sophia praises Minna's spontaneous revolutionary energy alongside Inglebrecht's qualities, "resolute, discreet, self-contained, alert," with Sophia as the site of their synthesis. In line with Lenin's tendency toward the consciousness side of the dialectic, it is the latter set of characteristics that make Sophia an ideal worker for the Communists, for whom she begins to transport scrap metal to be made into bullets. The Communists' armory is hidden beneath a laundry, and Sophia is chosen because, as an Englishwoman and a lady, she would attract little attention. Her English "eccentricity" would account for her taking her washing to the laundry rather than have a servant deliver it, while her class position would add to the respectability of the front; as the proprietress remarks, "one can see from a glance that you would not be connected with anything – with anything unusual" (277).

Musing on this covert work, Sophia notes that prudence has reasserted itself with her new tasks, indeed that she has come to view order and regularity "with an almost mystical admiration." She continues:

And yet, though it was destruction she served, it was a purposed destruction, something foreseen and deliberated; and here, if she could only get herself into the well-scrubbed fortress of the Alpine Laundry, become one of those Communists instead of an eccentric Englishwoman carrying a laundry-basket, might be a safety for the mind. (282)

Here is Sophia's transformation into an agent of Communism, "serving" something "foreseen and deliberated," an orderly form of destruction of which she now approves. She also wishes for a tighter integration with Communist praxis and everyday life, to be more than a merely instrumentalized "eccentric Englishwoman." In fact, as Inglebrecht had observed on their very first meeting (203), Sophia is supremely suited to a serious role in the Communist movement, which she soon comes to realize, pondering that "more and more clearly during those summer evenings, shone out her air of technique, of being a professional amongst amateurs" (284).

While Sophia, Minna, and Inglebrecht make up an eccentric cell, a Communist social unit encompassing queer partnership and non-reproductive futurity, *Summer Will Show* also features an abject figure of revolutionary exclusion. We meet Sophia's illegitimate biracial nephew Caspar early on in the narrative, when he comes to visit her in England, livening up her country life with his exoticized presence before he is sent to boarding school, having angered the village with his physical perfection in something of a cliché of biraciality. Much to Sophia's irritation, Caspar later appears in Minna's apartment in Paris; again he is sent away, apparently to boarding school. But instead it turns out that Frederick enlisted the unwanted youth in the Gardes Mobile, the counter-revolutionary force deployed against the revolutionaries in the June Days uprising which spelled the victory of reaction.

Caspar is the paradigmatic figure of the racialized, feminized lumpenproletarian in Marx's and Engels's writings. As the illegitimate son of a plantation owner, he is a remainder of the old class order, part of the "dregs, refuse, and scum of all classes" as Marx condemns the lumpenproletariat; feckless and buffeted by circumstances beyond his control, he is manipulated into becoming a foot soldier of the forces of reaction.[64] Indeed, Caspar's role in the Gardes Mobile fixes him at the most intense site of Marx's development of the concept of the lumpenproletariat, in his account of Bonaparte's coup of 1851 in *The Eighteenth Brumaire of Louis Napoleon* (1852) – an analysis of the aftermath of the very events depicted in the novel. Marx argues that Bonaparte was crucially supported by a rag-tag army of misfits and outcasts. In a famous, curiously lyrical passage he lists a series of types who make up the lumpenproletarian rabble:

> From the aristocracy there were bankrupted roués of doubtful means and dubious provenance, from the bourgeoisie there were degenerate wastrels on the take, vagabonds, demobbed soldiers, discharged convicts, runaway galley slaves, swindlers and cheats, thugs, pickpockets, conjurers, card-sharps, pimps, brothel keepers, porters, day-labourers, organ grinders, scrap dealers, knife grinders, tinkers and beggars, in short, the whole amorphous, jumbled mass of flotsam and jetsam that the French term bohemian.[65]

Marx's racializing polemic ends with a telling identification between the lumpenproletarian and the unconventional artist, an association that was gathering force in mid-nineteenth-century France through the life and work of Georges Sand (another pioneer of forms of female masculinity), and today perhaps best known from Bizet's *Carmen* (1876).[66] In *Summer Will Show*, Sophia remarks to herself that Minna "is an artist, what they call a Bohemian. And I, in this strange holiday from my natural self, am being a Bohemian too, she thought with pride" (132); later on, Minna mock-chastises herself for "hauling you [Sophia] down into this shabby Bohemia," to which Sophia briskly replies "I have never been so happy in my life and you know it" (263). Throughout the narrative, Minna's stable of romantic revolutionaries and artists are figured as paradigmatic bohemians, an ethnically diverse group of drifters and artists living an unconventional politics of everyday life whose radical élan must be sublated by orderly revolution.

Caspar functions as an abject remainder to this formation, a rejected body whose exclusion pharmakologically resolves the problem of the heterogeneous revolutionary collective. He is thus a site of overdetermination, as the novel's tragic denouement prominently figures. As Sophia stands on a crumbling barricade overrun by Gardes Mobile troops, she muses, "Caspar is one of these," and then, "with the certainty of a bad dream, there, when she looked up, was Caspar's profile outlined against the smoky dusk" (310). There follows a scene of double recognition and violent reaction: first, "she saw Caspar recognize her [Sophia], and for an instant his face wore a look of sheepish devotion"; then Minna greets Caspar with her "inveterately hospitable" voice (310). Caspar responds by stabbing Minna with the words "'Drab!' [...] 'Jewess! This is the end of you,'" and Sophia shoots Caspar in the mouth "as though she would have struck that mouth with her hand" (311). Radical unity between the Jewish bohemian and the lumpenproletarian colonial subject is brutally occluded, and the circuit of reaction completed by Sophia – although a queer Communist in volition, finally drawn into committing an act of imperial murder.[67]

Chapter 1 examined Isherwood's negotiation of the lumpenproletariat, arguing that *The Berlin Stories* offer a radical vision of lumpen revolutionary agency in the figure of the queer sex worker, while *Journey to a War* forecloses this capacious collective through an Orientalist gaze on the Chinese "coolie." *Summer Will Show* encompasses these two movements – outwards, encompassing the abjectly excluded lumpen, then inwards, away from the racialized subject as holding revolutionary potential. It is beyond the scope of this book to evaluate the broader contours of the British left's attitude toward the lumpenproletariat in any detail, an endeavor that would necessarily involve a complex decolonial history. The point for this present study is that the queer reception and transformation of key debates within the Marxist intellectual canon can provide radical new departures for both queer studies and Marxist theory. Both Isherwood and Townsend Warner offer complex, troubled articulations of the figure of the lumpenproletarian within the revolutionary body that resist a static opposition of condemnation or embrace that has often characterized the figure in political theory.

Following the deaths of Minna, Caspar, and Inglebrecht, Sophia falls into a catatonic depression. She struggles through this, however, and the final pages of the novel see her reading the opening of *The Communist Manifesto*, one of the pamphlets she had been distributing for Inglebrecht in another task she performed for the Communist cause. This moment articulates a classic trope of mid-century leftist fiction: the glimmer of hope in the moment of defeat, as seen in novels such as (to name but a few), Edward Upward's *Journey to the Border* (1938), Isherwood's *Goodbye to Berlin* (1939), Anna Seghers's *The Seventh Cross* (1945), Alexander Fadeyev's *The Young*

Guard (1946), or indeed Townsend Warner's own *After the Death of Don Juan* (1938). Strikingly, however, as opposed to how these moments usually operate, hope lies in theory; rather than the grim determination on the face of a condemned man, we have Sophia, "reading, obdurately attentive and by degrees absorbed" (329). In other words, a Communist counterpublic has begun to materialize through a text that is at once repellent to some observers and yet awaiting an eager readership; the novel itself, in the characteristic feedback loop of the counterpublic, mediates this process as another such text. Put another way, the close of the novel articulates in no uncertain terms that revolution requires a tightly integrated conception of theory and praxis. Inglebrecht and Minna are both killed, but Sophia is seated with the foundational text of Marxism at the novel's close – she is finally figured as a site of sublation, and as such necessarily full of potentiality.

I hope it is clear that by this reading I do not mean to suggest that *Summer Will Show* offers a straightforwardly progressive or utopian narrative (it is rather dialectical and serpentine), nor to claim that despair or regret are absent from the affective register of the text, but rather to reconstruct the novel's pull in the opposite direction. Considering Townsend Warner's and Ackland's positioning in the Dorset backwaters, Love's conception of "impossibility" does have a further sense of traction; yet the response called forth by this situation is more bracingly future-oriented than despairing. Moreover, while Love is surely right to claim that the ending of *Summer Will Show* "suggest[s] that one's relation to a collectivity might be based on the model of erotic love," what is missing from her account is how erotic love could emerge from a shared relation to radical collectivity.[68]

Queer typicality

Chapter 1 argued that Isherwood's *Berlin Stories* offers a critique of Lukács on two different levels. By revalorizing instrumentalization through an engagement with Tretiakov, Isherwood refuses the residual Kantianism in Lukács's ban on objectification in *History and Class Consciousness*, thus refusing property ownership and legitimizing queer erotic practice. At the same time, Isherwood's playful depiction of Arthur Norris empties out realist typicality, subverting the sleek dialectical reflection of history through character that Lukács suggests in his writings of the 1930s. With Townsend Warner, however, clearly something rather different is going on. Indeed, it is very tempting to read her historical novels as paradigmatically Lukácsian – a designation that might be applied not only to her 1930s texts *Summer Will Show* and *After the Death of Don Juan* (1938), but also, and perhaps more accurately, to two other novels she would go on to write in the coming years, *The Corner That Held Them* (1948) and *The Flint Anchor* (1954). *The Corner That Held Them*, for instance, depicts a convent during the years between the Black Death and the Peasants' Revolt, carefully drawing out historical change through a set of characters with a semi-peripheral relationship to major historical events, as Lukács famously urged in *The Historical Novel*. Although I have found no direct reference to Lukács in Townsend Warner's unpublished and published correspondence or diaries, her archive does contain a copy of *International Literature* from 1939; not the same issue in which the first English translations of *The Historical Novel* appeared, but very close to it.[69] Moreover, there were discussions about whether *Summer Will Show* might be translated and serialized in the Russian-language edition of *International Literature* – this appears not to have transpired, but it does indicate that Townsend Warner was in contact with the publication, and might reasonably be assumed to have read it.[70] It seems very likely that from the late 1930s onwards Townsend Warner became acquainted with at least the main contours of Lukács's major literary-critical positions – which is not to maintain that novels such as *The Corner That Held Them* are derivative, but rather that they perhaps bear some trace of influence.

The case of *Summer Will Show* is perhaps more intriguing. Townsend Warner had conceived of the character of Sophia some fifteen years before the novel was published, as she famously wrote in a note to the novel:

> It must have been in 1920 or 21 [. . .] that I said to a young man called Robert Firebrace that I had invented a person: an early Victorian young lady of means with a secret passion for pugilism; she attended prize-fights dressed as a man and kept a punching-ball under lock and key in her dressing-room. He asked what she looked like and I replied

without hesitation: "Smooth fair hair, tall, reserved, very ladylike. She's called Sophia Willoughby.[71]

Townsend Warner's invention of Sophia clearly anticipates the full-forced blow dealt to her husband in *Summer Will Show*, as well as her physical description; the possibility of Sophia actually becoming a pugilist is raised by Minna in the novel, but not followed through (225). The original Sophia's sexual object choice does not appear to be a concern as such in the above description, and was perhaps only articulated when Townsend Warner came to start writing the novel in 1932–3. This depiction delights in the starkly dichotomous: on the one hand, a thoroughgoing antinormativity – the prize fights, the cross-dressing, the punching ball – on the other hand, the most respectable and elegant of upper-class "very ladylike" appearances. This interaction of surfaces and passions foreshadows Sophia's transformation in *Summer Will Show*, particularly her role as a respectable-looking courier whose upper-class exterior would be above suspicion, a ruse expressive of the usefulness of her bourgeois mental furniture for orderly Communist organization.

In its depiction of this highly original historical creation, the most salient aspect of this passage is the way in which Townsend Warner is already at play with typicality. Sophia is simultaneously a typical representation of her class and gender at a specific moment in history – "*early* Victorian" and "ladylike" – and yet she heralds forms of female masculinity that were to become increasingly prominent in the interwar period, almost 100 years later. It is worth recalling Engels's much-cited definition of typicality as expressed in his letter to Margaret Harkness from 1888, a key text for Lukácsian realism first widely available in England through *International Literature* in 1933, not least because it was around this time that Townsend Warner began to formulate the narrative of *Summer Will Show* and commence her engagement with Communism. Engels famously argued that "realism implies, to my mind, besides depiction of detail, the truthful reproduction of typical characters under typical circumstances," before going on to praise "old Balzac" who, despite his monarchism, clearly foresaw the ascendency of the "men of the future" in the rising bourgeoisie.[72]

Like Isherwood and Edward Upward, Townsend Warner was wary of "taking Balzac and decanting new content into it," as can be seen from later on in the note to *Summer Will Show* where she archly observes that in writing the novel she "tried to avoid the French novelists."⁷³ Yet it's hard not to see Sophia as a reconfiguration of Balzac's "men of the future," a typical character whose narrative journey is proleptic of future developments in social and political history. Sophia's Toryism, moreover, might profitably be read alongside Balzac's monarchism, transposed from writer to character, then transmogrified in her movement toward Communism, a transformation that tropes Marx's, Engels's, and Lukács's repurposing of politically conservative forms of nineteenth-century realism for radical ends. Her "eccentricity" – indeed her queerness – might, however, appear to pose a problem here, for surely such central aspects of Sophia's character, and indeed the novel as a whole, militate against typicality in the full sense of the term? Indeed, in his polemic against decadence, "Healthy Art or Sick Art," Lukács fulminated against "decadence" in obviously heteronormative terms, as an "abnormality" and "deformity" as opposed to the social health of realism.⁷⁴

It is worth pausing, however, before designating Lukácsian realism as characterized at root by normativity in its strong sense. In "The Intellectual Physiognomy of Literary Characters," first published in English by *International Literature* in August 1936, Lukács argues at length against the naturalist concept of everyday reality, which leads him to a critique of the concept of the "average" in Zola:

> It is tacitly assumed as a matter of course that "life" is average everyday life, which is actually simpler than the world of Stendhal or of Balzac [. . .] Thus the illusion can very easily arise that the average is just as much an objective "element" of social reality as say, the elements of chemistry.⁷⁵

This is a crucial passage, for Lukács in no uncertain terms rejects the idea of the "average" as a literary optic onto social reality, thereby sharply distinguishing realist typicality from the governing epistemology of the norm. This naturalist error is presented as complementary to the excesses of modernism:

> Endeavors to portray the "exceptional" man, the eccentric man, even the "superman," that have arisen in the apparently violent struggle against naturalism remain within the magic circle of style that begins with the naturalist movement. The eccentric individual, "isolated"

from everyday reality, and the average man are two complementary poles in literature and in life.[76]

The "eccentric" appears as the other side of the coin to the "average man," polarities that skip the mediations of typicality and fall into similarly constituted forms of error. Returning to Balzac's letter, the problem here is that neither modernist eccentricity nor the naturalist "average man" can produce the "men of the future," in that they both fail to articulate and anticipate the narrative of history. Indeed, such "men of the future" are for Lukács "exceptional," if not eccentric – and in fact sometimes women. Later on in the essay, Lukács takes the classic example of Maxim Gorky's *Mother*, a novel which depicts the growth to class consciousness of an elderly woman and her son; the titular woman, he argues, "is expressly portrayed as an exceptional case [...] this very exceptional element makes Nilovna's road so profoundly typical."[77]

The significance of this moment in Lukács for the possibility of queer typicality in *Summer Will Show* and beyond cannot be underestimated, for there is no reason to presume that the fundamental structure of typicality cannot work in terms of queer history – Halberstam's reminder that types are not necessarily the same as stereotypes is worth bearing in mind here (to say nothing of what one might observe in everyday life).[78] Not average nor necessarily eccentric, but *exceptionally typical*, figuring the development of future social forms: this structure might well be applied to the protagonists of a number of canonical novels in gay and lesbian literary history, whether or not the style of the text is recognizably realist. This genealogy might include the following: Thomas Mann's *Death in Venice* (1912); André Gide's *Corydon* (1924); John Henry Mackay's *The Hustler* (1926); Forster's *Maurice* (1970; composed 1912/32), Hall's *The Well of Loneliness* (1928); John Rechy's *City of Night* (1963); Isherwood's *A Single Man* (1964); Andrew Holleran's *Dancer from the Dance* (1978); Edmund White's trilogy beginning *A Boy's Own Story* (1982/1988/1997); Abdellah Taïa's *Salvation Army* (2007); and Sarah Waters's *Tipping the Velvet* (2010). Such a largely Anglo-American, mainly white list is necessarily marked by a great number of omissions. But the point is that these particular canonical authors present a variety of typical experiences in widely divergent styles, which become an important terrain upon which a major line of gay and lesbian literary history emerges – imbued with creative energy, and yet also undeniably marked by racialized exclusion. Moreover, the validity of this schema for non-Anglophone or Germanophone queer literature is beyond my competency, and may or may not prove fruitful ground for scholars better versed in diverse languages.

Nevertheless, it is worth underlining that typicality opens up a vision of non-reproductivist social change that has no need to resort to heterosexual procreation in order to figure and embody the future. It might perhaps be objected that this is rather too broad a generic category; indeed, that historically and socially informed literary production as such comes under the rubric of Lukácsian typicality on this reading – but that would be to erase the distinctive forms of queer literary production, always reaching beyond themselves toward new, open-ended configurations of the social simultaneously as they constitute a series of identity types. As Muñoz has argued, queerness is at once "not yet here" and yet insistently present in utopian performance, and, likewise, queer literary history must always be concerned with constructing the people of the future as it writes the history of its present. Part of Townsend Warner's significance lies in the extent to which she was situated very close, politically and historically, to the canonical Anglophone elaboration of the concept of typicality, and through its method *Summer Will Show* sets out quite explicitly to explore its historical possibilities for a queerness to come.

In differing ways, both Townsend Warner and Isherwood demonstrate the importance of Soviet Marxism as a vital, transformative site in the queer literary history of the 1930s. Typicality, vanguardism, proletarian objectivism: however imbricated with reproductive heterosexuality these concepts may have been in the dominant leftist imaginary, they are no more necessarily heteronormative (indeed perhaps less so at points) than the various forms of western modernist literary practice – collage, indeterminacy, experiment, and so on – often thought of as holding radically queer potential. This is not to offer a final polemic against the ideology of modernism à la Lukács, but rather to contend that Soviet Marxism, that supposedly most sexually conservative and aesthetically reactionary body of thought and culture, offered vital resources for queer writing that have resonances to this day. The literary and cultural history of the Popular Front, however, reveals a less hopeful genealogy of the left's sexual politics. Responding to the supposed sexual aberrance of fascism, Popular Front literary producers insistently shaped a cultural field through which liberal humanism, nationalism, and heterosexual reproduction became mutually constitutive of the idealized sexual subject, even as more and more queer writers and artists were drawn into antifascist movements. It is to this juncture of cruel optimism that Chapter 3 will now turn.

Chapter 3

The Hymning of Heterosexuality: Katharine Burdekin and the Popular Front

Katharine Burdekin's dystopian novel, *Swastika Night* (1937), is set 700 hundred years after total Axis victory. The Jews have been extirpated, Nazis and Japanese fascists rule supreme over the entire world, and women have become reproductive chattel: forced to shave their heads, held in prison camps, they are no longer the objects of male sexual or romantic interest, which is turned in on itself in a violently masculinist homoeroticism. The novel opens with a speculative identification of Nazi triumphalism with queer male desire:

> The Knight turned towards the Holy Hitler chapel which in the orientation of this church lay in the western arm of the Swastika, and with the customary loud impressive chords on the organ and a long roll on the sacred drums, the Creed began. Hermann was sitting in the Goebbels chapel in the northern arm, whence he could conveniently watch the handsome boy with the long fair silky hair, who had been singing the solos. He had to turn towards the west when the Knight turned. He could no longer see the boy except with a sidelong glance, and though gazing at lovely youths in church was not even conventionally condemned, any position during the singing of the Creed except that of attention-eyes-front was sacrilegious.[1]

This passage – and Burdekin's project in the novel as a whole – may initially appear strange in its intertwining of a notoriously homophobic regime with the queer male gaze. However, it is in fact paradigmatic of mid- to late 1930s British dystopian visions of fascism, and of the sexual politics of Popular Front literature more broadly. From the fantastic dystopias of Rex Warner and Ruthven Todd to more sober critiques of fascism by Winifred Holtby or Storm Jameson, Popular Front literary production incessantly deployed a vigilant homophobia as a key weapon in the antifascist struggle.[2]

That the dystopian novel should prove a particularly important genre for the development of this heteronormative sexual politics is perhaps unsurprising. For the shock of the antifascist dystopia is, at core, the shock of the aberrant, the pathological that relies upon an implicit sense of social and sexual normality. This powerful normativity is at work even as dystopias more often than not see such normality as desperately unattainable even in non-fascist – or pseudo-fascist – domestic society, as can be seen in the psychopathology of Pinkie in Graham Greene's *Brighton Rock* (1936) or the despairing yearning for normality in the phantasmagoric critiques of English life in Edward Upward's *Journey to the Border* (1938) or Patrick Hamilton's *Hangover Square* (1941). In their dogged, even desperate, pursuit of the normal, 1930s dystopias function as inaugural documents of a much broader mid-century backlash against interwar queer culture that can be traced forward via Orwell to The Movement and certain aspects of first-generation Cultural Studies; more locally, they register a tactical moment in the left's ideological fight against fascism which reached its peak in the mid- to late 1930s.

More surprising is the role of Katharine Burdekin (1896–1963) in this formation. An enigmatic, elusive figure, Burdekin was a prolific but neglected queer feminist writer whose authorship ranged from children's stories to speculative dystopian fiction, and more realist narratives, much of it written under the male pen-name Murray Constantine. Largely unread and out of print until the 1980s, her work has been the subject of increasing attention in recent years, fueled by the publication of a trio of her speculative fictions by The Feminist Press (UK) and the Feminist Press at CUNY, all edited by Daphne Patai: *Swastika Night* (1985; first pub. 1937); *Proud Man* (1993; first pub. 1934); and *The End of This Day's Business* (unpublished until 1993).[3] One of Patai's central claims is that Burdekin's 1930s fictions represent an important progenitor to Orwell's better-known dystopia, *Nineteen Eighty-Four* (1949); moreover, Patai and others such as Andy Croft argue, Burdekin's dystopian and utopian fictions offer a uniquely comprehensive critique of mid-century authoritarianism as they are, apparently alone among 1930s and 1940s dystopias, acutely aware of the central role played by misogyny in fascist and imperial ideologies.[4]

The recuperative work of Patai and others has been invaluable in re-establishing this neglected figure as an important 1930s feminist writer, but until very recently the question of queer sexuality in Burdekin's work has been elided or ignored, and it was not until Elizabeth English's 2015 study, *Lesbian Modernism: Censorship, Sexuality and Genre Fiction* that the first sustained queer reading of Burdekin emerged. Drawing on archival materials, including manuscripts of Burdekin's unpublished novels and correspondence with important figures such as H.D., Gertrude Stein, and Havelock Ellis, *Lesbian Modernism* examines how "Burdekin's speculative fiction is populated by what H.D. terms 'other people', or sexually dissident identities."[5] Specifically, English traces the sexological figure of the "invert" – subtending and imbricated with but not identical to the category of the "homosexual" – through Burdekin's published and unpublished works, contending that "for Burdekin, like [Edward] Carpenter, the invert is a venerated, utopian figure elevated above the throng of (heterosexual) humanity by his or her heterodox nature, acutely perceptive of the structures of society and endowed with the ability to enact social revolution."[6]

English offers a robust case for this argument, particularly in her readings of *Proud Man* and *The End of This Day's Business*, which both feature invert protagonists with revolutionary gifts of perception, empathy, and intelligence. And yet, her study's implicit stress on the positive valorization of queer and/or dissident sexualities in Burdekin rings false for *Swastika Night*, for it fails to fully take into account the frankly disgusted attitude this text has to male homoeroticism as fascist perversion.[7] Even more striking than *Swastika Night*'s condemnation of male homoeroticism – which is partially explicable if not excusable as an "extension" of Burdekin's critique of "male dominance," as English points out – is the text's investment in the recuperative power of conventional heterosexuality.[8] Against the Nazis' queer misogyny the novel aims to recover heterosexual desire, thus locating the possibility of victory against Nazi dominion in the restitution of "normal" sexual and affective relations, a word that appears repeatedly throughout the narrative, always heavily valorized. This aspect of Burdekin's development is rendered still more troubling when we consider an unpublished novel yet to be discussed in the literature on Burdekin. The ironically titled *No Compromise* (c. 1933–5) is a Communist retelling of *Lady Chatterley's Lover*

(1928), a heterosexual romance between a masculine Party firebrand and a rather weak young aristocratic woman. In its central coupling Burdekin's novel at points achieves the dubious honor of being more masculinist than Lawrence's novel, as the "silly" young woman is insistently compared to the steadfast male Communist.

It is from this strange juncture that the following chapter takes its departure point. Why would Burdekin move from a Carpenterian position of the invert's superior revolutionary potential to a condemnation of male homoeroticism, a hymning of heterosexuality, and praise of the masculine ideals of proletarian fiction? How does this movement reveal the extent to which Popular Front antifascism demanded a strategic heteronormalization of the left, even for queer writers such as Burdekin? And how might we situate this problematic in a longer history of mid-century sexual politics taking in the vision of national heterosexuality engendered during the "People's War" and feeding into the sexually conservative ethos of postwar Britain? In what follows I first outline the contours of Popular Front heteronormativity in relation to the Soviet Union's "homophobic turn," the Nazi accession, and a broader set of leftist cultures. I then turn to *Swastika Night* in order to interrogate the ways in which Burdekin's development in the mid- to late 1930s can be seen as paradigmatic for the heteronormalization of Popular Front sexual politics. Finally, I further situate and complicate this reading by putting it into dialogue with *No Compromise*, arguing that read together these texts reveal the fraught manner by which a local, tactical antifascist antihomosexual rhetoric ossifies into a strategic heteronormalization with lasting consequences for the sexual politics of the left.

Homo-fascism

Between 1931 and 1934, a series of crucial encounters between leftists and fascists set the scene for a major series of deployments of antihomosexual discourse on the international stage.[9] In charting the development of this discourse it quickly becomes apparent how the deployment of homophobic rhetoric by the left emerged in direct tactical reaction to major events in the rise of fascism. The first major scandal was the so-called "Röhm affair." In 1931 and 1932, when SA muscle was still a major force in the bloody everyday of German politics, the social democratic press acquired a number of letters written by the head of the SA, Ernst Röhm, in which the leading Nazi unashamedly proclaimed his homosexuality. The letters, printed in 1932, revealed, moreover, that he was a member of the prominent homosexual organization, the *Bund für Menschenrechte*, and that his sexuality was well known and even accepted within the Nazi Party. The Social Democratic Party (SPD) seized upon these letters and began a lurid propaganda campaign against Nazism as inextricably bound up with a virulent homosexual culture. The KPD was initially more circumspect, influenced by the 1917 decriminalization of homosexuality in the Soviet Union and committed to the abolition of Paragraph 175, the German statute prohibiting male homosexuality. However, by April 1932, it too had joined in the chorus of leftist homophobic voices, while continuing, somewhat incoherently, to support the abolition of Paragraph 175 (as is well known, following the purge of Röhm in 1934, the Nazis were themselves to mobilize this discourse, leading up to their tightening of anti-sodomy legislation in 1935).[10]

The next signal event was the Berlin Reichstag Fire on February 29, 1933. With the arrest of the ex-Communist Marinus van der Lubbe for the arson, the Nazis famously blamed the Communists for the fire. Communists responded by focusing on van der Lubbe's homosexuality in order to discredit him and disassociate him from the left; claiming that he was under the direct influence of Röhm himself, they produced a widely read pamphlet detailing these charges.[11] At the same time as these developments were occurring in Germany, the Soviet Union was undergoing what Dan Healey has called a "homophobic turn," leading up to its recriminalization of male homosexuality in a decree of March 1934. One British Communist working as a journalist in Moscow, Harry Whyte, wrote a brave letter to Stalin, arguing coherently against the new legislation on orthodox Marxist-Leninist grounds.[12] Perhaps in direct response to this letter (and certainly in support of the new law), Maxim Gorky produced his brutal essay "Proletarian Humanism," published in May 1934. Gorky's essay attributed a wide range of perversions to fascism, including but not limited to homosexuality. As Healey convincingly argues, in the causal genocidal logic of Gorky's slogan, "Destroy the homosexuals – Fascism will disappear," homosexuality was undoubtedly the most prominent and worrying of the fascist perversions.[13] As can be seen in a broader set of antifascist texts, the homosexual fascist's recruitment and corruption of young men was of particular concern to Gorky and others, and was widely deployed in anti-Nazi rhetoric.[14] The coincidence of the Soviet Union's "homophobic turn" with the Nazi accession represents a moment when a tactical maneuver in a war of movement against fascism became a strategic position occupied by leftists throughout Europe.

Antifascists were also able to draw on aspects of a variegated history of German male homosexual advocacy in their attacks on the perversions of Nazism. Alongside the better-known liberal left of the homosexual emancipation movement embodied in the figure of Magnus Hirschfeld, what might be called a right wing of the movement also existed in the years leading up to the Nazi accession. As Andrew Hewitt, Jack Halberstam, and others have pointed out, figures such as Adolf Brand, Friedrich Radzuweit, and Hans Blüher offered a masculinist vision of homosexual community that simultaneously drew on the *Männerbund* ethos of German comradeship and a misogynistic Hellenizing discourse, and was thus far more amenable to *völkish* and even Nazi politics than Hirschfeld's better-known project (to which, unsurprisingly, these figures were directly opposed).[15] Blüher, for instance, held to a nationalist version of heroic male homosexuality, and defended Röhm against attacks in the social democratic press; Adolf Brand's journal, meanwhile, *Die Eigene (The Personalist)*, "praised manliness, condemned femininity and toyed with anti-Semitism."[16] Antifascists including Wilhelm Reich and Erich Fromm were thus able to mobilize against the concept of a reactionary *Männerbund* in their attacks on Nazi perversion, leading to further strategic entrenchment of leftist heteronormativity.[17]

As Halberstam has urged, it is important not to erase the participation of homosexual men in the Nazi regime nor to deny the continuing draw of fascist aesthetics for some queers.[18] I do not dispute this, but a few remarks are in order here. The immanent relations between Nazism and homosexuality have been relentlessly overestimated, particularly with reference to the SS and the SA. While not denying the homoerotic draw of these organizations, historians of National Socialism have increasingly argued that the relationship was far more contingent than has usually been assumed. Geoffrey Giles has recently contended that, while much higher than

Himmler admitted, the incidence of homosexuality in the SS has been subsequently wildly inflated.[19] And Andrew Wackerfuss's study *Stormtrooper Families* (2015) extensively details the homoerotic bonds between SA men, but also underlines that there is no historical basis for the claim that Röhm's clique in the SA leadership was primarily organized by homosexuality.[20] Röhm picked the SA leadership for a shared investment in violent masculinism, not a common sexual orientation; to reduce the latter to the former is completely inaccurate. Halberstam is right to point out that Sedgwick evades the issue by claiming that "only one Nazi leader was homosexual," but his counter-claim, "Roehm was known to preside over a stable of homosexual stormtroopers" is more the stuff of antifascist myth than historical record.[21]

Moreover, the homoeroticism of aesthetic forms associated with fascism – most obviously the idealized male, soldierly body – obviously did not originate with Nazism, nor even with its close antecedents such as *Männerbund* formations; it goes without saying that classical aesthetics were a major precedent. These forms were indeed powerfully mobilized by fascist aesthetics, and were later taken up by a number of queer writers, artists, and filmmakers, but this means that it is more accurate to say that fascism mediated certain strains of queer aesthetics, rather than motivated or "fascinated" it, as Susan Sontag put it. For instance, both Auden and Isherwood were frank about how fascism could have a certain draw for queer bourgeois men of their generation; however their work does not so much draw on fascism, but rather shows how both fascist and queer aesthetics have roots in common.[22] Relatedly, there's a relatively long history of black leather, submission and control, and the pleasures of pain that was historically implicated with fascism to a degree, but never entirely reducible to nor even primarily mediated by it (nor of course by any means limited to male-on-male sex).

The work of Andrew Hewitt and William Spurlin addresses the exhaustive identification of fascism with homosexuality through the concept of "homo-fascism":

> a term not referring to individual homosexuals who also happened to be fascist, but to the discursive reduction of homosexuality to fascism, or to the location of homosexuality as fascism's source. More precisely, homo-fascism is the conflation of sexual with political

deviance, whereby homosexuality is pathologized as a fascistic fascination with the erotics of power, and fascism is reduced to a psychosexual manifestation of homosexual narcissism, as put forth in some of the psychopolitical writings by the Frankfurt School (Hewitt, *Political Inversions* 39).[23]

This is a vital distinction. What many antifascists proclaimed – and Halberstam's critique implicitly slides into with reference to the SA – is the mutual constitution of fascism and homosexuality. It is necessary to acknowledge the homoerotics at work in fascism; to make clear, as Halberstam points out, that some gay movements have overestimated Nazi persecution of homosexuals; and to note that a number of queer men participated in its brutal regime. But this is quite distinct from the conflation described by Spulin, which simultaneously sees fascism as the source of homosexuality, and homosexuality the origin of fascism. This "ideological linkage between homosexuality and fascism" is a well-established feature of twentieth-century cultural and social history: scholarly literature on homosexuality in the Soviet Union and in Nazi Germany has long acknowledged this important development in the propaganda wars between Nazism and Communism; the re-emergence of these tropes in Italian cinema of the 1970s has been the subject of a controversy sparked by Sontag's much-cited essay, "Fascinating Fascism"; and discussion of what has come to be known as "homo-fascism" has also been prominent in work on Adorno, Genet, and other major figures.[24]

There has, however, been no discussion of this specific discourse in British literature of the period.[25] Moreover, there has been no attempt to date to link this formation to the broad emergence of Popular Front culture across Europe in the mid- to late 1930s. This is surprising for two main reasons. First, the key events involved are very obviously central to the development of a Popular Front strategy, in particular the Reichstag Fire Trial of 1933. The hero of the trial for international Communism was the Bulgarian Communist Georgi Dimitrov, whose defense and release led to his elevation as the head of the Communist International in 1934, a post from which he announced the adoption of the Popular Front strategy in his famous address later that year. Set against the weak, "perverted" van der Lubbe was Dimitrov's towering figure (literally so, in John

Heartfield's famous photomontage), the new icon for international leftism in the mid- to late 1930s. This double movement can clearly be seen in a key work of British Marxist literary theory, Ralph Fox's *The Novel and The People* (1937). Fox's study sets up Dimitrov as the rough-and-ready man of the hour and devoted husband, while rehearsing the homophobic line concerning the "dull-witted, perverted pyromaniac" van der Lubbe's corruption by "homosexual storm-troopers."[26] In other words, if the pre-eminent hero of the Popular Front emerges in opposition to a queer villain, then homofascism must be, *via negativa*, of significance to Popular Front culture at large. As Dimitrov himself asserted in a 1935 speech in Moscow translated into English in the pages of *International Literature*:

> Take the figure of Van der Lubbe. With him it could be shown how a worker can become a tool of his class enemy. On the negative example of van der Lubbe thousands of young workers could be educated and a struggle conducted against the influence of fascism against youth.[27]

Second, the Popular Front offered a broad program of normalization on a number of different fronts, an over-correction to the failings of the class-against-class policy in late 1920s and early 1930s Germany in particular. Designed to broaden the appeal of the Communist left to a set of increasingly antifascist socialist and liberal publics, Popular Front propagandists and literary producers set about redeploying and revalorizing a series of tropes – "progress," "humanism," and "patriotism" being the most prominent – in order to garner widespread appeal for an antifascist politics of "common decency," and the antihomosexual discourse incited by the scandals of Röhm and van der Lubbe was central to this appeal. This new stress on leftist patriotism designed to counter the fascist claim to speak for the nation was outlined by Dimitrov in his announcement of the Popular Front strategy. As discussed in the Introduction, this new patriotism was stressed as the cornerstone of a new leftist internationalism, always respectful of national tradition and comprised of a number of different nations all fighting fascism with their own autochthonous radical traditions. This reinscription of the nation produced a discourse of organic community powerfully intertwined with normative reproductive heterosexuality. The Popular Front thus stressed an alliance of normal, earthy heterosexual nations against the queered "false patriotism" of fascism, as can be seen in a wide variety of texts of the period. The promotion of this vision of national sexuality went hand in hand with the development of a series of depictions of the psychopathology of fascism, two mutually constitutive aspects of Popular Front cultural politics that can be seen clearly in a number of British antifascist texts from the mid-1930s to late 1930s.

Rex Warner's dystopian fantasy *The Wild Goose Chase* (1937) offers a particularly salient example of this tendency. I have written elsewhere on how Warner's novel stakes out the nation as a crucial battleground in the war against fascism, part of an insistence that, as Jack Lindsay put it, "Communism is English."[28] Anticipating the films of Pasolini and Visconti, *The Wild Goose Chase* also offers a horrified vision of fascist perversion in its depiction of the ironically named "Convent," the university of the fascist metropole (there is also a clear sense here that Oxford is another of Warner's targets). George, the stoutly heterosexual and very English hero, destroys this institution as a crucial step on the road to revolution. All members of the cultish university must undergo an operation rendering them intersex, and much of their research is directed toward the experimental pursuit of sexual pleasure. When George and his revolutionary army finally conquer the town, they discover terrible sadist excesses deep in the "Research Department" of the Convent, which are seen as the logical conclusion of its mandatory destabilizing of gender norms. George blows up the "Research Department," immolating the sadomasochists it contains without trial or even speaking to most of them, and decrees that all surviving members of the Convent must decide on their gender.

Warner's novel also stridently proclaims the transformative potential of normative heterosexuality. Opposing the intersex sadists of the "Convent" is the novel's touchstone of sexual authenticity, the coupling of George with a revolutionary farmer's daughter, Joan, whose importance for the narrative is immediately signaled in purple prose:

> Interested in the sight of visitors the girl stood still with basket in hand, bearing butter and eggs. Hair like butter, but corn-furry, lay smooth glistening on back and side of head, on forehead stayed in wisps, a low forehead, sweat-pearled, beneath which began a straight

nose, a short one, set between fresh cheeks, sweet apple flesh, and then the calling soft mouth, retentive chin – soft material, no more plastic than the sea.[29]

This sub-Joycean accumulation of conventional images introduces Joan as an object of natural desire, to whom George is immediately drawn. Arriving with produce from the farm, the English rose appears as the personification of both organic national community and natural heterosexual desire. George and Joan have sex the same night, which is described in equally gushing language: "their manifold of joy," the reader is assured, "rose to a broad breaking wave."[30] After this transformative experience, Joan tells George that she invites many men who pass through her village into her bed, although she adds, "I was getting tired of it, and was so glad to see you to-night. You're much the nicest, and I want to marry and settle down."[31] While registered as completely natural, George's and Joan's heterosexual performance is simultaneously seen as a triumphant achievement set against the deviant sexual practices of the Convent. *The Wild Goose Chase* is a paradigmatic example of how Popular Front sexual politics offered a vision of what I am calling *transformative normalcy*: the bizarre yet widely-held belief that the restitution of normative sexual relations within the bounds of the nation is itself a revolutionary act.

Winifred Holtby's and Norman Ginsbury's 1935 play, *Take Back Your Freedom*, focuses on another central aspect of the Popular Front's heteronormalizing sexual politics: the psychopathology of the dictator, prominent in the work of the Frankfurt School and in Jean-Paul Sartre's antifascist texts.[32] In her Introduction to the 1939 edition of the play, Vera Brittain confidently asserts that "it is, I believe, generally accepted by psychologists that a pathological quality determines the careers of most dictators."[33] Featuring a repressed homosexual don turned English dictator, Arnold Clayton, brought up by an overbearing mother and in thrall to his manly school friend, the appropriately named Dick Lawrence, the play is an extended meditation upon this axiom.[34] While less sensationalist than Warner's novel, *Take Back Your Freedom* is marked by a series of knowing asides concerning the Leader's sexuality. A running joke throughout the play is how a foolish fascist-supporting woman, Lady Carter, cannot persuade Clayton into bed, as he prefers to spend time with his right-hand man. The culmination of insinuations through the first two acts comes when Lawrence persuades Clayton to use an exercise bike:

> C: It was you who first told me to go, you know. (*mounts machine*) What's that clock thing?
> L: That measures how fast you would have gone if you'd gone at all. That's right. God, man! Did you never ride a bicycle at Oxford? I thought all dons *lived* on 'em. Both feet equally – now – push away. Put some pep in it. Come on. Imagine Lady Carter's after you. That's better.[35]

As if the sweaty homoeroticism of the scene was not sufficiently legible to the audience, a few pages on the stage direction appears: "CLAYTON *sees* LAWRENCE *putting on his belt which he had loosened during the cycling episode*," followed by an outburst from Clayton who childishly upbraids his friend for not respecting "his Leader" enough.[36] Later on, Clayton kills his beloved Lawrence in a fit of rage, which occasions a breakdown into "hysterics" only finally put to rest as the young dictator is in turn killed by his own mother, horrified at what she has created by her hothouse parenting. The play thus insists upon a particular reading of fascist machismo as failed masculinity that was later to be elaborated by Theodor Adorno in *Minima Moralia* (1951), and which has become a common trope in writing on the sexuality of fascism influenced by the Frankfurt School. As Spurlin notes, "the so-called 'tough guys' within a totalitarian regime, according to Adorno, are really effeminate and need those who are weak or disempowered as their victims so as to prove they are not similar to them."[37]

Although *Take Back Your Freedom* is far from subtle in its portrayal of the queer dictator, it also cites an instance of antifascist homophobia, when Lawrence describes a counter-demonstration by the left: "Out of a side street came a band of Reds. They'd got wind of what we were doing – and *they* had posters saying 'Pansy's Paper says "Plan or Perish"'."[38] Coming in a play far more liberal-humanist than leftist, this moment can be considered as a snipe at the direct vulgarity of Communist propaganda as opposed to its own apparently more nuanced psychopathology, but it is nonetheless indicative of a moment of self-consciousness in the play's deployment of sexuality. *Take Back Your Freedom* also insists on the possibility of a specifically English fascism and resolutely refuses to cast queerness as a foreign disease. Indeed, as Vera Brittain's Introduction slyly implies – "knowing something of Oxford" is apparently key for Holtby's diagnosis of the dictator's malady – the play could actually be read as implying that English fascism would be the queerest of all.[39] For all its homophobia *Take Back Your Freedom* can at least be excused of the worst nationalist excesses that mar many cultural products of the Popular Front including *The Wild Goose Chase*, George Orwell's wartime essays, and Burdekin's *Swastika Night*. In contrast to Holtby's play, Burdekin's novel firmly insists upon the queerness of German fascism and the heterosexuality of Englishness, centrally embodied in its opposition between the novel's "normal" English hero Alfred, and his macho yet spiritually weak queer German friend, Hermann (22, 166, *inter alia*). Drawing together a series of homo-fascist tropes, the novel insistently locates revolutionary possibility in Anglocentric heterosexuality and moral degeneracy in Nazi perversion.

Hermann's homoeroticism

To return, then, to the opening of the novel: the scene in the Hitler Chapel juxtaposes official Nazi worship with Hermann's desire for the chorister in an antiphonal structure that comes to stand for the novel's presentation of the relationship between homosexuality and fascism:

> *And I believe in pride, in courage, in violence, in brutality, in bloodshed, in ruthlessness, and all other soldierly and heroic virtues. Heil Hitler.*
> The Knight turned round again. Hermann turned round and sat down gratefully to resume his contemplation of the golden-haired chorister. He was a big boy to have still an unbroken voice. He must be above fourteen. But not a hint of golden down had yet appeared on his apple-cheeks. He had a wonderful voice. Good enough for a Munich church, yes, good enough for a church in the Holy City, where the Sacred Hangar was, and in it the Sacred Aeroplane, towards which all the Swastika churches in Hitlerdom were oriented, so that the Hitler arm was in the direct line with the Aeroplane in Munich, even though thousands of miles lay between the Little Model in the Hitler chapel and the Thing Itself. (6)

While Hermann is anxious for the incantation to end so that he can gaze directly at the choirboy, here the official ideology is seen to call forth his desiring gaze, even as it punctures it. Indeed, the whole of the first scene of the novel is set up as a study in interpellation and its slippages, curiously anticipating post-constructionist theories of gender and sexuality. After Hermann leaves the church with the other men, eager to catch up with the youth so he can pull his hair, "not to hurt him much, just to make him mind" (7), women file in and are treated to a vicious harangue about their lowliness and necessary submission. The aristocratic Nazi reading the lesson, however, slips up and lets out a state secret. Not enough female babies are being born, and in a moment of unguarded honesty, he urges the women to bear daughters as opposed to the ideologically correct lesson that they should bear sons.

As he leaves the church, Hermann chances upon an old friend, the Englishman Alfred, whom he had met when on national service in England. Hermann worships Alfred sexually and romantically, who in turn maintains a humorous and stolidly non-sexual friendly attitude toward his German acquaintance, whom he urges to "come round to a normal attitude towards women" (22). As Alfred rests in a meadow after the two friends have been hiking and bathing, Hermann is caught in a strange reverie when he considers that his beloved is English and therefore below him as a German:

> Oh, if only Alfred had by some miracle been born a German and of knightly class, how he, Hermann, would have adored to serve him, to be his slave, to set his body, his strong bones and willing hard muscles, between Knight Alfred and all harm – to die for him ... Hermann's phantasy faded in a heat of shame. Even to think of an Englishman being a Knight was a sin against the Blood. (31)

The scene is set as a tableau of the homoerotics of Nazi aesthetic ideology. Friends hike through a forest, bathe in a secluded pool, rest in a quiet place; as one sleeps, the other gazes upon the sleeping, idealized form as knightly figure, which doubles back in unthinking narcissism upon his own physical perfection even as he contemplates his own masochistic enslavement. Burdekin's crudely homophobic writing in this passage is superbly adequate to Popular Front sexual politics; Hermann's tortured fantasy has been perfectly scripted by the antifascist injunction against Nazi homoeroticism.

Hermann's lust is further inflamed when he catches sight of his other object of desire, the young chorister. The angelic choirboy was also in the woods, attempting to rape a twelve-year-old Christian girl. Christians are viewed as subhuman by Nazi doctrine in the novel, and rape is only permitted once girls reach the age of fourteen. Hermann is filled with jealous anger: "Hermann's whole body filled with delicious thundering warming floods of rage. He loathed the boy for being even interested in girls – with his lovely face, his unmasculine immaturity – Hermann was physically jealous; he was shamed" (33). Hermann in his rage insists upon the exclusivity of the male object of desire – we also learn, a few pages before this passage, how he "can't stand" women and has failed to have sex with any; this is repeated shortly after the passage (21, 47). Predictably, Hermann's anger turns to sadistic violence, as he realizes that a savage beating would be ideologically coherent: "here was something at last that he could smash and tear and make bleed and utterly destroy" (33). The circuit of fascist sexuality is completed as he beats the boy senseless:

> He reached the struggling young animal with two jumps and seizing the boy by his long yellow hair he pulled him off the girl with such force that his neck was nearly broken. He then picked him up and threw him with every ounce of his strength at the nearest tree trunk [...] Hermann jumped at him again, and with his fists beat him into insensibility. He took special pleasure in spoiling his face. When the boy was lying unconscious at his feet he started to kick him, in the ribs, on the head, anywhere, and would most probably have left him, not unconscious, but dead, had not Alfred, who had at last awakened and come to the scene, intervened. (33–4)

This febrile scene is only interrupted by the sensible intervention of the Englishman, who saves the boy's life by insisting they take him to seek medical help. Alfred sees through Hermann's protestations of ideological innocence to his queer motives beneath: the *ne plus ultra* of perversion, an intergenerational homoeroticism. While Hermann claims to rage against the shame of the rape of an underage Christian girl – and thus maintains the legitimacy of the beating – Alfred knows better. "'I suppose you aren't at all annoyed because the *boy* is under age?' asked Alfred sarcastically. 'Because he's a pretty lad who ought only to be interested in *men*?'" (35). Alfred's knowing penetration of Hermann's motives provides a complementary conflation of fascism with queerness compared to the opening passage of the novel. For while the antiphonal relation between creed and desire in the chapel scene offers a reading of the symptomatic creation of homosexuality by the violent misogyny of Nazi ideology, here the tenets of fascist orthodoxy are motivated by queer desire. The concept of homofascism as elaborated by Hewitt and Spurlin is particularly useful to understand Burdekin's articulation of Hermann's violent desires, which are the embodiment of how homosexuality "is pathologized as a fascistic fascination with the erotics of power" by certain strains of antifascist writing.[40]

Indeed, Hermann turns out to be precisely the figure Adorno cites as paradigmatically fascist in his sneering "Tough baby" section of *Minima Moralia*: an outwardly "tough guy" whose macho exterior is a compensation for an effeminate lack of inner strength.[41] As the novel progresses, Hermann's physical capabilities are increasingly counterpoised to his inner immaturity or femininity: he is a "shrinking, shaking *coward*" (77; emphasis in original), with "a weakness, a strong desire for personal dependency" (91), possessed of a "weak soul, a baby soul" – all this in one who "works like a dynamo," indeed both works and fights with superhuman strength; he appears to be and yet ultimately is not a "real" man (91, 101, 130). The novel extends this view of failed masculinity to all German men, of whom Hermann is merely taken as an extreme example. When the revolutionary Alfred first announces seditious plans to Hermann, he declares that "no German ever has been or ever can be a man" (27), predictably provoking a threat of physical violence from his German friend. This charge is then reiterated throughout the narrative as Alfred and Hermann are educated by the dissident Nazi Knight who read the lesson in the opening scene, von Hess, who muses on the incompatibility of fascistic rule and true masculinity, arguing that Germans "cannot be *men* while they are still under discipline of any kind" (146; emphasis in original). The general extent of homosexuality under German rule is stressed by von Hess, most tellingly perhaps when it is invoked as a cover story for Alfred's seditious activities. When he entrusts the Englishman with a book detailing the last known scraps of non-Nazi history, the Knight advises Alfred to cry queer if challenged with his important package: "If they ask you why you, an Englishman, were chosen to be Knight's messenger, you'll say that I took a fancy to you, which isn't quite such a lie" (139). Here a general and accepted homosexuality among high-ranking Nazis is presupposed in order for the cover story to function; at the same time, there is a slippage between the homosocial and the homoerotic as the Knight acknowledges the bond he has with the younger man: even the novel's most noble German cannot help but slide into queer desire.

Alongside the book that the von Hess family had compiled and guarded for posterity, the Knight shows Hermann and Alfred a revelatory photograph. First to catch their eyes is a figure identified as Adolf Hitler. The dictator's short stature and dark hair is a great shock to Hermann, who fervently believed in the myth of Hitler as a marvelous, seven-foot-tall giant; but more startling still is a figure he and Alfred initially identify as a pretty youth, who was actually a young woman: "'A girl!' Alfred breathed softly. A girl as lovely as any boy, with a boy's hair and a boy's noble carriage, and a boy's direct and fearless gaze" (68). This revelation is the hinge of the whole narrative's presentation of gender and sexuality. At first, a radical sense of the construction of gender appears to be at work. In this moment, femininity and masculinity are entirely produced by hairstyle, clothing, gesture; by, in other words, bodily performance. And yet, as the passage continues, the lost practice of heterosexual monogamy emerges as a revolutionary postulate. Von Hess introduces the flabbergasted pair to the concept of marriage, "a lost word [. . .] being married means living with one woman and your children and going on living continually with her until one of you dies. It sounds fantastic, doesn't it? That men ever *lived* with women. But they did" (69; emphasis Burdekin's). While this uncovering sends Hermann into a deep depression, the Englishman is enlivened by the thought of lovable, desirable women and family life, in a yearning for the normal that comes to instantiate his revolutionary potential.

As normal as possible

Invigorated by the possibility of family life, Alfred is thrust into direct opposition to the morass of failed German masculinity, functioning as a symbol of heroic Englishness and relatively normal masculinity – he is, at least, "as normal as possible for a man to be in such a society" (166). Alfred repeatedly repudiates any homoerotic desire throughout the text while stressing his place in a line of noble English rebels. As if the resonance of his name with Saxon history were not sufficiently clear, Alfred proclaims to Hermann:

> There's a legend about a great English leader called Alfred, who had a huge statue in Winchester (you remember Winchester, we went there once together); it was as big as the hill behind, and he had a knife and a shrapnel helmet, but he wasn't only a soldier, because he wrote a book. Now if I had *that* to compare with Hitler's! And a man called Alfred is to deliver England from the Germans. (30)

Alfred's memory of England's mythical past refers to the statue of Alfred the Great by Hamo Thornycroft that was erected in 1899 for the millenary commemoration of the king's death, and to Alfred's reputation as a learned leader. King Alfred successfully repelled the Viking invasions of the late ninth century, and Burdekin clearly sets up a comparison between the bloodthirsty Vikings and Nazi rule. Further on in the same passage, Alfred goes on to state that he is "not only going to deliver *England* from the Germans," but the whole world; he explains that this is possible because "I am the repository, the place where a very old human idea is kept" (30; emphasis in original). Saliently positioning *Swastika Night* within British Popular Front cultural politics, Alfred articulates a narrative of autochthonous English radicalism that was beginning to gain ground on the British left in the 1930s as a specific national response to Dimitrov's call to reintroduce the nation to progressive discourse – a leftist iteration of what Jed Esty has called mid-century England's "redemptive Anglocentrisms."[42] As I outline in the Introduction, in their promotion of the idea that "Communism is English," leftists reconstructed a "radical patriotism," which they traced back to Saxon resistance to the "Norman yoke," through the "English Revolution," and on to Chartism and modern socialism. Later in the text Alfred has to choose a surname to sign his name as a keeper of the last volume of history – all non-aristocrats are not allowed a surname under Nazi rule – and he picks the somewhat comical "Alfred Alfredson," firmly articulating himself within a patriarchal line of Saxon succession reconfigured as Anglocentric radicalism.

Alfred's "normality," consistently underlined throughout the novel, serves not only in opposition to Hermann's fascist deviance, but also, like George's coupling with Joan in *The Wild Goose Chase*, as a form of transformative normalcy. In touch with the natural, "human" love of freedom, Alfred contains the promise of the overthrow of Nazism, both through his revolutionary activities, and in his willingness to assume his proper place in the future reproductive nation, as a fond father who attempts to forge bonds with the mother of his children. Alfred's heroic attempt to re-found heterosexuality is, indeed, the cornerstone of his revolutionary potential. One of his first acts when he returns from Germany is to visit his current woman in her prison camp, and make the first steps toward articulating a recognizably heterosexual family unit. For a moment, Alfred starts to envy his homosexual son, Thomas, only to realize that his favorite son, Fred, was worth all the trouble:

> *He* wouldn't be in the sickening atmosphere of the Women's quarters, worrying about his baby daughter and being sorely tempted to beat up Army Knights. He'd be off with the friend of the moment, free to go where they would, with the whole clean night-country before them. But then as he looked at Fred, studious, absorbed, patient, with only his father knew what a solid gritty character behind his intelligence, he ceased to envy Thomas entirely. A son like Fred was worth any frets and difficulties. (166; emphasis in original)

Predictably, the favored son Fred continues the work of rebellion after Alfred's death at the close of the novel, continuing the line of popular radicalism of a "solid, gritty character" which the novel sees as the only hope for the overthrow of fascism. This father-son succession complicates claims of the novel's feminism, to put it mildly. Like some other strains of homo-fascist theory (including, for instance, Sontag's), Burdekin's homophobia in *Swastika Night* is only fully explicable within a feminist critique of the phallic masculinity of fascism, according to which the violent expulsion of the principle of femininity results in a vicious, macho homosexuality.[43] And yet, such is the force of the heteronormativity encoded within this critique, patrilineal succession resurfaces as a desirable goal for revolutionary struggle.

By the close of the novel, Hermann has joined Alfred and his son in their revolutionary activities, which might appear to somewhat leaven the novel's homophobia. But Hermann has no real change of heart, merely blindly following his beloved Alfred, who himself took his German friend back to England because he feared Hermann might kill himself at the continuing shock of von Hess's revelations. Hermann dies alongside Alfred heroically fighting off German soldiers so that Fred can escape; an individually redemptive death, to be sure, but not one that overturns the novel's insistent identification of queer male desire with Nazism. Ultimately, Hermann continues as he began – a dumb brute slavishly in love with his English friend, and his brave death functions pharmakologically, representing the beginning of the purgation of queer Nazism necessary for heterosexual English revolution.

The homophobia of Burdekin's novel is not merely a tactical antifascist maneuver, nor simply an unfortunate symptom of its critique of masculinity, but rather part of a strategic heteronormativity at its core. This is not only expressed negatively as the denigration of fascist perversion, but positively, as the construction of the autochthonous subject of popular national radicalism. *Swastika Night* offers a vision of antifascist resistance that is simultaneously resolutely Anglocentric and thoroughly heteronormative, centering on the transformative restitution of the national family, a formulation that prefigures George Orwell's famous vision of English community in essays such as *The Lion and the Unicorn* (1941). Indeed, given *Swastika Night*'s insistence on heroic Englishness as the sole hope for antifascist resistance (and particularly its gushing praise of English "moral fibre" [114]), it is unsurprising that it was reprinted the year before Orwell's essay by the Left Book Club, complete with a preface reassuring readers that the author now believes that fascism will be defeated in rather less than seven centuries: "the picture painted must be considered symbolic rather than prophetic [...] the author has changed his mind about the Nazi *power* to make the *world* evil [...] Nazism is too bad to be permanent."[44] This republication of a signature text of the Popular Front in 1940 indicates how, as I explore further in Chapter 4, the heteronational imaginary of the "People's War" should be seen not as a break with 1930s leftist culture, but rather as the persistence and in some sense a fulfillment of certain strains of Popular Front cultural politics.

Always there in England

For all the novel's strident heteronormativity, Alfred's heterosexuality remains embryonic in *Swastika Night*: he is only "as normal as possible for a man to be in such a society," and while he loves his sons he only makes the first steps toward reinstating a normative family unit, for the thoroughgoing misogyny of Nazi rule will take generations to overturn and for women to become lovable again. However, in the unpublished novel *No Compromise* Burdekin offers a more complete vision of antifascist heterosexuality. Written in the early to mid-1930s, *No Compromise* is set only a few years in the future, in 1940, when political contradictions have intensified and a pitched battle between Communists and fascists is being played out on the streets of England. The first half of the novel is a rewrite of *Lady Chatterley's Lover* from a leftist perspective, as a young aristocratic woman, Romona Lowell, meets a working-class man, Adam Fletcher, who was employed as her family's chauffeur. Initially revolted by his rough exterior and even frightened of him, Romona comes to love Adam, who had been admiring her vulnerability from early on in their acquaintance. When they declare their love for one another, Adam reveals that he is a Communist organizer, and had been writing a book for the Party while working for the Lowell family. Romona's mother, a strong woman and Communist sympathizer, has no objection to their marriage, and her husband, a choleric Colonel and honest Tory, is won over by the revelation that the bloodthirsty Bolshevik is at heart a better man than he. The novel's central coupling thus articulates the central premise of the Popular Front: an implicitly heterosexual alliance between the activist proletarian and his bourgeois helpmeet.

Throughout this part of the narrative, Romona is continually mocked for her hysteria, utter silliness, and failure to "be a person" as the novel curiously puts it; completely unaware of her own sexuality and mental processes, she is depicted in thoroughly and traditionally misogynistic terms.[45] For instance, in the scene immediately preceding the new couple's declaration of mutual love, she runs away from Adam in frigid fear of his sensual masculinity. They had paused on a car journey to pick flowers (shades of Mellors and Chatterley), and then suddenly Romona takes flight:

> But no sooner had she turned her back on him all semblance of reason left her; she was reduced to the mindless condition of an animal. She dropped all her primroses, screamed, and began to run. In three seconds she was in full stride, going so fast that though there was no wind the air fairly whistled past her ears [. . .] she hardly knew who or

what she was, only that she was an animal with legs which must run and run until it was caught. (71–2)

Here an unarticulated fear of rape appears to motivate Romona's flight; and yet she is granted no cognizance of herself as human subject in this moment – yet more troublingly, perhaps, this "animal's" capture is taken to be a predetermined end. And indeed, Adam catches up with her; cradling her gently in his arms, he occasions a change of heart in the young woman. "Romona was crying, from reaction after her hysterical fear, from extreme physical distress, and also from a slow delicious ecstasy which was beginning to pervade her, coming up from the ground under her feet and down from Adam's hand which stroked her head" (73). Almost immediately following Romona's recovery from her "hysteria" the couple declares their undying love for one another; they are soon married. While Adam is away for a few days prior to their wedding, they write to one another, and again Romona's foolishness is stressed, as she goes "about reading Adam's letters in a dream of happiness tinged with regret, reading Adam's letters in all the most sacred and haunted places in the garden [. . .] like any girl she had a faint hope that he might be in love with her forever" (108). Romona's silliness is attributed to her "mother fixation," as she is caught in abject admiration of her strong-willed, intelligent, and politically aware mother (a character who does somewhat leaven the novel's sexism).

In stark contrast to Romona, Adam's level-headed masculinity is stressed throughout, and his moral beauty is immediately noted by the shrewd Mrs. Lowell in the opening scene of the novel, who claims that she is "interested" in the new chauffeur "because he is so good" and rebukes her "silly" daughter for her initial inability to see past his rough exterior to a heart of gold (8). As the narrative progresses, Adam gains in stature to become a paragon of Communist masculinity, possessed of almost superhuman physical strength, an iron will, a keen intelligence, and gentleness behind his rough exterior. The adoring Romona articulates this perfection with an Anglocentric line of heroic rebels, embodying the genealogy of radical Englishness put forward by Popular Front leftists in the mid- to late 1930s. Following a discussion of the possibility of the birth of the "new man" under Communism, Adam puns that he is actually an old man, given his name, and Romona responds:

'I like it best," she said rebelliously. "I don't want any new human beings. If men were all like you the whole race would be happy. And I adore your commonness and oldness. You were at the Battle of Hastings under Harold's flag, and in the Parliamentary army and among the Chartists. You've always been there, in England, and you always must be." (181; emphasis in original)

Despite Adam's sardonic reply that in that case he's had "three sound drubbings to one win," the novel itself continually identifies him, like Alfred in *Swastika Night*, as a particularly English rebel, even as he is cast as a committed internationalist. During one of the novel's many political set pieces, Adam has dinner with several Communist comrades, including a German Jew and an Irishman, in a scene that reads like a programmatic exposition of Popular Front internationalism, as each individual's doughty national characteristics are praised in turn (110). Later on, in an equally programmatic moment, Adam, quoting *Hamlet*, describes to Romona how he came to be a Communist, locating his political biography in a desire to avenge the death of his father on the Western Front in World War I. Adam thus corrects the weakness of the relationship of national labor movements to the Second International in his Third International Communism, and articulates his political awakening in patrilineal terms. Adam voices this commitment to Communism in unmistakably – if strangely diminutive – phallic terms, referring to himself as a "hard little battering ram against capitalism," to which Romona dutifully yet slyly responds "nothing could be harder" (152).

No Compromise is less lurid in its depiction of the homoerotics of fascism than *Swastika Night*. The main queer figure in the novel is Romona's brother, Wade, who is depicted as a decadent but not politically dangerous homosexual aesthete whose disposition is tolerated by Adam and his family.[46] Meanwhile, Romona's other brother, Arthur, is a fascist soldier who is vain and hates women; one might argue that these two brothers together represent a homo-fascist formation, but neither quite fits the full stereotype. The supposed queerness of fascism is nevertheless unmistakably present throughout the text. Most importantly, the central plot device of the second half of the narrative hinges on a sadistic homoerotic subtext involving a van der Lubbe figure. After their marriage, Romona and Adam settle in Westbridge, where he is the town's Communist leader. Not long after they arrive, strife hits the Party in the form of a "hooligan" defector to the fascists, who is murdered by an "excitable" Scottish Communist, Linklater (his "highland" excitability and residual "clan loyalty" are stressed throughout with an Anglocentric gaze upon the primitive Celt). During Linklater's trial for the murder it emerges that the "rat" offered Linklater extreme provocation, in the form of a boast about what would happen to Adam when the fascists took over. In a homo-fascist version of "the love that dare not speak its name," Linklater refuses to reveal the details of this boast, only confiding to Adam that the "rat" had taunted him with the

> most dretful and horrible things about what they would do when they had their machority in the country, what they would do to you, Adam. The Potempa murder was nothing, nothing to what he said they would do to you, and it was not fit for me to tell you what it wass, or for any man to think or speak of, it wass so dirty and so cruel. (219)

Quite clearly, "dirty and cruel," coupled with the namelessness of the boast indicates some form of sadistic torture, most probably a rape (the Potempa murder was a case in 1932 when a group of SA men trampled a Communist to death in front of his mother). Burdekin's attempt at Scottish intonation provides a further gloss, "machority" being perhaps a pun on the hyper-masculinity of the fascist takeover. Later on, Adam is captured by the fascists and is overtaken with fear, voiced in terms which make explicit the nature of the torture alluded to by Linklater, as he "thinks of what Linkie had not told him," and therefore "understand[s] what Rom felt when she was running through the wood" – the fear of rape (240).

Adam is not raped, however, and it turns out that the most important fascist in the text, Major Hardruff, is not in any way queer, his campy name notwithstanding. Hardruff turns out to be a relatively well-mannered, English sort of fascist – an authoritarian and a misogynist, to be sure, but no sadist and a gentleman in his dealings with other men. Indeed, he develops a great respect for Adam and does not torture him or anyone else. Instead, with cold calculation but no pleasure, he tells Adam not to stand for Parliament in the next election, then murders him with a clean gunshot wound to the head when he refuses, having given Adam some time to consider. Hardruff's comparative decency and respect for Adam echoes

Romona's father's attitude toward the great-souled revolutionary. Colonel Lowell consents to his daughter's marriage, and acknowledges Adam's inner superiority to himself, yet (or perhaps unsurprisingly) as the two men part they reveal that if they saw each other in the street, armed, they would shoot each other (104). In some senses a prequel to *Swastika Night*, Burdekin's unpublished novel appears to mourn the passing of the comparatively civilized forms of non-fascist masculinity associated with British capitalist modernity. Throughout *No Compromise* both Adam and Mrs. Lowell, the two wisest characters in the text, continually reiterate the prediction of a fascist period of history to come before Communism's victory; the macho duel-like face-offs between Adam and Colonel Lowell and Adam and Hardruff thus appear strangely quaint compared to the horrors to come.

Don't take much account of fucking

For all his apparently conventional masculinity and his punning protests that he is an old-fashioned sort of man, Adam is actually far less orthodox in his masculinity than he first appears. In a long discussion about his past with Romona, Adam reveals that his mother died when he was very young, and he was brought up by his father; consequently, he "learned to do everything in the house like a girl" (154). Indeed, Adam is house-proud, a nourishing cook, and a keen knitter; as Romona teases him, "you're not very manly, dear, with all your feminine accomplishments" (172). Adam is also sexually diffident and shy. Shortly after they are married and move in together, the clearly amorous Romona suggests they "sit in the same chair to be warmer"; Adam can only "look modestly down at a pile of sandwiches" – ones he just made himself (143). Moreover, he later states that he "don't take much account of ---" (160): here the novel performs a complete reversal of Lawrence's text, playing on the censorship of "fucking" or "cunt" in order to overturn its importance. Indeed, Adam is almost completely sexless, as is underlined at various other points in the novel. Upon reading her brother's novels, he complains to Romona, for instance, that they "make too much" of sex which he doesn't see as "serious" (145); he displays great compassion for the plight of prostitutes in the town, but an absolutely pristine inability to be even remotely intrigued by them (158–66).

What, then, is to be made of Adam's strange blend of normative masculinity, sexlessness, and "feminine accomplishments"? His asexuality might be explained by Burdekin playing on the common stereotype of the puritanism of Communists already operative by the mid-1930s (particularly in England), but this is somewhat mitigated by his use of earthy language throughout, even as it is placed under erasure. More importantly, as English has convincingly contended, Burdekin argues consistently in her work for celibacy as an important practice for exceptional individuals, and even as a common goal for humanity in general. Especially for Burdekin's heroic inverts, a transcendence of sexual desire is central to her imaginative project of radical human evolution, as is particularly salient in her depiction of the so-called "Person" in *Proud Man* (1934). The Person is a strikingly beautiful post-human who visits present-day Earth and is flabbergasted by the flailing morass of failed, desiring humanity they find there. The Person is completely intersex, humanity having evolved beyond gender, and utterly asexual, desire having been eliminated in the perfectly harmonious society they inhabit, but decides to pass as a female invert as that would be the closest approximation to their asexual perfection. In a turn of phrase more troubling than English's generally sympathetic reading of Burdekin would allow, the Person incessantly refers to Earth's inhabitants as "subhumans."[47]

In the Person, Burdekin appears to have anticipated later radical feminist formulations of the necessary abolition of gender, viewing the female invert as the next best thing to the post-gender Person, anticipating Valerie Solanas's transmogrified women of the future. This formulation goes some way to explaining the strange ambivalence of *No Compromise* toward its male protagonist – Adam, too, is presented as a staging-post, a next-best gendered being in a fallen world. The term "person" is deployed in a marked fashion at certain points in *No Compromise*: it will be recalled that the childish Romona is "not yet" a person; by contrast, Adam's personhood is literally underlined in a conversation Romona has with her mother. As Romona talks of her utter subservience to Adam, she argues that "it isn't just because he is a man. He's such a good person" (136; emphasis Burdekin's). The conundrum posed by Adam, however, remains, crystallized in this remark. Why build up this masculine figure only to problematize his gender identity? Why draw such a foolish female character in order to set such a figure in high relief? Why, in fact, is Adam killed off in the text, his funeral making up the final scene of the novel?

What produces Adam Fletcher – and indeed the strange tenor of Burdekin's work in the mid- to late 1930s more broadly – is the fraught relationship between strategy and tactics posed in a particularly acute way by Popular Front sexual politics. It is as if, somewhat against her will, Burdekin felt the pressing need to create a popular Communist romance, complete with manly hero and shrinking heroine, but yet was somehow unable to go through completely with the project, concerned at the longer-term ramifications of such a narrative. The strange blend of the radical and the heterosexist that marks both *Swastika Night* and *No Compromise* is a symptom of a profound uneasiness with the left's deployment of normative sexuality even as they are in part wholehearted tactical expositions of it. Picking up Laurent Berlant's term, in the Introduction I identified the "cruel optimism" of the Popular Front for queer writers, the harsh way in which an apparently inclusive formation turned out to be relentlessly antihomosexual. *Swastika Night* and *No Compromise* are signature documents of this problematic, as Burdekin mobilizes gender against sexuality in the name of the Popular Front's reproductive nation.

The Popular Front's social accomplishments are not to be disputed, the postwar welfare state being the most obvious. And yet, the harm its normalizations did to the left's sexual politics, encoded in these very institutions, was as lasting as its most famous achievement – quite precisely, given the coincidence of the emergence of second wave feminism, gay liberation, and the beginnings of the Fordist settlement's breakdown, all at the turn of the 1960s and 1970s. This lasting damage becomes clearer still when we move into World War II and interrogate England's most famous essayist. If Burdekin was a curiously positioned exponent of Popular Front sexual politics, George Orwell was, unwittingly perhaps, its most important and most convinced advocate.

Chapter 4

Orwell's Hope in the Proles

George Orwell's characterization of England as a "family" in *The Lion and the Unicorn: Socialism and the English Genius* (1941) must surely rank among his most infamous statements of Anglocentric *Gemeinschaft* peddling.[1] Perhaps aware of this, later in life Orwell listed this text as one of a list of four book-length works he did not want republished, alongside *A Clergyman's Daughter* (1934), *Keep the Aspidistra Flying* (1936), and *The English People* (1947).[2] It might seem an act of critical churlishness to pay too much attention to this list; it is also important, as Stefan Collini cautions, not to set too much store by Orwell's most famous patriotic pronouncements in *The Lion and the Unicorn*.[3] And yet, attending to Orwell's reproductive anxieties may prove telling in more ways than one. Read alongside lesser-known materials from the *Complete Works*, and his famous assertion that "if there was hope, it lay in the proles" (original Latin usage: offspring), these texts reveal a deep-seated preoccupation rarely commented on in Orwell studies: the national birth rate.[4] From the eponymous clergyman's daughter's pathologized asexuality, Gordon Comstock's obsessive hatred of birth control in *Keep the Aspidistra Flying*, to *The English People*'s brutal recommendation for the government to "make childlessness as painful an economic burden as a big family is now," Orwell persistently frets over the reproductive capabilities of the English nation.[5]

The modern nation state always requires ideologies and practices of population, necessarily synthesizing forms of national and sexual normativity in its ongoing process of self-constitution. The key episode in Britain pre-dating Orwell's working life was the combination of homosexual panic and reproductive anxieties in the late nineteenth and early twentieth centuries, driven by degeneration theory,

Boer War jingoism, and the Wilde trial; the longer, broader history of these imbrications could be traced through the development of Foucault's concept of population, a line of inquiry adumbrated in *Security, Territory, Population* (1977–8), and continued in his famous analyses of biopolitics.[6] What is distinctive about Orwell's particular synthesis of patriotism and reproductivist heterosexuality is that it is made on behalf of a specifically English "democratic socialism" ranged against both Communism and moribund Toryism, and thus must be seen as an important precursor to the national imaginary of postwar welfare-state Britain – the definitive moment of pronatalist patriotism in twentieth-century British history.

Any critique of Orwell is faced with a distinct challenge. From the start of his posthumous reception, Orwell's admirers have set him up as a paragon of exemplary ordinariness, an outsider figure with a radical commitment to continuity, a writer whose intellectual inconsistency is a mark of moral authority.[7] The tricky question of Orwell studies is, then, how one mounts a critique without either sounding hysterical – I use the term advisedly – about something commonplace, "of its time" as the cliché goes; or, on the other hand, simplifying an eternal outsider or "radical eccentric" as Kristen Bluemel has mythologized Orwell.[8] Moreover, dissent from Orwell's myth is adduced as evidence for his judgments, as the suppression of native English decency, i.e. disagreement with Orwell, is precisely the mark of a decadent, Europeanized intellectual, totalitarian stooge, or jargon-spouting professor.[9] At the same time, from the position of a theoretically-informed critical field, Orwell might appear all too easy a target, his naïve epistemology of language and cultural conservatism being easy game for anyone familiar with, say, Jameson, Foucault, or Butler. Christopher Norris's Derridean critique of Orwell's "home-spun empiricism," for instance, has the feel of a sledgehammer being brought to bear on a philosophically indefensible nut; conversely, Alex Woloch's recent attempt to find dialectical nuance in Orwell's every pronouncement seems equally misplaced.[10]

These problems loom especially large for scholars of gender and sexuality who seek to interrogate Orwell. For a theoretically sophisticated field drawing extensively on continental thought and opposed by definition to Orwell's palpable misogyny and homophobia, what, one might ask, is the point in drawing attention to this figure beyond mere condemnation? Daphne Patai's feminist critique *The Orwell*

Mystique (1984) made a series of important interventions, and yet from a certain perspective might be seen to overstate its biographical case, imputing the misogyny of capitalist modernity at large too paradigmatically to Orwell; it remains, tellingly, the only book-length feminist study of Orwell.[11] Focusing on Orwell's homophobia *per se*, meanwhile, no longer seems intellectually generative, often leading to a weak biographical reading of his repressed homosexual desires (I am similarly uninterested in Eric Blair's personal belief that he was unable to have biological children).[12]

Faced with these difficulties, focusing on Orwell's obsession with national reproduction has a particular advantage. For Orwell was surely not only a hidebound social conservative who "reverted to type" as Raymond Williams has argued, but also clearly committed to a certain fatally flawed vision of an egalitarian future.[13] To complete this chapter's opening quotation, "England is a family," Orwell writes, but continues, "with the wrong members in control." What is most salient about Orwell's sexual politics is not his undeniable misogyny and homophobia, but rather his desperate attempts to renegotiate and reinvigorate reproductivist heterosexuality and national masculinity in line with his Anglocentric "democratic socialism."[14] This is most obvious in Orwell's wartime essays, which incessantly stress the need for "deblimping": his term for the way in which the nation needs to purge the decayed old guard of upper-class military men and political leaders. These moribund figures are not to be replaced with revolutionary proletarians, nor with women, still less with elements from the existing leftist intelligentsia or sexual dissidents, but with the vigorous rising men of the working and lower middle classes: "intelligent mechanics" and determined men of "indeterminate social class."[15]

From an antiheteronormative standpoint the horrors of such a meritocratic imaginary are clear – not least because to an extent Orwell's positive vision actually "came true," as liberal commentators are given to describing his later despairing predictions. The sexual-political implications of "Orwell's victory" are clearly legible in the social and literary history of postwar Britain, a period during which the persecution of queers rose dramatically, women were pressured to return to the domestic sphere, and in which such working- and lower-middle-class writers as John Osborne, Alan Sillitoe, Kingsley Amis, and John Braine rose to prominence alongside the construction of the welfare state.¹⁶ It is important not to overstate Orwell's agency in the development of postwar Britain's distinctive texture of sexual conservatism and statist redistribution of wealth. One has to concede, after all, that the Beveridge Report (1942), not *The Lion and the Unicorn*, was the founding document of the postwar settlement; as Owen Hatherley has pointed out, Orwell's pamphlet was not that widely read at the time compared to the work of J. B. Priestly and Robert Tressell.¹⁷ Manifold other forces were also manifestly at work. Richard Hornsey has suggestively argued that the architectural imaginary of postwar Britain was shaped amidst fears of unruly working-class queer life in the period.¹⁸ But Orwell's reproductivism did play a crucial role in mid-century social history, part of the series of uneasy articulations between the shifting sexual politics of the 1930s left, the homophobia of anti-Communism, and the statism of the postwar regime.

Chapter 3 advanced a concept central to the imaginary of Popular Front sexual politics: transformative normalcy, a term that names how a formation of apparently revolutionary recuperative heterosexuality comes to dominate leftist antifascism in response to the supposed queerness of fascism. Focusing on the texts Orwell sought to banish from his own canon, this chapter argues that transformative normalcy is the guiding turn in Orwell's imaginary, not only the way in which he recoiled from the queer, but also the tool with which he attempted to cut the Gordian knot of anti-futurist socialism. A constitutive problem for Orwell, as for other instinctively conservative socialists, and increasingly for Communists in the mid- to late 1930s, was how to adapt a socialist idea of the future to incorporate a critique of the horrors of cultural modernity, one of which is futurism, itself implicated in socialism (I use the term "futurism" here not only to denote the artistic movement, but also a broader complex of attitudes oriented toward the continuance of technological modernity and new social forms). Throughout his authorship Orwell rails against the gleaming technological utopias of George Bernard Shaw's and H. G. Wells's "progressivism" as well as Soviet Communism's "machine worship" – but this is only the most obvious symptom. A triangulation between sexual perversity, sterility, and the statism of Soviet Communism lies at the core of Orwell's deep-seated fear of the future, expressed paradigmatically as a hatred for the queer leftism of the Auden circle, of Communism at large, and of birth control, strongly associated with feminism and queer sexual practice. Orwell's response to this anxiety was to reconstitute a vision of hard-won fecund normality: the English working-class hearth, teeming with children and well stocked with nourishing food, whose prevalence could only come about through socialist transformation. In a famous passage in *The Road to Wigan Pier*, Orwell waxes lyrical on the "perfect symmetry" of the English working-class home: "Especially on winter evenings after tea, when the fire glows in the open range and dances mirrored in the steel fender, when Father, in shirt sleeves, sits in the rocking chair at one side of the fire reading the racing finals, and Mother sits on the other with her sewing, and the children are happy with a pennorth of mint humbugs" – a cloying vision indeed.[19]

Orwell's purple passages of domestic bliss are easy to mock. But my intention here is to draw attention to the overlooked importance of how such moments operate within the sexual history of the left, and the ways in which they were formed by and themselves shaped the broader contours of English mid-century social and literary history. This process of mutual constitution was, it must be granted, surely painful for Orwell, as his later authorship registers the acute birth pangs of the welfare state. For what becomes apparent when Orwell's advocacy of an English *Gemeinschaft* reaches its peak, in his pamphlet *The English People*, is the paradox that only a statist – cognately for Orwell a perverse – formation can bring about his vision of organic normalcy. This paradoxical formulation is necessarily foundational for the modern nation state, but Orwell's is a lastingly influential iteration of this tension in mid-century Britain. His uneasy realization of this paradox was further compounded by the marked similarities between Orwell's patriotic cultural politics and those of the CPGB from the late 1930s onwards.[20] The fact, moreover, that *The English People* was commissioned by the Ministry of Information adds a certain irony to this moment, and the infamous list of Communists Orwell gave to MI5 on his deathbed must be viewed in the context of a longer, if less transparently egregious, collaboration with the British state. Indeed, as I argue at this chapter's conclusion, the particular despair of *Nineteen Eighty-Four* derives from Orwell's looming realization that what he had been calling for all along necessarily entailed precisely what he decried.[21]

Silly potboilers

As war drew to a close in 1945 Orwell drafted a set of notes for his literary executor. Emphatically stating that *Keep the Aspidistra Flying* and *A Clergyman's Daughter* should not be republished, he described these two early novels as "silly potboilers which I ought not to have published in the first place" (CW XVII, 114). He seemed to have been rather uneasy with the genre from the start, as both novels feature prominent moments directly subverting the potboiler's function. In *Keep The Aspidistra Flying*, the protagonist, failed poet Gordon Comstock, works in a series of bookshops and lending libraries, and is confronted by customers who seek titillation only to be disappointed even by the most salacious-sounding titles.[22] This is even more pronounced in *A Clergyman's Daughter*, for the novel's plot mechanics might be described as anti-potboiler: the eponymous, sexless anti-hero, Dorothy, disappears in a fugue state having resisted the somewhat listless advances of a balding middle-aged semi-rake, and is viciously slandered by the village gossip, only to return home at the novel's close as the gossip was sued for libel and thus no longer credible. Rita Felski and Terry Eagleton have both called these novels "lower-middle class" – an acute designation on first glance perhaps, given not only the novels' social milieu and halting critiques of sophistication, but also their apparent unease with sexuality as such.[23]

However, on closer inspection, one of the most telling aspects of these novels' sexual politics is a thoroughly bourgeois polemic against the dangers of sexual repression, seen in quite orthodox Freudian terms as the great psychosocial danger that leads to perversion. To classify Orwell as a Freudian is to read against the grain somewhat, given the dearth of references to Freud in his work and his avowed anti-psychoanalytic position. The only mention of "Freud" listed in the *Complete Works* is anti-Freudian: in "Raffles and Miss Blandish," Orwell decries the way in which "Freud and Machiavelli have reached the outer suburbs" in the perversions of the modern detective novel – a rejection that forms part of his insistence on the value of English hypocrisy in keeping society "decent."[24] However, it is clearly rather hard to understand *Nineteen Eighty-Four* outside of the dynamics of repression. In fact, from very early on in his career

Orwell's understanding of sexuality was rooted in some version of the concept, as can be seen in his Hop Picking Diary from 1931, which was to provide material for part of *A Clergyman's Daughter*. Orwell notes with disgust the sexually explicit conversation of the homeless: "Merely lecherous people are all right, but people who would like to be lecherous, but don't get the chance, are horribly degraded by it. They remind me of the dogs that hang enviously round while two other dogs are copulating" (CW XX, 218).

Orwell further develops this thought in a lower-middle-class register in the first instance of titillation-seeking behavior from *Keep the Aspidistra Flying*. A "decentish middle-aged man" lingers outside a bookshop, "wear[ing] a guilty look," his eyes are drawn to D. H. Lawrence's novels, and the protagonist Gordon, an impoverished poet and bookshop assistant, triumphantly diagnoses him:

> Ah! So that was it! Pining for a bit of smut, of course. He had heard of D. H. Lawrence afar off. A bad face he had, Gordon thought. Pale, heavy, downy, with bad contours. Welsh, by the look of him – Nonconformist, anyway. He had the regular Dissenting pouches round the corners of his mouth. At home, president of the local Purity League or Seaside Vigilance Committee (rubber-soled slippers and electric torch, spotting kissing couples along the beach parade), and now up in town on the razzle. (CN, 579)

Imbricated with this passage's traditional skewering of hypocrisy and racist physiognomy is a more contemporary, psychoanalytic dynamic, according to which the suppression of sexuality results in its irruption into perversion. And indeed, the "Welsh solicitor" as Gordon decides to call him, will "doubtless tonight, when darkness hid his blushes [. . .] slink into one of the rubber-shops and buy *High Jinks in a Parisian Convent* by Sadie Blackeyes" (CN, 580), completing the repressed man's descent into voyeuristic, sadistic perversion, expressed concisely through the transformation of his "rubber-soled slippers" into the rubber-shops.

A Clergyman's Daughter presents a complementary perspective. Rather than a furtively sadistic voyeur like Gordon's shady customer, Dorothy is a frigid masochist, downtrodden by an emotionally abusive father. The opening sequence details her unpleasant morning routine, entirely dedicated to his whims and beset by worries about debts, and the novel's opening passages are certainly sympathetic to

Dorothy. Soon, however, it becomes clear that there is something "abnormal" about her. "She made it a rule, whenever she caught herself not attending to her prayers, to prick her arm hard enough to make blood come. It was her chosen form of self-discipline, her guard against irreverence and sacrilegious thoughts" (CN, 259). Dorothy's perverse response to irreverence is, appropriately, brought forth through a gaze upon her father, whose garments she lovingly stiches: "With a shock Dorothy discovered herself gazing vaingloriously at the pleats of her father's surplice, which she herself had sewn two years ago. She set her teeth and drove the pin an eighth of an inch into her arm" (CN, 259). This Freudian structure is further developed in her complete refusal to engage in sexual relations with men, which "even in memory or imagination [. . .] made her wince. It was her especial secret, the especial, incurable disability that she carried through life" (CN, 310). The predictable source of her frigidity was "certain dreadful scenes between her father and her mother – scenes that she had witnessed when she was no more than nine years old [. . .] And then a little later she had been frightened by some old steel engravings of nymphs pursued by satyrs" (CN, 302–3). Dorothy's "sexual coldness" is framed not only in terms of her witnessing a primal scene of parental intercourse, but also that of a failed or perverted pastoral – a recurring theme for Orwell from these novels, through *Coming Up For Air* (1939), right up to its overturning in Winston and Julia's defiant open-air sex in *Nineteen Eighty-Four*.

In fact, Dorothy does have her own bucolic pleasures, but they are solitary, with only vegetation for company. Stopping to rest in a field on a hot summer's day, she "pulled a frond of the fennel against her face and breathes in the strong sweet scent." She is soon "overwhelmed" by its "lovely, lovely scent – scent of summer days, scent of childhood joys, scent of spice-drenched islands in the warm foam of Oriental seas!" (CN, 297). Here "warm foam" operates as a heavy-handed figure for arousal, as do the luxuriant connotations of "Oriental." The novel goes on to describe her pagan ecstasies in a curiously salacious passage that heavily implies orgasm, treating the reader to a half-glimpsed image of female masturbation:

> Her heart swelled with sudden joy. It was that mystical joy in the beauty of the earth and the very nature of things that she recognised, perhaps mistakenly, as the love of God. As she knelt there in the heat,

the sweet odour and the drowsy hum of insects, it seemed to her that she could momentarily hear the mighty anthem of praise that the earth and all created things send up everlastingly to their maker. All vegetation, leaves, flowers, grass, shining, vibrating, crying out in their joy. Larks also chanting, choirs of larks invisible, dripping music from the sky. All the riches of summer, the warmth of the earth, the song of the birds, the fume of cows, the droning of countless bees, mingling and ascending like the smoke of ever-burning altars. Therefore with Angels and Archangels! She began to pray, and for a moment she prayed ardently, blissfully, forgetting herself in the joy of her worship. Then, less than a minute later, she discovered that she was kissing the frond of the fennel that was still against her face. (CN, 297)

The implications of "sudden joy [. . .] dripping music [. . .] forgetting herself" are hard to miss, but what is perhaps most important here is the irony of Dorothy's solitary – and thus sterile – pleasure in the midst of a scene of heavy fecundity. This juxtaposition continues later in the novel in a famous sequence when Dorothy, now destitute and experiencing an extended blackout, goes hop-picking; at this point, she has also lost her faith and thus, without her former alibi of prayer, is presumably unable to masturbate in the fields. Her lack of productivity is compared not only to the late-summer atmosphere of drooping hops, but also to the earthy sexual license of her down-at-heel companions, simultaneously more adroit at picking hops and enjoying themselves during the long summer evenings than the feckless rector's daughter (CN, 318–22).

Keep the Aspidistra Flying also centrally features a scene of failed pastoral sex, the centerpiece of a narrative that is insistently organized around reproductive anxieties. The novel follows the life of a young failed poet, Gordon Comstock, who "declares war on money" and leaves his relatively well-paid job as an advertising copywriter to become an impoverished second-hand bookshop assistant (CN, 726). Following a drunken misadventure, Gordon sinks even lower, losing his job at a fairly reputable West End bookshop, and moving from his Hampstead lodgings to a slum in Waterloo. Now working at a wretched mobile library and paid extremely low wages, Gordon sinks into apathy, stops writing poetry, and, wallowing in his poverty, finds grim satisfaction at this successful flight from lower-middle-class respectability. At this point, however, Gordon's girlfriend Rosemary reveals that she is pregnant, and Gordon gives up his self-willed downward spiral. He gets his old job at the advertising firm back, and the couple marry, with Gordon's acquiescence in petit-bourgeois respectability figured at the narrative's close by his demand that they purchase an aspidistra, the novel's symbol of humdrum lower-middle-class domesticity.

Keep the Aspidistra Flying is considered one of Orwell's weakest novels, with even his most ardent admirers criticizing the novel's conclusion as "doubtful" and "not Orwell's most innovative fictional resolution."[25] Yet the novel's denouement is meticulously prepared throughout the narrative, as Gordon's disgust at birth control is the central organizing device of the whole plot, an aspect curiously overlooked in critical accounts of the novel.[26] From the very start, Gordon's jaundiced critique of contemporary capitalism is voiced as an obsessive hatred of birth control. In the novel's opening sequence, Gordon gazes at an inane advertising billboard, and despairs of modern civilization:

> Desolation, emptiness, prophecies of doom. For can you not see, if you know how to look, that behind that slick self-satisfaction, that tittering fat-bellied triviality, there is nothing but a frightful emptiness, a secret despair? The great death-wish of the modern world. Suicide pacts. Heads stuck in gas-ovens in lonely maisonettes. French letters and Amen Pills. And the reverberations of future wars. Enemy aeroplanes flying over London; the deep threatening hum of the propellers, the shattering thunder of the bombs. (CN, 586)

Birth control is part of the "great death-wish of the modern world," in a series of associations which link the emptiness of everyday modern life to historical crisis, placed in between "suicides in lonely maisonettes" and "the reverberations of future wars." This connotative chain is reiterated throughout the narrative, as Gordon insistently connects contraception with violence and decay. Seizing on the same advertisement, Gordon later exclaims to his friend Ravelston, "'the imbecility, the emptiness, the desolation! You can't look at it without thinking of French letters and machine guns.'" Such is the strength of his disgust at these threats to life that he claims to wish for war: "do you know the other day I was actually wishing war would break out? I was longing for it – praying for it, almost" (CN, 630). The same pairing of "French letters and machine guns" appears again later in the text, the constant motif of Gordon's anomie (CN, 679–80). In fact, Gordon's abhorrence of birth control does not appear to be exclusively related to contemporary capitalism, but rather a rejection of a more broadly conceived modernity, including socialism, which he sees as "some kind of Aldous Huxley *Brave New World*: only not so amusing. Four hours a day in a model factory, tightening up bolt number 6003 [...] Free abortion clinics on all the corners" (*CN*, 632). Mirroring Orwell's well-known polemics against the dehumanizing "machine-worship" of the left, here Gordon attacks socialism for its evacuation of life of meaning and purpose, with legalized abortion seen as part of this process.[27] Failed artistic production is similarly implicated, as Gordon morosely contemplates his "forty or fifty drab, dead little poems, each like a little abortion in its labelled jar [...] dead as a blasted foetus in a bottle" (*CN*, 628–9). Throughout the novel, abortion and birth control dominate Gordon's imagination as the master-tropes for a corrupt and decadent civilization, to which neither art nor politics can offer a response.

The root of Gordon's obsessive disgust with birth control and abortion is a particular reaction to his decayed class position. Gordon's grandfather had made a great deal of money, and produced a large number of offspring, but Gordon's parents' generation, completely mired in apathy and inertia, had failed to breed (apart from producing Gordon and his sister): "It was noticeable even then that they had lost all impulse to reproduce themselves. Really vital people, whether they have money or whether they haven't, multiply almost as automatically as animals" (*CN*, 600). Gordon's response to his sterile middle-class family is to celebrate the apparently unthinking philoprogenitivism of the working class: "How right the lower classes are! Hats off to the factory lad who with fourpence in his pocket puts his girl in the family way! At least he's got blood and not money in his veins" (*CN*, 603). Far from being merely an illustration of Gordon's unappetizing character, this sentiment is echoed very precisely in Orwell's own voice in *The Road to Wigan Pier* (1937), where he argues that the working class's habit of "getting married on the dole" is "proof of their essential good sense."[28]

Matters come to an awkward anticlimax during a scene of failed pastoral reproduction, when on a trip to the country Rosemary refuses to have sex with Gordon in a field without a condom. The frustrated would-be lover is furious, arguing that Rosemary's only concern is financial, and launching yet another polemic against birth control as a mode of oppressive capitalist control: "This birth-control business! It's just another way they've found out of bullying us. And you want to acquiesce in it, apparently" (*CN*, 667). Gordon's outburst figures birth control as part of the corrupt money-world, in which lower-middle-class women are apparently the most thoroughly complicit subjects. As in *A Clergyman's Daughter*, heterosexual reproduction and masculine vitality are under threat; however, they are here imperiled by capitalist modernity and feminine caution rather than decayed patriarchal authority and female frigidity. Gordon and Rosemary are not, moreover, doomed to sterility like Dorothy. Rosemary does in the end decide to have sex with Gordon without demanding contraception, and they joylessly conceive a child at his slum lodgings in Waterloo. When Rosemary later visits to tell him she is pregnant, Gordon initially cannot take in the news, but once she mentions the possibility of abortion, his course of action and their love become dramatically apparent:

> That pulled him up. For the first time he grasped, with the only kind of knowledge that matters, what they were really talking about. The words 'a baby' took on a new significance. They did not mean any longer a mere abstract disaster, they meant a bud of flesh, a bit of himself, down there in her belly, alive and growing. His eyes met hers. They had a strange moment of sympathy such as they had never had before. For a moment he did feel that in some mysterious way they were one flesh. Though they were feet apart he felt as though they were joined together – as through some invisible living cord stretched from her entrails to his. He knew then that it was a dreadful thing they were contemplating – a blasphemy, if that word had any meaning. Yet if it had been put otherwise he might not have recoiled from it. It was the squalid detail of the five pounds that brought it home.
> 'No fear!' he said. 'Whatever happens we're not going to do *that*. It's disgusting.'
> 'I know it is. But I can't have the baby without being married.'
> 'No! If that's the alternative I'll marry you. I'd sooner cut my right hand off than do a thing like that.' (*CN*, 723)

A "disgusting" threat to unborn life prompts a sudden, joyous realization of reproductive heterosexuality – their production of a fetus makes Gordon and Rosemary "in some mysterious way [...] one flesh." Their course for the rest of the narrative is now clear. Gordon rushes off to look at pictures of unborn babies in a public library, realizes that he no longer wishes for war, and the couple are married, the novel closing on a lyrical passage depicting the unborn baby's first kicks, the movement of the fetus occasioning the quietly triumphal final line, "well, once again things were happening in the Comstock family" (*CN*, 729). Here, as Gordon gives up his poetic aspirations and settles down, reproduction is made to stand for activity *tout court* in a pervasive pronatalist synecdoche that relegates political and artistic life – and indeed the social itself – to second-order modes of production. It is, in other words, an obsession with the fetus, not the aspidistra, which insistently structures Orwell's novel.

It will be clear from the first half of this book that I do not endorse Lee Edelman's thoroughgoing conflation of political futurity with reproductivist heterosexuality. Townsend Warner's novel of queer revolution, *Summer Will Show*, surely offers a compelling vision of non-reproductivist futurity; similarly, Isherwood's transformation of the family structure into a queer red front belies the strong iteration of Edelman's thesis. However, Orwell's novel is superbly adequate to Edelman's argument – perhaps more than any other left-wing novel of the 1930s, in *Keep the Aspidistra* the future *is* the child. While, along with the documentary film I discuss in the Introduction, *A Diary for Timothy*, this text is admittedly an extreme case, Orwell was not alone on the left in these totalizing claims for sexual reproduction, which should be viewed in terms of a broader movement within the Popular Front, toward what I have been calling a transformative normalcy.

Orwell and the Popular Front

As I argue in Chapter 3, writers as diverse as Katharine Burdekin, Rex Warner, and Winifred Holtby offered a vision of recuperative heterosexuality as a bulwark against fascism and the threat of the coming war, a precarious norm seen as desperately under threat that thus emerges as a revolutionary postulate. It is therefore worth briefly considering how the explicitly sexual-political aspects of Orwell's work in the 1930s form part of what has been identified by Nick Hubble and Philip Bounds as Orwell's convergence with Communist cultural politics in the period – in particular what Hubble has astutely identified as Orwell's project of "satiris[ing]

Popular Front cultural politics while simultaneously participating in them."²⁹ I would go further to suggest that, for all his polemics, Orwell was not merely a participant in but a paradigmatic figure of Popular Front cultural politics.

Writing in 1937, Orwell described the Popular Front as "a combination with about as much vitality, and about as much right to exist, as a pig with two heads or some other Burnham [sic] and Bailey monstrosity" (CW XI, 42–3).³⁰ Orwell's polemics against the Popular Front are well known, but what is most telling about this exclamation is his deployment of the idea of congenital deformity – Barnum and Bailey were circus impresarios, well known for their "freak shows." Orwell designates his target as perverse, an outrage to common decency, and opposed to the natural order. The underlying irony is that key Popular Front cultural producers were themselves assiduously instrumentalizing this opposition between decency and perversion in an attempt to broaden the appeal of leftist antifascism. Orwell's consistently urgent attempt to reach out to the lower middle classes, moreover, is a characteristic gesture of Popular Front political engagement. To take the most famous example: the final section of his *Road to Wigan Pier* appeals to an impoverished but politically timid middle class, with "nothing to lose but our aitches," as the text famously concludes.³¹ Orwell's concern here is remarkably close to that of the Communist-led factions of the Popular Front. Taking their cue from Dimitrov's announcement of the Popular Front in 1935, a significant part of the project of publications such as *Left Review* or *International Literature* during the period was to draw petit-bourgeois intellectuals into the antifascist fray.³²

Orwell's explicitly sexually oriented front of this specific class-based appeal is, unsurprisingly, opened out in a polemic against D. H. Lawrence. Orwell complains that Lawrence's work "expresses the same thought over and over again," namely, that the bourgeoisie are "a race of eunuchs." This apparently illustrates "the danger of the 'proletarian' cant [. . .] the terrible antagonism that it is capable of arousing." Orwell continues:

> For when you come up against an accusation like this, you are up against a blank wall. Lawrence tells me that because I have been to a public school I am a eunuch. Well, what about it? I can produce

medical evidence to the contrary, but what good will that do? Lawrence's condemnation remains. If you tell me I am a scoundrel I may mend my ways, but if you tell me I am a eunuch you are tempting me to hit back in any way that seems feasible. If you want to make an enemy of a man, tell him that his ills are incurable.[33]

Orwell's movement toward a recognizably Popular Frontist position pivots on his reproductive anxieties, as well as his nationalism and desire to reach out to the petite bourgeoisie. "Proletarian cant" was very precisely the target of Popular Front policy, part of its overreaction to the "class against class" policy of proletarianization dominant in the late 1920s and early 1930s. As I argue in the Introduction, while proletarianism has often been castigated for its masculinism, the Popular Front reaction was in many ways more sexually conservative, and most certainly more concerned with heterosexual reproduction. Here Orwell amplifies and draws together the most conservative aspects of the formation, insisting on healthy bourgeois manhood as a core element of the socialist project. For Orwell, the accusation of failed bourgeois reproduction in the name of proletarian glorification was one of the gravest dangers to the prospect of a united left, a concern that continued in his famous wartime essays.

Another convergence between Orwell and the Popular Front closely imbricated with the sexual-political is a shared investment in socialist nationalism. As Bounds points out, the whole concept of "revolutionary patriotism" that is usually seen as typically, eccentrically Orwell's, was actually a dominant strain of CPGB thinking during the period as figures such as Jack Lindsay promoted the idea that "Communism is English."[34] Moreover, as Bounds and Hubble have argued, Orwell's supposedly abrupt turn to patriotism in 1940 was thus legible in his writing of the 1930s; somewhat counterintuitively, *Homage to Catalonia* (1937) is the major site of this foreshadowing. Orwell's internationalist commitments are figured in nationalist terms throughout his account, as a series of national clichés are praised as each nation's unique contribution to the broad fight against fascism. *Homage to Catalonia* is a classic example of what I have called elsewhere "transnational provincialism." This term names how Popular Front internationalism was deeply marked by a Herderian conception of unique national culture, a defensive formation of national integrity deployed on a broad front against the fascist claim to speak for the nation.³⁵ Throughout Orwell's text, national tradition constitutes and yet threatens to overwhelm a precarious internationalist imaginary, as a series of passionate identifications with soldiers of other nationalities is couched in terms of the clichés of national tradition, culminating strangely yet inexorably in Orwell's curious desire for the Spanish to "drive all the foreigners out of Spain."³⁶

By the close of *Homage to Catalonia*, Orwell is no longer advocating a coalitional provincialism, but rather dwelling in an entirely Anglocentric utopia. Describing his journey back from Spain, Orwell provides a lyrical description of the southern English landscape, with which the text ends:

> And then England – southern England, probably the sleekest landscape in the world. It is difficult when you pass that way, especially when you are peacefully recovering from sea-sickness with the plush cushions of a boat-train carriage underneath you, to believe that anything is really happening anywhere. Earthquakes in Japan, famines in China, revolutions in Mexico?
>
> Don't worry, the milk will be on the doorstep tomorrow morning, the *New Statesman* will come out on Friday. The industrial towns were far away, a smudge of smoke and misery hidden by the curve of the earth's surface. Down here it was still the England I had known in my childhood: the railway-cuttings smothered in wild flowers, the deep meadows where the great shining horses browse and meditate, the slow-moving streams bordered by willows, the green blossoms of the elms, the larkspurs in the cottage gardens; and then the huge peaceful wilderness of outer London, the barges on the misty river, the familiar streets, the posters telling of cricket matches and Royal weddings, the men in bowler hats, the pigeons in Trafalgar Square, the red buses, the blue policemen – all sleeping the deep, deep sleep of England, from which I sometimes fear that we shall never wake till we are jerked out of it by the roar of bombs.³⁷

This passage initially claims to be decrying the "deep, deep sleep of England," bemoaning the lack of internationalism shown by the English people. Yet the rhetorical effect is not to chastise insular English patriotism, but in fact to support and produce it. Despite Orwell's caveats concerning the industrial north, the phrase "The England I had known in my childhood" immediately lulls the putative middle-class English reader into stupefied complicity, which the long list of provincial scenes proceeds to exploit. The length of this list and its gentle appositional structure prepare the shock of the final line, which might appear to be a reversal of middle-English complacency. But when the "roar of bombs" arrives, the reader has been so saturated by Englishness that such bombs can only be seen as a threat to the pastoral idyll, which now emerges not as sickeningly complacent, but entirely worthy of protection. In the signature move of nationalist rhetoric, England is imagined through the threat of attack, rendered vulnerable and thus valorized by the very bombs that might appear to shatter its complacency. And yet there is work to be done – the work of national awakening, the master trope of the nationalist lexicon since the early nineteenth century.[38]

We are now seated in a landscape recognizable as that of the famous wartime patriotic essays: the England of the shires George Bowling searches for in Orwell's 1939 novel, *Coming Up For Air*, and Orwell finds in essays such as *The Lion and the Unicorn*. Orwell's misty-eyed vision of southern England is a major iteration of what Patrick Wright and Angus Calder have influentially identified as "Deep England," the softened landscape that was a central image in World War II propaganda.[39] In a range of propagandistic cultural products, a sentimental southern English country scene was depicted as the national fabric under threat from fascism, as the title of a famous Frank Newbould poster put it: "Your Britain: Fight for It Now."

De-blimping and the "People's War"

The "England Your England" section of *The Lion and the Unicorn* is today perhaps the most famous example of this Deep English project, offering Orwell's best-known statements of national identity as organic community. The subtitle itself densely encodes a national literary history beginning with the high imperialist William Ernest Henley's 1892 "Pro Rege Nostro," where the line "England My England" appears as a patriotic refrain, through D. H. Lawrence's reworking in his 1922 short story featuring a futile death in World War I, "England, My England," Cyril Connolly's sardonic 1928 essay, "England, not my England," and finally – perhaps most tellingly – to Jack Lindsay's 1939 work of radical populism, *England, My England*. A sedimentation of Englishness is at work here, and Orwell's essay goes on to boldly address the reader as part of a mystical national community:

> And above all, it is *your* civilization, it is *you*. However much you hate it or laugh at it, you will never be happy away from it for any length of time. The suet puddings and the red pillar-boxes have entered into your soul. Good or evil, it is yours, and this side of the grave you will never get away from the marks it has given you. (*CW XII*, 393; emphasis Orwell's)

The opening section of "England Your England" is able to set up this vision by following the historical dialectic encoded in its title, between negative and positive national characteristics. Orwell's vision of national community thus insulates itself from the charge of nationalism – as Orwell repeatedly claims in "Notes on Nationalism," apparently a pathological mindset characterized by an inability to recognize national failings (*CW XVII*, 141–55). This is the fundamental structure of Orwellian nationalism, its lasting seductive appeal. Apparently softening and yet more importantly preserving what Stuart Hall has called the "inexcusably casual brutalist phrase" of "My Country Left or Right," Orwell's text sets the English reader free to take almost any national cliché, feel reassured in a brief moment of self-criticism, and then proceed with a clear conscience to an uncomplicated statement of national superiority.[40]

Take, for instance, the famed English hatred of intellectuals. Orwell asserts again and again that this anti-intellectualism evinces a healthy skepticism about the totalitarian dangers of European theorizing. English hypocrisy, meanwhile, is revalorized by Orwell as the foundation for English cultural unity, part of an English "species of instinct" and "ability to pull together at moments of supreme crisis." Even bad dental health is somehow recuperated by Orwell, bound up in "England Your England" with a specifically English gentleness: "the crowds in the big towns, with their mild knobby faces, their bad teeth and gentle manners, are different from a European crowd" (*CW XII*, 392). The apogee of this process comes in Orwell's reclamation of the "hanging judge" as "one of the symbolic figures of England." This "evil old man" is completely out of touch, "nothing short of dynamite will ever teach him which century he is living in," and yet "will at any rate interpret the law according to the books and will in no circumstances take a money bribe." Indeed, Orwell goes on to argue that "he is a symbol of the strange mixture of reality and illusion, democracy and privilege, humbug and decency, the subtle network of compromises, by which the nation keeps itself in its familiar shape" (*CW XII*, 397). Orwell's judge becomes a powerful synecdoche for the English nation: riddled with contradictions, to be sure, but in the end a symbol of incorruptible decency, even as he is marked as "evil." Here the brutal functioning of state power is legitimized as a means of national cohesion in this most unlikely of figures, who is in turn described in terms bordering on affection, "humbug and decency." Finally, then, we come to England as family:

> England is not the jeweled isle of Shakespeare's much-quoted passage, nor is it the inferno depicted by Dr. Goebbels. More than either it resembles a family, a rather stuffy Victorian family, with not many black sheep in it but with all its cupboards bursting with skeletons. It has rich relations who have to be kow-towed to and poor relations who are horribly sat upon, and there is a deep conspiracy of silence about the source of the family income. It is a family in which the young are generally thwarted and most of the power is in the hands of irresponsible uncles and bedridden aunts. Still, it is a family. It has its private language and its common memories, and at the approach of an enemy it closes its ranks. A family with the wrong members in control – that, perhaps, is as near as one can come to describing England in a phrase. (*CW XII*, 401)

In this passage Orwell's nationalist dialectic comes to fruition, Shakespeare's praise and Goebbels's condemnation leading strangely yet inexorably to the master trope of the whole essay, England as a family. Even here the process of give and take remains at work, as this valorization is qualified by England's family issues, problems that articulate Orwell's deep-seated reproductivist fears for the future of the English nation. Class difference is naturalized through this family metaphor, reduced to the homely concerns of demanding "rich relations" and then transposed into the more worrying perversity of "irresponsible uncles and bedridden aunts." These last two personages clearly stand in for the queer man and the sexless spinster, a pervasive duo of threats to the reproductive order. As ever, left-wing intellectuals, coded as queer, are also at fault; Orwell later notes that they are categorized by their "hedonism," and cautions against this unproductive attitude in no uncertain terms, "a nation trained to think hedonistically cannot survive amidst peoples who work like slaves and breed like rabbits" (*CW XII*, 428). Here reproductive anxieties are made yet more explicit, with non-procreative sexuality seen as a direct threat to England's war aims.

In order to fully interrogate Orwell's anxieties in this essay, it is necessary to examine his glimpses of a solution to the problem of national reproduction. These recommendations are expressed paradigmatically through Orwell's investment in the Home Guard, a commitment that centrally shaped his vision of revolutionary patriotism. Turned down for military service, Orwell became deeply involved with the organization, not only volunteering but also lecturing on defensive warfare. In article after article, Orwell proclaims the Home Guard as a vital force not only for protection against possible invasion, but as the model for a distinctively English – and perhaps revolutionary – socialism. This initially seems rather quixotic, partly as the Home Guard was later to be famously satirized as "Dad's Army" in the popular television series of that name; Collini, for instance, wryly observes that it "constantly threatened to attain the dignity of service in a civilian militia" in Orwell's imagination.[41] But, however implausible as it may seem in hindsight, Orwell was not alone in this perception. From its earliest inception, this apparently risible organization was a crucial battleground in home front politics, a site of contestation between advocates of a "People's War" and more traditional voices within the military and political establishment. Central to this debate was the training center set up at Osterly Park by another veteran of the Spanish Civil War, Tom Winteringham, where the ex-Communist taught guerilla tactics he had learnt in Spain to Home Guard recruits.[42] Lacking an official mandate, it was eventually shut down, but for Orwell, who attended for a time, it was the symbol of the possibility of a genuinely popular approach to fighting the war that could revolutionize English society.

Many of the arguments Orwell advances in his promotion of the Home Guard are developed in an article he wrote for the *Evening Standard* in January 1941, "Don't Let Colonel Blimp Ruin the Home Guard." The article opens by noting the great numbers of volunteers (famously over a million when the first call went out), evaluates the organization as a defensive force, then quickly shifts gears to argue that "the greatest importance of the Home Guard hitherto has been as a political symbol [. . .] it has demonstrated what the common people of this island feel about Naziism [sic]" (*CW XII*, 363). It then becomes apparent that the Home Guard embodies the lost promise of the Popular Front, an "antifascist force" that respects the traditions of "British democracy." Standing in the way, however, is Colonel Blimp, the popular fictional figure of moribund military authority. Orwell explicitly opposes Colonel Blimp to the "spirit of Osterly Park" and cautions against the danger that the antiquated authoritarianism of his predominance will "drive working-class recruits away" (*CW XII*, 364). As the title indicates, "Don't Let Colonel Blimp" is the most programmatic exposition of Orwell's "deblimping," but his concerns are voiced over a wide number of published and unpublished sources, each time with very similar emphasis.[43]

Colonel Blimp is not Orwell's creation. Best known today from the Powell and Pressburger film *The Life and Death of Colonel Blimp* (1943), this character was first imagined by the cartoonist David Low in 1934. Blimp's name is taken from the moniker given to barrage balloons in World War I, and in Low's cartoons, Blimp, a retired colonel, often appears in a Turkish bath, his rotund form naked apart from a towel around his waist, pontificating nonsensically about contemporary politics. Blimp's appearance in this state is most obviously a comment on his soft living conditions; yet it is surely significant that this figure of decayed masculinity should be depicted in a steamy all-male setting – by the 1930s long associated not only with its bourgeois homosocial function as "an extension of the gentleman's club" but also with a distinct homosexual presence.[44]

In a 1940 entry in his Wartime Diary, Orwell writes of the Blimpish officers he meets on a Home Guard exercise that they are "so degenerate in everything except physical courage," a remark that opens up a reading of this figure as, if not quite perverse then certainly as a threat to the health of the reproductive nation (*CW XII*, 241). It is therefore worth reconsidering Orwell's famous opposition between the Blimp and the Highbrow, the two figures he identifies as threats to national morale in *The Lion and the Unicorn*, published a few weeks after his article in the *Evening Standard*. As Collini identifies, these two personalities appear in dialectical opposition in Orwell's essay, and the obvious way to interpret this structure sexually would be to oppose the effete homosexuality of the "Bloomsbury Highbrow" to the stout heterosexuality of the retired Colonel.[45] But the tightness of Orwell's imbrication suggests another reading – not to say that the Blimp is coded as homosexual like the Highbrow, but rather that they present joint threats to national masculinity and their dialectical unity might indeed prove rather queer. Orwell writes of "these two important sub-sections of the middle class":

> These two seemingly hostile types, symbolic opposites – the halfpay colonel with his bull neck and diminutive brain, like a dinosaur, the highbrow with his domed forehead and stalk-like neck – are mentally linked together and constantly interact upon one another; in any case they are born to a considerable extent into the same families. (CW XII, 405)

Here Orwell's use of "seemingly" immediately destabilizes the terms of opposition, and joins together these uneasy bedfellows who are "mentally linked together and constantly interact upon one another." This is not quite to open up a phantasmagoric vista of different gay types fucking away in Orwell's tortured imagination – however tempting such a conjecture may be – but rather to suggest that these two perverse figures are in unwitting cahoots against the possibility of a healthy national manhood. This unwitting alliance is echoed in "Notes on Nationalism," in which both the English nationalism of the Blimpish Tory and what Orwell calls the "transferred" nationalisms of the pro-Communist intellectual are castigated as complementary psychopathologies (CW XVII, 149–51). Over the course of the war, the Blimp and the Highbrow come to completely dominate Orwell's imagination of failed masculinity. Indeed, aside from passing remarks such as his approving review of Holtby's depiction of the queer dictator in *Take Back Your Freedom*, Orwell is curiously uninterested in the perversity of fascism. His particular brand of transformative normalcy is a thorough domestication of Popular Front heteronormativity, the home front of the fight against degeneration in the name of the nation.

What, then, is the positive content of Orwell's vision of healthy national masculinity above and beyond the most obvious figure of "the working man with two or three medals on his chest"?[46] Who, in other words, is to take the place of the Blimp and the Highbrow? In *The Lion and The Unicorn* he suggests that what is required for the national war effort is a meeting of patriotism and intelligence, denied by Blimp and Highbrow alike. "Patriotism and intelligence will have to come together again. It is the fact that we are fighting a war, and a very peculiar kind of war, that may make this possible" (*CW XII*, 407). This is the somewhat self-evident resolution to the Blimp/Highbrow dilemma – a meeting of patriotism, physical courage, and intelligence. But the group in which Orwell finds such qualities is striking. Immediately following this passage, the next section of *The Lion and the Unicorn* is concerned with "the upward and downward extension of the middle class." Proceeding from a critique of Marx's immiseration thesis – "the tendency of advanced capitalism has therefore been to enlarge the middle class and not to wipe it out as it once seemed likely to do" – Orwell goes on to analyze the "new civilization" of "people of indeterminate social class" who are to be found "in the light industry areas and along the arterial roads":

> To that civilization belong the people who are most at home and most definitely *of* the modern world, the technicians and the higher-paid skilled workers, the airmen and their mechanics, the radio experts, film producers, popular journalists and industrial chemists. They are the indeterminate stratum at which the older class distinctions are beginning to break down. (*CW XII*, 408; emphasis Orwell's)

Orwell initially criticizes this new formation as a "rather cultureless, restless life, centering around tinned food, *Picture Post*, and the internal combustion engine" (*CW XII*, 408), but as *The Lion and the Unicorn* progresses from its descriptive project in "England Your England" to its urgently prescriptive later sections, a very different picture of these men of the future emerges.

In Part II, "Shopkeepers at War," Orwell argues that "what this war has demonstrated is that private capitalism [...] does not work" (*CW XII*, 409), for "it is a system in which all the forces are pulling in opposite directions and the interests of the individual are as often as not totally opposed to those of the State" (*CW XII*, 411). Socialism is desirable both as a moral end and as the only means to win the war, with Orwell placing the stress on the system's efficiency. This also requires "new blood, new men, new ideas – in the true sense of the word, a revolution" (*CW XII*, 413). Accordingly, in the final section, "The English Revolution," Orwell sets out his program for English Socialism, outlining how efficient new blood will infuse his mystical national community:

> It will not be doctrinaire, nor even logical. It will abolish the House of Lords, but quite probably will not abolish the Monarchy. It will

leave anachronisms and loose ends everywhere, the judge in his ridiculous horsehair wig and the lion and the unicorn on the soldier's cap-buttons. It will not set up any explicit class dictatorship. It will group itself round the old Labour Party and its mass following will be in the Trade Unions, but it will draw in most of the middle class and many of the younger sons of the bourgeoisie. Most of its directing brains will come from the new indeterminate class of skilled workers, technical experts, airmen, scientists, architects, and journalists, the people who feel at home in the radio and ferro-concrete age. But it will never lose touch with the tradition of compromise and the belief in a law that is above the State. (*CW XII*, 427)

Orwell's reverence for British institutions and his insistence that they would remain under socialism are well known. More striking in this passage, perhaps, is the final juxtaposition between the new "directing brains" and Orwell's immediate concern for the rule of law. This juxtaposition appears to indicate that Orwell is immediately aware that what he is advocating is a technocracy (albeit a traditionalist one), and thus dangerously close to what he saw as the horrors predicted by James Burnham.[47] In *The Managerial Revolution* (1941), the ex-Trotskyist Burnham famously argued that capitalism was giving way to a new period of world history, in which the manager would reign supreme. Citing Nazi Germany, the Soviet Union, and Roosevelt's New Deal as precursors to this new epoch, Burnham contended that it was control, not ownership of the means of production, that would determine the formation of the elites of the future. Orwell conducted an ongoing polemical argument with what he saw as Burnham's inhumane technocratic vision, sometimes wholly condemning, sometimes grudgingly acknowledging Burnham's descriptive acuity, but always deploring the possibilities he predicts. And yet *The Lion and the Unicorn* unequivocally advocates the rule of the manager, tempered only by the rule of law. This paradox – that was to finally result in the horrified vision of *Nineteen Eighty-Four* – was amplified by Orwell's growing collaboration with the British state.

The future of the English people

The English People is in many ways a reappraisal of *The Lion and the Unicorn* from the viewpoint of the later years of the war when victory was in sight; largely composed in 1943, it appeared in revised form in 1947. Commissioned for a series masterminded by the Ministry of Information, "Britain in Pictures," Orwell's later pamphlet follows a similar structure to his earlier polemic, beginning with a discussion of "national characteristics" before moving to a set of prescriptions for English society. As in *The Lion and the Unicorn*, a patriotic dialectic of positive and negative national traits is set up – more soberly now that Orwell's hope for an English Revolution had died down – which gives way to a series of recommendations drawn from those traits. In the final section, titled somewhat portentously "The Future of the English People," Orwell's revolutionary exhilaration in his earlier pamphlet gives way to a no less urgent concern with England's new role as a lesser world power. Translated into a number of different languages, *The English People* is an important document of what Andrew Rubin has identified as Orwell's role in the handover of imperial power from Britain to the US, which Rubin traces through the dissemination of translations of *Animal Farm* (1945) in states threatening decolonial revolution. Lacking the accessible fabular structure and anti-Communist heft of his more famous work of the period, *The English People* was never to be deployed on such a scale, but its didactic tone and insistent predictions function at points rather similarly.

What the English apparently have to offer in the coming world of Soviet and American dominance is "a moral quality which must be vaguely described as decency" (*CW XVI*, 209); in other words, "the habit of not killing one another" (*CW XVI*, 220). Once Orwell seizes on this favorite trait of "decency" – one of the master tropes of his whole authorship, as has often been pointed out – he rather overconfidently predicts a future when the excellence of English democratic habits might make them "the political leaders of western Europe, and probably some other parts of the world as well" (*CW XVI*, 222). However, once more circling back into a moment of self-criticism, Orwell immediately makes clear that no such thing can happen unless the English reform their behavior:

> But to play a leading part they have got to know what they are doing, and they have got to retain their vitality. For this, several developments are needed in the next decade. They are a rising birthrate, more social equality, less centralisation, and more respect for the intellect. (*CW XVI*, 222)

Orwell's ten-year plan is unequivocal: decentralization, pronatalism, some social leveling, and more intelligence. He is particularly stern about the need to promote the "dwindling birthrate," a concern raised earlier in the pamphlet in a curiously disgusted passage that reads pet ownership symptomatically as taking the place of healthy family life (CW XVI, 202). The causes of this worrying trend are identified as primarily economic, for large families will result in tightened living conditions for all but the very rich. It is then that Orwell switches gear into full statist mode:

> People should be better off for having children, just as they are in a peasant community, instead of financially crippled, as they are in ours. Any government, by a few strokes of the pen, could make childlessness as unbearable an economic burden as a big family is now: but no government has chosen to do so, because of the ignorant idea that a bigger population means more unemployed. Far more drastically than anyone has proposed hitherto, taxation will have to be graded so as to encourage child-bearing and to save women with young children from being obliged to work outside the home. (CW XVI, 223)

The homophobia and misogyny of this passage are clear as childlessness must be made "unbearable" and women economically coerced back to the hearth. What I want to draw attention to is the dialectic underlying such prescriptions, as Orwell veers between nostalgia and futurity, offering the strange possibility of the creation of aspects of a "peasant community [. . .] by a few strokes of the pen." It is this constitutive paradox of state *Gemeinschaft* that anticipates the ethos of the postwar welfare state in formation at the time of publication. The obvious contemporary comparison is with the Beveridge Report, which Orwell mentions in passing earlier in the text – but such a managed organicism is the effect that central tenets of Popular Front cultural politics had on British mid-century society, crucially transmitted through Orwell's growing authority in postwar Britain. As I suggested at the close of Chapter 3, the particular achievement – and failure – of broad-based 1930s antifascist leftism was the conservative-socialist consensus that helped produce the National Health Service, increased council housing, the cult of mid-century motherhood, and a mounting persecution of queers. Orwell was the most consistent advocate of this social imaginary in the 1940s.

Justifiably, Orwell is particularly concerned with housing. *The English People* goes on to argue for "the building of bigger and more convenient houses," lamenting that "when the government designs a prefabricated house, it produces a house with only two bedrooms – with room, that is to say, for two children at the most" (*CW XVI*, 223). The tone here, and indeed throughout the essay, is tellingly close to that of postwar planners such as Patrick Abercrombie. In a 1945 Ministry of Information film (the same ministry that commissioned Orwell's pamphlet two years earlier) entitled *Proud City*, Abercrombie outlines his famous plans for London, which were never to be fully realized. Abercrombie and fellow planner J. H. Forshaw are earnestly concerned about working-class living conditions. The tenor of the film is not only relentlessly paternalistic, but at points descends into a bizarre rhetoric. Perched over the more soberly reflective Forshaw, Abercrombie's first lines in the film lay bare the sheer strangeness of his concept of population:

> Yes, it is rather like the way you plan a garden. You've got to give the plants air and sunshine. And then also you've got to give them shelter from wet and cold. And they've got to have room to grow. And I tell you what, there mustn't be any overcrowding.[48]

Orwell was too astute a stylist to compare people to plants in quite this way, but his pamphlet participates in the same ideological networks of population production illuminated by Abercrombie's rambling metaphor. They both, for instance, offer strikingly similar attempts to blend organicist aspirations with large-scale state action – while Orwell called for the return to aspects of a "peasant community," the Abercrombie Plan sought to restore "village life" in its reconstruction of London. As Richard Hornsey has argued, this moment of planning was complexly articulated with a widespread fear of unruly queer life in the city, which would be expunged from or at least tamed by a new orderly pronatalist city.[49] Orwell's demand that the English people "must breed faster, work harder, and probably live more simply" (*CW XVI*, 227) is an explicit demand for this heteronormative world, and his pamphlet a crucial document of postwar planning. Taking Orwell's work as a whole, Stuart Hall is surely correct to underline that he had a fundamentally contradictory relationship to the state, but in *The English People* the message is unequivocal, and its sexual politics all too legible.[50] Rather than confronting statist organicism as a paradox or contradiction, Orwell's essay asserts that the state can be the vehicle for the reconstruction of the national *Gemeinschaft* – a formulation that draws together and intensifies contradictory forms of heteronormativity into a dialectic of absolute refusal of non-normative sexuality. In its management of desire, the famous name Orwell applied to the organ of state torture, "The Ministry of Love," could not be more adequate to his own vision of the production of intimacy; at the same time, the radical possibilities of this formulation in the Soviet Union, running from Alexandra Kollontai's Department for Women up to the recommendations for lesbian marriage in 1929, are entirely foreclosed.

Obvious figures of perversity do not, however, make an appearance in *The English People* as they do in earlier writings, other than the rather cryptic personage of the individual excessively fond of their pet. We might speculate on various reasons for this: the sense of quiet triumph following Allied victory; Orwell's earnest focus on social and sexual reproduction rather than on threats to their flourishing; the text not wanting to name its enemies for fear of demoralization; the complete closure that the dialectic of state and community creates, and so on. But the most compelling explanation at the level of the text's political unconscious is the worrying possibility that personal identification with state action is itself a perversion – certainly un-English, dangerously close to Communism, and ultimately sadomasochistic.

Monstrous mothers and Big Brothers

It has become a cliché of Orwell studies to diagnose the sources of the despair of *Nineteen Eighty-Four* with reference to Orwell's life. I do not intend to add to such biographical considerations here, but rather to offer a few brief observations about how this text reveals the roots of Orwell's particular brand of sexual politics in what I have been calling the transformative normalcy of the Popular Front. Overturning the failed pastorals of his early novels, *Nineteen Eighty-Four* contains Orwell's only scene of enjoyable, valorized sex. As we have seen, *A Clergyman's Daughter* features a perverse masturbation scene, and *Keep the Aspidistra Flying* a rather different sort of pastoral encounter. To these may be added the sensual but guilt-ridden and monetized colonial coupling between Flory and his Burmese mistress in *Burmese Days* (1935), the attraction-less marriage of George and Hilda Bowling in *Coming Up For Air* (1939), and Orwell's obvious reluctance to depict animal copulation in *Animal Farm*. But for Winston and Julia, their first sexual encounter in the woods and subsequent relationship are truly transformative experiences; in a much-cited line, "a political act" (*CN*, 818).

The relationship is at first figured as a defiantly filthy affair compared to the puritanism of Party politics. During their initial sexual encounter, Winston is drawn to Julia's coarse language as a "symptom of her revolt against the Party," its worryingly unladylike aspects immediately softened as they are normalized as "natural and healthy, like the sneeze of a horse that smells bad hay" (*CN*, 815). Winston goes on to celebrate Julia's "corruption," even proclaiming that "the more men you've had the more I love you [. . .] I hate purity, I hate goodness! I don't want any virtue to exist anywhere. I want everyone to be corrupt to the bones" (*CN*, 817). Winston's ardent desire to see the Party crumble extends to a desire to infect "the whole lot of them with leprosy or syphilis," and he revels in Julia's wide sexual experience – immediately figured as diseased – as metonymically expressive of the same spirit of revolt (*CN*, 817). Again there is a psychoanalytic dynamic at work, here right at the moment of sexual consummation, as Winston enjoys a brief moment of polymorphous perversity: "Not merely the love of one person but the animal instinct, the simple undifferentiated desire: that was the force that would tear the Party to pieces" (*CN*, 817). However, the troublingly non-normative aspects of this formulation are quickly foreclosed as the couple form asserts itself – as much as it can in the inauspicious circumstance of Orwell's dystopia.

After this first joyous coupling, Winston and Julia attempt to catch snatches of conventional domestic life. In the room they rent above an antiques shop, the couple recreate a homely atmosphere of mid-century heterosexuality, the ghost of Orwell's famous lines in *The Road to Wigan Pier*. Julia brings the usually unobtainable real tea and coffee, white bread and jam; ever the "rebel from the waist downwards," she puts on make-up and scent:

'Yes, dear, scent too. And do you know what I'm going to do next? I'm going to get hold of a real woman's frock from somewhere and wear it instead of these bloody trousers. I'll wear silk stockings and high-heeled shoes! In this room I'm going to be a woman, not a Party comrade.' (CN, 828)

In this passage Orwell's vision of normal sexiness is exultantly transformative, overcoming the perversity of Party dress, and closely paralleling the revelatory moment in *Swastika Night*. As I argue in Chapter 3, Burdekin's novel hinges upon a scene in which the Knight reveals to a stunned Alfred and Hermann that women were once conventionally feminine by showing them a photo featuring a young woman from the Hitler Youth. Daphne Patai and Andy Croft have speculated about whether Orwell was directly influenced by Burdekin's earlier dystopia; but my concern is rather with the genealogy of the Popular Front's sexual politics, how a transformative normalcy is articulated in Burdekin, and in some ways reaches its completion here in Orwell.[51] Burdekin deploys this formation as part of a flawed feminist critique of fascism, but Orwell's later rendering is ranged against the perversity of Communist totalitarianism; indeed, one might say, against a queer Marxism – for the Party's overalls must surely be seen not only as part of its apparent denial of sexuality and fetishized proletarianism, but also, when donned by women, of gender non-conformity in the service of the Communist state. As Chapter 2 argued with particular reference to Valentine Ackland, tolerant and even valorizing Soviet attitudes toward some versions of female masculinity in the late 1920s may prove overlooked aspects of the formation of lesbian identity in interwar Britain. Julia's gender performance is an explicit rejection of this formation, and here again Jack Halberstam's formulation of a "sartorial semiotic" is useful.[52] What Ackland called her "liberating" trousers become Julia's "bloody trousers" (obviously troping menstruation) which must be torn off and make-up, silk stockings, and high heels deployed, as she "is going to be a woman, not a Party comrade." Orwell's sartorial semiotic forecloses the queer possibilities of Communism through a triumphant outburst of gender and sexual conformity.

Just before they are taken by the police, Julia's and Winston's attempts to recreate heterosexual domesticity are complemented by another desperate vision of fetishized normalcy. Gazing out of the window from their room, the pair glimpse "with a sort of fascination" a middle-aged proletarian woman, hanging diapers on a clothes line, who is rendered "beautiful" by childbearing and hard work, "blown up to monstrous dimensions by childbearing, then hardened, roughened by work till it was coarse in the grain like an over-ripe turnip" (CN, 867). The passage continues:

> The woman down there had no mind, she had only strong arms, a warm heart, and a fertile belly. He wondered how many children she had given birth to. It might easily have been fifteen. She had had her momentary flowering, a year, perhaps, of wild rose beauty, and then she had suddenly swollen like a fertilized fruit and grown hard and red and coarse, and then her life had been laundering, scrubbing, darning, cooking, sweeping, polishing, mending, scrubbing, laundering, first for children, then for grand-children, over thirty unbroken years. (CN, 868)

Following this celebration of female hardship, Winston ponders the possibility of revolt against the Party given that working-class people around the world are all "very much the same" and therefore may be able to overcome the repressive governments that pitted each continent against the other. He is then led, transfixed, to the famous declaration, "if there was hope, it lay in the proles!" This line has been taken to signify Orwell's continuing commitment to working-class revolution – but as Orwell was well aware, before becoming a metonymic term for the common people, the Latin word originally referred to offspring and thence to the plebeians whose only function was to bear children. It is perhaps no accident, then, that Winston's declaration of hope is occasioned by a fetishized image of reproduction, what Orwell called in *The Road to Wigan Pier* the "essential good sense" of the proletariat to reproduce against all the odds. Tellingly, the fecund woman Winston observes apparently has "no mind," and, as has often been pointed out, Orwell rarely seems to believe the British proletariat capable of any form of revolutionary consciousness whatsoever. Instead, they can bear children, their ultimate function in Orwell's imaginary. Just as much as in the original Latin usage, reproduction is ontologically exhaustive for Orwell's proletarians – their proles are everything that is the case, their reproductive capabilities the source of all hope.

Shortly after this vision of working-class fecundity, the pair are captured, and Winston falls into the hands of the sadistic statist, O'Brien. The extended torture scene forming the climax of the novel is intensely homoerotic, as Winston comes to enjoy his torment at the hands of O'Brien, who manifests a number of moments of relenting kindness in a movement characteristic of sexual praxes of control and domination. Unsurprisingly, critics have seized upon this extended scene of male-on-male sadomasochism to draw the obvious biographical inference.[53] But it would be misplaced to merely attribute this long sequence to some form of repressed personal sexuality on Orwell's part, not least as such a reading would uphold, albeit ironically, Orwell's own repression thesis in the text and elsewhere. Rather, while *Nineteen Eighty-Four* ostensibly offers a picture of a totalizingly repressive society that tries to "abolish the orgasm" (CN, 898) in an all-out attack on sexuality itself, what actually goes on in the famous final sequence is an education in masochistic desire.

The biographical impulse is understandable here, for the novel's depiction of Winston's torture is an extremely vivid, compelling picture of BDSM sexual practice (without, of course, the element of consent). "Don't worry," O'Brien reassures Winston, "you are in my keeping" (CN, 883); speaking in a "gentle and patient" voice, like "a teacher taking pains with a wayward but promising child," he calls for an "act of submission" (CN, 884–6); alternately tightening and loosening Winston's bonds, O'Brien promises that the Party will "squeeze you empty then fill you with ourselves" (CN, 891). For his part, soothed as O'Brien cradles him like a child, Winston realizes that "he loved him so deeply" (CN, 888) and is rewarded with a moment of agency: "your mind appeals to me [. . .] you can ask me a few questions, if you choose" (CN, 892). Still, O'Brien will not relent, for "progress will be progress towards more pain" (CN, 898), and he screams a characteristic rhetorical question at a disobedient Winston: "what are you? A bag of filth" (CN, 901). Winston finally grows to become a well-trained submissive, responding correctly to O'Brien's questions, and surrendering more and more completely to his master's will. O'Brien then explains his and the Party's intentions, in some of the novel's most famous lines:

> All competing pleasures will be destroyed. But always – do not forget this, Winston – always there will be the intoxication of power,

constantly increasing and constantly growing subtler. Always, at every moment, there will be the thrill of victory, the sensation of trampling on an enemy who is helpless. If you want a picture of the future, imagine a boot stamping on a human face – for ever. (CN, 898)

Despite having earlier boasted that "the sex instinct will be eradicated" O'Brien reveals the central role of pleasure in the Party's political practice and ideology, a sadistic pleasure constantly refining itself in ever-expanding whorls of libertine desire. It is not sexuality itself, but reproductive heterosexuality that will be destroyed, the bonds between man and wife, child and parent, as seen in Winston's colleague's denunciation by his own children, and Winston's own loveless marriage. Winston's submission is therefore incomplete, for he has one last renunciation to make. In Room 101, Winston is petrified into this last betrayal:

> Everything had gone black. For an instant he was insane, a screaming animal. Yet he came out of the blackness clutching an idea. There was one and only one way to save himself. He must interpose another human being, the *body* of another human being, between himself and the rats. (CN, 909; emphasis Orwell's)

Winston's insane fear provokes him into the telling articulation of the interposition of another body between himself and the rats. This formulation recalls the famously queer riposte attributed to Lytton Strachey when asked by a military tribunal what he would do if he saw a German soldier raping his sister: "I would interpose my body between them." Curiously, the major published source for Strachey's remark puts it slightly differently. In Robert Graves's *Goodbye to All That* (1929), Strachey says "I would try to get between them," and it is unclear when and where the alternate version of the quote originated.[54] It is quite possible, in fact, that Orwell's novel played some part in the source of the variant; the language may also be drawn from Byron's famous declaration that there is a moral imperative to "interpose" oneself between the Greeks and the Turks. In any case, as Laura Frost has argued, Strachey's remark crystallizes a series of associations between German military aggression and homosexual constructions of sexual identity in Britain that link (and, I contend, reduce) queer desire to the erotics of fascism – associations that, as Chapter 3 has argued, become paradigmatic for antifascist homophobia in the 1930s.⁵⁵ Winston's erotic education recalls these homo-fascist polemics. Transposing Popular Front homophobia to his anti-Communist dystopia, Orwell recapitulates the antihomosexual discourse mobilized against Ernst Röhm; rather than Hitler's brutal pawn and sometime friend, apparently a demonic figure presiding over a wide network of disciplining agents assiduously molding German youth in their own perverted image. In the febrile imagination of some antifascists, and for Orwell's equally lurid anti-Communism, this perverted politics spells the imminent destruction of heterosexuality itself, supposedly only possible in flickering utopian moments of transformative normalcy.

Here a cycle is complete. There are many moments that might be seen to signal the "end of the 1930s" – the most convenient being the Nazi-Soviet Pact and outbreak of World War II, which closely coincide with what the queer literary historian might plausibly see as an ending, the departure of Auden and Isherwood for America in 1939. But these dates are far too neat. Why not, for instance, the end of World War II, the conflict prepared throughout the decade? Or perhaps one year later, with Churchill's "Iron Curtain" speech? Maybe the end of rationing in 1955? Orwell's death in 1950 might be another such placeholder for the end of this most reified of decades. The Coda to this study will resist this process, but for the moment perhaps the best way to foreclose our conception of this apparently "low, dishonest decade" might not lie in a date as such, but rather in a vision of anti-Communist, homophobic, incestuous despair: "He loved Big Brother." In these lines, Orwell's novel continues in inverted form the process of the left's mounting heteronormativity during the period, entirely intertwined in his anti-statist polemic with the fraught compromises of the postwar welfare state. In this way, *Nineteen Eighty-Four* encodes the two major intertwined discourses of the Popular Front's legacy, revealed through its most insistent of critics' final awareness that he was one of its most important exponents. And it was surely not only its widespread recruitment by cold warriors that made Orwell's allegory of Popular Front sexual politics a classic. For all this study's relative disinterest in literary value as such, Marx's fundamental postulate that great art must indelibly bear the imprint of its age must surely apply to *Nineteen Eighty-Four*. I'm not sure this is, however, a good thing in this case – but it does mean we must continue to read our Orwell.

Coda:
A Little Window for the Bourgeoisie

Accounts of the "failure" of 1930s radical politics often alight on Auden's famous lines from "September 1, 1939," "The clever hopes expire/Of a low dishonest decade."[1] Auden's apparent denunciation of the 1930s on the eve of war has been taken to index his despair at the failure of the political itself, his lines "not universal love/but to be loved alone" expressive of the necessary malfunctioning of any collectivist project in the face of individualism.[2] The supposed cowardice of Auden and Isherwood's move to the US in 1939, much decried at the time, has typically been mobilized in support of this view.[3] But there are a number of reasons for resisting reading these lines as a failure of the political *per se* – not least because in his hitherto unexplored unpublished diary of that week Auden laid out earnest plans for political reform through a form of socialist democracy.[4] Rather than delving into the wide-ranging debates about Auden, America, and the Political that have been the subject of so much scholarly focus, I would like to draw attention to the equally political modalities of queer life explored in this poem. Curiously, the poem's queer valences have remained relatively unexamined, even in Richard Bozorth's excellent study, *Auden's Games of Knowledge: Poetry and the Meanings of Homosexuality* (2001).[5]

The "dive" in which the poem is set was the Dizzy Club, which Auden visited on September 1, 1939. As he recorded in a diary entry: "Went to the Dizzy Club. A whiff of the old sad life. I want I want."[6] Here Auden complains about a certain form of queer sociality, cast as graspingly promiscuous, marked by sadness and the past. And yet, the previous month he had begun a relationship with Chester Kallman. Falling for the young American, Auden earnestly hoped that the relationship would prove monogamous and began to refer to it as a "marriage" (Auden's hopes of exclusiveness were not fulfilled, but the two men remained lifelong partners). While "September 1, 1939" might convey the sense of an ending, the expiration of the hopes of the 1930s, or indeed despair at the impossibility of queer life, its negations call forth an emergent mid-century sexual identity: the respectable homosexual. Surveying the dive, Auden notes that "Faces along the bar/Cling to their average day," deploying both the concept of the norm and the trope of the everyday as refuges for queers, lodged in a bar described as "a fort" that "conventions conspire" to fill with "the furniture of home." He continues:

> The windiest militant trash
> Important persons shout
> Is not so crude as our wish
> What mad Nijinsky wrote
> About Diaghilev
> Is true of the normal heart;
> The error in every bone
> Of each woman and each man
> Craves what it cannot have,
> Not universal love,
> But to be loved alone.[7]

Perhaps these lines' most immediately striking aspect is their alignment of the famous queer couple of Nijinsky and Diaghilev with "the normal heart," Auden's and others' usual term for heterosexuality that also indicated the possibility of the normalization of queer desire. Auden then offers a paradox between the universal and the particular that Bozorth, under the influence of Sedgwick, has identified as central to Auden's queer poetics.[8] Universal love is desired neither by queers nor "normal heart[s]," and yet the universal is implied in the very assertion that all men and women desire the same form of romantic commitment, defined by privacy and exclusiveness, "loved alone" clearly recalling "left alone" as well as the possessiveness of monogamy. It is far from my intention to decry the normalizations of these lines, which proclaim queer love at a time when decriminalization was a long way off. Moreover, Auden's series of negations are far from triumphant proclamations of the couple form. He casts all romantic love as an "error" and as impossible, something neither queer nor straight can ever fully attain; the possibility of queer community, "our wish" as well as the romance of the normal, is then aligned with the gramophone-politics of the "windiest militant trash." Bozorth's stress on the ongoing series of tensions and contradictions in Auden's poetic sexual politics is useful at this point – there are no easy answers in Auden. Yet here, at one of the supposed "ends of the 1930s," the nascent subjectivity of the respectable homosexual is glimpsed even as it is put under erasure.

Matt Houlbrook and Richard Hornsey have detailed the arrival of this figure in postwar Britain. Emerging at the time of the Wolfenden Report, this new personage was defined by monogamy, exclusive interest in their own gender, discretion, and bourgeois deportment; as I argue in the Introduction, the Report's recommendations bore marked similarities to the proposals of Soviet psychiatrists in the late 1920s. Houlbrook maintains, rightly in my view, that the rise of respectable homosexuality was at once an important moment of liberalization, and a foreclosure and erasure of certain modes of queer life.[9] One of the most important documents of this development was Peter Wildeblood's memoir *Against the Law* (1955). Wildeblood was an upper-middle-class journalist, one of three men convicted and sent to prison on trumped-up charges in a widely sensationalized case in 1954. His evidence in court bravely proclaimed that "I am a homosexual," which contributed to his harsh sentencing. Following his release from prison, Wildeblood published a memoir detailing the police's scandalous handling of the case, and made an impassioned plea for a change in the law. Wildeblood went on to be a prominent gay rights campaigner, and his memoir is striking as both an early coming out narrative, marked by a persistent register of truth telling, and as an account that centrally informed the exclusions and erasures of the respectability paradigm.[10]

In the US, the 1940s and 1950s were marked by a parallel process, the Homophile Movement, most prominently the Mattachine Society, led by Harry Hay. Again sometimes belittled from the later perspectives of gay rights and queer critique, the Homophile Movement was a secretive society that advocated for limited acceptance and equal rights. As Daniel Hurewitz has persuasively argued, Mattachine was not only deeply inflected by Communist organizational methods, but also drew on models of personal-political identity developed by US Communists in the interwar period – perhaps most importantly for our purposes, it was organized into cells.[11] Hurewitz focuses on the genealogy of modern identity politics and the secrecy of underground, semi-legal political organization; similarly, the Communist concept of the cell was vital to these mid-century movements and beyond, particularly in their embodiment in literary counterpublics. A similar, interrelated process was, then, occurring in both the US and Britain, the broader contours of which are beginning to be charted by David Minto.

Christopher Isherwood, John Lehmann, Stephen Spender, and W. H. Auden were complexly implicated in this Anglo-American social-historical development, as their later careers celebrated, instantiated, and resisted the uneven spread of respectability. Their authorships' mobile relationships between fact and fiction, novel and memoir register the constitutive paradoxes of the respectable homosexual, particularly this figure's dialectical emergence with and against his working-class sexual partners and the postwar British nation state. This process was marked by new transatlantic affiliations – not only Auden's and Isherwood's move to the US, but also Spender's new role as globe-trotting anti-Communist intellectual – and might initially appear to function in what has become known as a homonormative fashion. However, enlivened by the radical élan of gay liberation, Isherwood and Lehmann in fact resisted the respectability paradigm in their memoir-fictions of the period. *Christopher and His Kind* (1976) and *In the Purely Pagan Sense* (1976) focus on Berlin and Vienna respectively, both returning to the class-crossing queer practices of the 1930s, deeply inflected by both writers' engagement with Marxist cultures of the period. In a very different register, some of Townsend Warner's later work performs this vital mediation between the exigencies of normalization and the claims of resistance. An oblique yet unmistakable allegory of the closet, Townsend Warner's 1964 short story "The Love Match" ironically examines the containment of non-normative desire within the monogamous couple form; simultaneously celebrating and satirizing a deeply bourgeois incestuous couple's nesting in rural England, the story subtly probes the question of discretion and respectability. It is to these three texts and their mediation of the respectability problematic that this Coda will turn.

It goes without saying that there were massive, complex, and contradictory developments in queer and leftist history in Britain from the late 1960s to the 1970s, and in the troubled relation between the two. Indeed, this period of the emergence of the New Left, second wave feminism, and gay liberation is generally viewed as the central historical period for the development of twentieth-century radical politics. The historical leap I make here from 1964 to 1976 might therefore seem impetuous, but it is of course outside the scope of this present study to explore this history anew. However, there is another, less pragmatic reason for this leap-frogging approach. One of the major premises of this book has been that queer Communism has never been progressivist – or chrononormative, to use Elizabeth's Freeman's term – but rather operates in a series of tightly integrated dialectical moments all too often quickly foreclosed, which nevertheless offer us ways to think through contemporary problems in Marxism and queer studies.[12]

Bourgeois endogamy

If the usual assumption about Isherwood and Lehmann would be that they progressed into sedate middle age as respectable homosexuals and memoirists, then the parallel cliché about Sylvia Townsend Warner's later career would be that she disappeared as a queer radical writer and re-emerged as a quaint miniaturist.[13] After the publication of her final novel *The Flint Anchor* in 1954, Townsend Warner focused largely on short stories, many of which were published in *The New Yorker* for quite considerable sums – quite a change from *Left Review* and other similar publishing venues of the 1930s (although it should also be noted that her years with each publication overlapped for a short while).[14] Her active participation in the Communist movement ceased in the 1940s, but she never formally resigned as Ackland did in 1953; unlike Auden et al. she never renounced her former Communism, still praising Stalin in 1956 and up to the end of her life never apologizing for her political commitments of the 1930s.[15] Meanwhile, Townsend Warner's and Ackland's relationship continued but had been sorely tested by Ackland's affair with an American woman, Elizabeth Wade Wright, and the two women's later years were beset with illness and discord as well as mutual support and continuing love. The usual narrative here would be a cautionary tale of "left-wing melancholia" and the dangers of non-monogamy, but rather than lamenting the misplaced attachments of her later life, I would like to offer a brief discussion of how Townsend Warner's writing retained its critical edge in her 1964 short story "A Love Match."[16]

"A Love Match" charts the settled domesticity of an upper-middle-class brother and sister, Justin and Celia Tizard, who fell in love during World War I, up to their death during the Blitz in World War II. The story opens during or just after the Battle of the Somme, when Justin is on leave and visits the recently bereaved Celia, whose fiancé has just been killed in France. Justin is suffering from shell-shock; one night, Celia hastens to his bedside to comfort him and "they rushed into the escape of love like winter-starved cattle rushing into a spring pasture." They do not expect Justin to survive his next stint in France, and so feel themselves "mated for life."[17] Justin however survives, and brother and sister continue to live together as devoted sexual and romantic partners until their death, carefully guarding their secret from the outside world under the cover of their siblinghood itself. Following some time living in France just after the war, the pair settle in a quiet English country village in the 1920s, where they are generally undisturbed by their unsuspecting middle-class neighbors, with the exception of a young woman who falls in love with Justin. The narrative closes as they are killed by a bomb, and discovered in bed by villagers digging through the rubble of their house.

Simultaneously an allegory of the closet and a plea for the acceptance of consensual incest between adults (elsewhere Townsend Warner maintained that a less judgmental society would not find such incest "upsetting"), "A Love Match" nevertheless maintains a tone of ironic humor throughout.[18] This gentle comedy is directed not only at the Tizard's unsuspecting stuffy middle-class neighbors, but at the couple themselves as a paragon of bourgeois respectability. Early on in the narrative, Justin was disdainful of what he called *La Jeune France*, "ruefully" observing "two young men in pink trousers, riding through the town on donkeys" who later improvise a modernist ballet (2); upon their decision to return to England, Celia remarks that "we were both of us born for a sober, conventional, taxpaying life" (3). In a radicalization of the endogamy of bourgeois marriage, the pair are perfectly matched as they were "brought up to the same standard of behavior," and so have "no need to impress each other" (10). When the Tizards come back to England, their path to respectability is complete. The pair attend church, play whist, and become prematurely middle-aged when in company, if not when alone together:

> Returning from their sober junketings Justin and Celia, safe within their brick wall, cast off their weeds of middle age, laughed, chattered, and kissed with an intensified delight in their scandalous immunity from blame. They were a model couple, the most respectable couple in Hallowby, treading hand in hand the thornless path to fogeydom. (12)

When the English version of *La Jeune France* reaches "even to Hallowby," Celia is initially disdainful of the Bright Young Things' callow rebellion, mere ostentation compared to "the exultation of living in defiance of social prohibitions and the absorbing maneuvers of seeming in compliance with them" (13–14). And yet she grows to wish the young rebels well. Mindful of the stodginess that threatens to dampen her passionate incestuous love, she befriends them in order to vicariously experience their outward rebellion; in return the Bright Young Things callously drop her. Here, as throughout the story, there are a series of tensions at work – between the pain and the mitigated pleasures of the closet, between different forms of dissident life, and between respectability and desire, the couple's "scandalous immunity from blame" that gives their love an "intensified delight."

The narrative then moves into the 1930s. Celia throws herself into relief work, and "being totally inexperienced" she "exploded like a nova," her schemes so outlandish that they fail to trouble the authorities. On first glance, the story maintains a wry distance from Celia's activism, casting it as a mere "outlet" for her "smoldering resentment" (15). Yet this formulation also suggests the possibility of a symbiosis between non-normative sexuality and leftist engagement – not the most inspiring version, perhaps, relying on a sublimation of hidden desire into worthy causes, but nevertheless proposing clear links when all too often histories of the period see these forms of life as radically incompatible. As Celia's career in the movement progresses, a vanguardist dialectic emerges. Chapter 2 of this study has argued that Townsend Warner and Ackland maintained a fundamentally Leninist concept of revolutionary consciousness as they sought to catalyze the untutored radicalism of the rural poor; at the same time, as Lenin and others urged, such consciousness must constantly be informed by the instinctive class revolt of the masses. In

"A Love Match," Celia makes "the unemployed interested in their plight instead of dulled by it," an assertion that might initially appear as condescending. But a few lines later, we learn that "she was impressed by their arguments, and became political, and by 1936 she was marching in Communist demonstrations" (15); in other words, the worker and the bourgeois learn from each other in turn. The earlier satire of Celia's motives is thus preserved and negated: it turns out that she hadn't yet become political despite being heavily involved in relief work, but she then becomes committed following her contact with the proletariat and their reasoning. In the words of *The Communist Manifesto* much cited in the 1930s, she "goes over" to the side of the proletariat. Townsend Warner's presentation of this dialectical emergence is irreducible to the formulation of left melancholia that has become so prominent in recent scholarship; as in her remarks in later interviews there is no bitterness or regret here but rather a sober evaluation of the commitments of 1930s Communism.

Celia's engagements are however curtailed when she receives a series of poison pen letters threatening to expose the real nature of the Tizards' relationship. Previously the quieter of the couple, Justin leaps into action when he learns of the letters. Aware that they come from a woman who had been pursuing him, he "settles" her in an undisclosed fashion but with some suggestion of violence (17). It is then that the normalizations of the heterosexual couple finally overwhelm Justin's and Celia's relationship in the form of traditional gender roles. Following Justin's masterful handling of the situation, no scandal emerges and the couple can rest easy; but "the balance between Justin and Celia had shifted, and never returned to its former adjustment" (19). While Justin remains fundamentally irresponsible but assumes control, Celia now falls into a clichéd pattern of middle-aged femininity – putting on weight, losing her skill as a driver, reading novels before lunch, and needing small holidays to maintain her sanity (19–20). A neighbor puts this down to the menopause, but the real import of "the Change" is the final normalization inherent in the Tizards' relationship – the assumption of masculine power under the pressure of the male-female couple.

At this point "A Love Match" seems almost despairing of the possibility of non-normative partnership. But the story's moving closing lines heavily imply that the workers of the village had known all along about the Tizards' incest:

> The wavering torchlights wandered over the spectacle. There was a silence. Then young Foe spoke out. 'He must have come in to comfort her. That's my opinion.' The others concurred. Silently they disentangled Justin and Celia, and wrapped them in separate tarpaulin sheets. No word of what they had found got out. Foe's hypothesis was accepted by the coroner and became truth. (20)

There is a dual dialectic at work in this passage: simultaneously acknowledging and subverting the binary logic of the closet, the coroner's bourgeois ignorance is produced by working-class knowledge and discretion. "A Love Match" is not only a satire on bourgeois marriage and its powerful normalizations, able to smother even the most reviled and taboo sexual practices, but also a meditation on the relationship between sexual dissidence and class consciousness. Sexual knowledge, the story suggests, is directly occluded by bourgeois institutions, even as non-normative desire may be protected within them. As such, "A Love Match" stands as a compelling critique of the model of respectable homosexuality promoted by the Wolfenden Report and today prominent in debates around gay marriage.

Bloomsbury porn

In his pioneering cultural history *Literature, Politics and Culture in Postwar Britain* (1989) Alan Sinfield adumbrated some lines of inquiry into the dynamics of cross-class queer desire. Sinfield argues that in the 1940s and 1950s a hostile climate toward the privileged literary establishment involved not only a denunciation of their class privilege, but also a pervasive antihomosexual discourse that pitted the effete highbrow against the new, manly working- and lower-middle-class subjects of the postwar state. At the same time, members of the literary establishment recoiled in aesthetic horror from the new technocratic class mobility they saw as overwhelming civilized values centered on individual expression. However, Sinfield argues, both sides of this equation were problematized and perhaps subverted by literary queers' choice of working-class partners (he seems rather less interested in working-class men's choice of bourgeois literary types).[19] Sinfield's account is important, but he assumes that figures such as

Lehmann and Isherwood were exhaustively defined by their associations with Bloomsbury – throughout his account "Bloomsbury" is used as an overarching term for every bourgeois writer of the period, whatever their politics. Even as he argues that "cross-class liaisons problematized the personal relationships upon which Bloomsbury prided itself," Sinfield does not take into account the crucial shift that then occurs between these earlier modernists and the young queer writers of the 1930s.[20] As I argue in the Introduction, the literary counterpublics of 1930s writing cannot be adequately defined by their links to Bloomsbury, as Isherwood, Auden, and others insistently reached out for new modes of queer leftist public address quite distinct from the liberal hygiene between public and private practiced by Woolf and Forster. These new forms of literary and social address meant that the class-crossing sexual practices of these writers were radically different from those of the older generation, and their trips to Weimar Germany and Red Vienna were central to this process of differentiation – particularly in the case of Lehmann and Isherwood.

This has important ramifications for the question of respectability, given that Isherwood might plausibly be retroactively fitted into a normalizing narrative that draws on his work on the publication of Forster's *Maurice* following his friend and mentor's death and on the reception of his own most famous gay novel.[21] Indeed, Isherwood would appear to be the closest figure to the "respectable homosexual" of all his group. Never hiding his sexuality socially, but refusing to enact the speech act of coming out in interviews until the 1970s (surely uncoincidentally around the time of the publication of *Maurice*), Isherwood has often been cast as the quintessential bourgeois homosexual; a gay man who "led strongly from the middle," as Jonathan Fryer put it.[22] Taking place in one day in the life of a middle-class queer Englishman, dealing with the death of his lover and contemplating his life as an academic in the US, Isherwood's *A Single Man* (1964) would appear to follow this logic. But on a closer look, even this apparently most bourgeois of homosexual's identity is destabilized, emptied as "that non-entity we call George"; simultaneously a joke about moribund Englishness and a recognition of the limitations of middle-class gay male experience as an exclusive model for queer life.[23] Moreover, the text's reception history is so prominent as to itself constitute its own canon – the novel was selected as one of the texts in a famous symposium organized by George Whitmore in 1980 attended by figures such as Edmund White, Larry Kramer, and Andrew Holleran, who went on to be prominent members of the Violet Quill – and this genealogy has shaped a perception of the novel as less anti-bourgeois than might be the case.

Following the publication of *A Single Man* and the fast-paced development of gay print culture in the 1960s and 1970s Isherwood's reputation as a queer novelist quickly grew in the US. As Jamie Harker has documented, the press clippings and readers' letters housed in his archive stand as a remarkable record of these intertwined processes.[24] While undoubtedly pleased with these developments, Isherwood maintained an ironic stance toward his own place in the burgeoning gay rights movement. In a 1965 interview he remarked on the apparent modesty of his sexual-political aims:

> Whether I'm so optimistic to expect that anything I write will really change very many people's opinions, that's another matter. Everybody knows that you are lucky if you can just do the smallest thing. I often quote the remark that Norman Douglas made about D.H. Lawrence. He meant to slight Lawrence very much and he said Lawrence opened a little window for the *bourgeoisie*. And I always say, *My God*, imagine being able to open a little window for the *bourgeoisie*. That's enough for a hundred lifetimes.[25]

This passage moves, with characteristic sly wit, through an admission of the necessarily limited claims literature can make on the social, to a jibe made by a queer writer about Lawrence, and finally to a limiting statement of the possibilities of literary liberation in the mid-century. Like many of Isherwood's statements about his career, this should be taken with more than a pinch of salt.

Chapter 1 argued that *Christopher and His Kind* (1976) continues to mobilize the Marxist antihumanism Isherwood encountered in Weimar Berlin, embodying a thoroughgoing critique of humanist identity, even as it becomes paradigmatic for the bourgeois gay subject. Throughout the text, Isherwood disinstantiates himself by toggling between "Christopher," "he," and "I" – a technique that he had explored throughout his career, and which was vitally informed by Sergei Tretiakov's factography. Tretiakov infamously argued that the human subject must be instrumentalized by the literary text, just as the individual worker was sublated by the processes of revolutionary production. In *Christopher and His Kind* Isherwood relentlessly operationalizes himself in the service of gay subjectivity, precisely as that subjectivity was becoming solidified into an identity by the gay rights movement and thus increasingly seen in non-instrumental terms. While Isherwood repeatedly insists on the narrative as a coming out story – "describing his life as he had lived it" – his memoir undercuts the conception of a pre-existing gay identity upon which that narrative relies.[26]

In other words, Isherwood simultaneously embodies and resists the respectability paradigm. The closing passage of *Christopher and His Kind* makes explicit the social dynamics of this conceptual maneuver:

> Yes, my dears, each of you will find the person you came here to look for – the ideal companion to whom you can reveal yourself totally and yet be loved for what you are, not what you pretend to be. You, Wystan, will find him very soon, within three months. You, Christopher, will have to wait much longer for yours. He is already living in the city where you will settle. He will be near you for many years without your meeting. But it would be no good if you did meet him now. At present, he is only four years old.[27]

Initially this passage rather cozily assures the reader that they too will progress to gay coupledom under the sign of disclosure, an "ideal companion" to whom you may "reveal yourself totally." Isherwood had to wait for his perfect complement, who had been living close by without mutual recognition – so far so proto-homonormative – but then suddenly it becomes clear that Christopher isn't going to quite live up to such prim expectations. The memoir closes with a four-year-old Don Bachardy waiting in the wings for the thirty-one-year-old Isherwood, the memoir closing with a defiant defense of intergenerational queer love. Not only does Isherwood resist respectability with this parting shot, but we might also see his relationship with Bachardy as a synecdoche for the queer cultural and social history he and his peers embodied. Here is a deferred, anticipated intimacy, mirroring the gap between Isherwood's time in Berlin and the publication of his memoir, and troping the movements of queer history charted throughout this book. This is not a progressivist history, nor is it a dissolution of the historical itself, but rather a narrative of fits and starts, negations and sublations – of the dialectics of sex, to borrow a term from Marxist feminism.[28] Lehmann's novel embodies this history in a rather more explicit fashion.

On first glance, John Lehmann was the closest of any figure of his generation to Bloomsbury, working with the Woolfs on the Hogarth Press from 1936–8. He is today best known for this role, and as the "literary impresario" (as he called himself) who founded the influential leftist magazine *New Writing*; but in addition to his work as a publisher and editor he also produced a substantial body of writing, much of it autobiographical.[29] His voluminous memoir came out in three installments, and was collected in 1969 as *In My Own Time: Memoirs of a Literary Life*, followed in 1976 by a thinly-veiled autobiographical novel, *In the Purely Pagan Sense*. Sinfield has rightly observed that Lehmann essentially wrote parallel memoirs, the relentlessly sexually explicit *In the Purely Pagan Sense* the counterpart to his earlier literary autobiography.[30] However, as with the Forster-Isherwood relationship, a progressivist coming out narrative is inadequate to describe Lehmann's autobiographical writings. As I discuss in the Introduction, his 1938 novel *Evil Was Abroad* narrated what Isherwood called "a semi-erotic interest in the working classes," detailing its protagonist's love for a young unemployed Viennese man.[31] Admittedly, the novel is free of direct sexual reference, and does not explicitly present itself as autobiographical. But to anybody who happened to know anything about Lehmann, the novel is plainly based on his own experiences in Vienna during the period, and to any knowing reader is clearly about queer love. What follows in his memoirs of the postwar period is a retrenchment both of Bloomsbury concerns and of sexual discretion, simultaneously denouncing his former Communism, celebrating his contact with the Woolfs, his bourgeois aesthetic sensibilities, and so on.

This is blown apart by *In the Purely Pagan Sense*. One of the most extraordinary queer British novels of the 1970s, this romping text has received little critical attention, undoubtedly because of its utter transgression of modernist canons of literary value ironically explicitly supported by Lehmann himself. In the mode of a mid-century thriller, Lehmann's alter ego, Jack Marlowe, is a glamorous spy with incredible literary gifts, not only furiously signaled by his name, but also explicitly in his becoming "in a small way, a literary lion," and his secret work for the British government.[32] Needless to say, Marlowe also has good taste in food and wine, giving off the distinct impression of a gay James Bond.[33] Coupled with these aspirations, the prose is bare, with no pretensions to any sort of experiment whatever. The novel is also curiously completely devoid of effective humor despite the author's best intentions – one scene features the narrator pelting a sleeping guardsman with potatoes in an attempt to rouse his would-be conquest (163–4), an inherently comic idea that in its execution merely gives the impression of Lehmann gamely trying to raise a laugh (this lack of humor may also account to a degree for this novel's neglect). As Foucault famously described Don Juan, Lehmann's protagonist moves across Europe driven by "the somber madness of sex."[34]

A completely unashamed narrator, Marlowe's sexual career operates in constant tension with his prose, a joyous celebration of the experimental creative energies of queer desire catalogued with sober seriousness. It starts out quite vanilla, with schoolboy crushes and mutual masturbation, but the narrative quickly mounts in excitement, cataloguing a panoply of perversions, proudly and carefully detailing the narrator's adventures across Europe in the 1930s and 1940s, including sadomasochism (166), intergenerational incestuous desire (171), exhibitionism and voyeurism (187–8), and public group sex (182, 201–2). For good measure, Marlowe even beds an aristocratic Frenchwoman, but decides it isn't for him. Underlying all of this is cross-class desire, the constant tenor of Marlowe's sex, whatever the acts, and wherever the setting; a large part of the cross-class sex is also transactional, with Marlowe paying his working-class sex partners money or gifts. All the while, the writing remains completely free of any pretense to experiment or high literary lyricism. Here is a representative sample of the text's depictions of sex between the narrator and one of the many young servicemen he meets:

> As I accelerated the rhythm and took the cock deeper into my mouth, all the time surrounding it with the flicker of my tongue, he began to wriggle and groan as if he were under torture. I soon sensed that the climax was coming, and could feel him involuntarily withdraw. I gripped his bottom to prevent this, and pushed it towards me. A moment later I felt his love-juice jetting into my mouth [. . .] 'Divine, Jack, divine!' he murmured almost brokenly, and then began violently to kiss my spunk-wet mouth again. (248)

Here the writing is frankly pornographic – and I say this with more than a little approval. With its glamorous hero and insistent sexual explicitness, Lehmann's novel might be profitably compared to gay pulp, the vital genre of the 1960s that opened up gay male sexual self-understanding to a mass readership. And there could be nothing less Bloomsbury than *In the Purely Pagan Sense*, nothing less cautious, less refined, less aesthetically experimental – in a word, less respectable – than this joyous mutual instrumentalization by bourgeois and proletarian. It might immediately be objected that this is all too easy an access to the utopian; as Leo Bersani pointed out some time ago, the location of utopia in gay male sex *per se* is deeply problematic.[35] Moreover, the transactional aspects of Marlowe's sex life may jar on some readers as vitiating the radical potential of his embrace of the proletarian. And indeed, *In the Purely Pagan Sense* is far from devoid of snobbishness. Toward the end of the novel, Marlowe meditates on the difficulties inherent in cross-class sexual relationships, going on to ponder in a distinctly sneering tone what a growing breakdown of class barriers may bring:

> It is, I think, possible to envisage a time, and in the not so very distant future either, when the differences in cultural background that still prevail will have narrowed almost to vanishing point. Your doughty guardsman my [sic] be as ardent an *aficionado* of the ballet as his gentleman friend, and will compare notes with him on the latest middlebrow bestseller. The guardsman will, perhaps, provide his friend with the rare sporting print or Rowlandson he needs to fill the gap in that enchanting series on the staircase; and offer, when the friend is down on his luck, to take him for a package tour among the Greek islands. (251–2)

Here is the recoil from postwar leveling diagnosed by Sinfield, a series of reversals that drip with contempt for the "middlebrow bestseller" and the implausible turn of the guardsman to the ballet – to say nothing of the horrified glimpse of a "package tour." Marlowe's disgust for petit-bourgeois pleasures is undeniable; but Lehmann's pulpy text itself repeatedly and triumphantly violates the aesthetic principles underlying his explicit dismissal. Moreover, to read these lines entirely as a foreclosure of utopian modes of non-normative desire would be mistaken, for they are immediately followed with a defiant critique of the process of normalization:

> When that moment comes, the relationship will have few if any of the tensions I have been describing, and which have saddened so many of my friends who were not content with the whirligig of promiscuous one-night stands, that 'expense of spirit in a waste of shame' so briefly delightful to youth. Instead, the civilian (no longer indeed to be described as a 'gentleman friend') and the soldier will have simply to face the hazards inherent in any married state. Allowing for the absence of children and family life, their relationship will be no more insecure, or productive of emotional discord, than that between a 'straight' husband and his wife; which is not saying much. (252)

The obvious reading here would be that Marlowe (and, apparently transparently, Lehmann) merely wants to retain class privilege, and there is some truth in this. Marlowe laments the loss of the soldier-gentleman pairing, even as he appears to decry the "whirligig of promiscuous one-night stands" (liaisons that have, in any case, formed a great part of his narrative, and to which he tellingly refers as saddening to his friends, not himself). But merely denouncing Lehmann's bourgeois privilege is a flattening reading that glosses over the compromises inherent in the postwar settlement. While it jealously guards class status, this passage mourns the loss of queer life inherent in the normalization of a marriage of "equals" – in other words, the central ideological fulcrum of heteronormativity is implicated in the supposed dissolution of class boundaries. What is lost here is difference itself, dissolved into anodyne complementarity by the couple form.

Reading against the grain somewhat – but with a strong warrant from Lehmann's Communist past – this passage also unconsciously implies that class struggle is evaded by the supposed leveling of the postwar state and the normalization of queer life. The key term here is the "tensions" that define cross-class sexual encounters, and which Lehmann, Isherwood, Auden, and others saw as points of access not just to proletarian bodies but to the processes of revolutionary socialism. To argue that these two aspects are mutually exclusive is not only to foreclose queer instrumentalizations of the body, but to erase working-class desire and uphold property ownership through a blanket ban on human objectification. Lehmann's catalogue of cross-class transactional sex is in fact less ideologically propertied than the position that ethical instrumentalization is impossible (to say nothing of this position's ignorance or evasion and erasure of the complex pleasures of interwar queer male life). For Lehmann as for Isherwood, each sexual encounter does not simply or inherently encode radical politics in itself, but is rather determined by the social contact made between bourgeois and proletarian, a play of class consciousness operating in dialectical tension with the joyful immediacy of the sex. Needless to say, the movement of this dialectic is foreclosed by the ideology of monogamous intra-class domesticity – gay or straight – if not always by actually existing coupledom.

The problematic of respectability raised by Lehmann's novel recapitulates the question with which this study began: how to practice an effective queer Marxist cultural politics against bourgeois ethics and aesthetics? *Queer Communism* has argued that the answer does not lie in modernist literary experimentalism nor in antinormativity *per se*; that vanguardism and proletarianism aren't quite such false friends for queers as first might be presumed; and that any attempt to broaden the appeal of these forms of radical life by appeal to a putative popular sentiment must always be resisted. It should go without saying that all revolutionary formations must necessarily reject the idealized family unit and the nation state *tout court*: any attempt to recapture this ground from fascism is a futile endeavor. And yet such quixotic commonsense reappears time and time again. For in the face of strategic defeats, the temptation of overcorrection is always lurking in the form of populism – "the bad side which produces the movement that makes history, by providing a struggle."[36] The lesson of the thirties is to resist this tendency.

Notes

Introduction

1. Thomas de Quincey, *Confessions of an English Opium Eater* (London: Bibliolis, 2010), p. 3.
2. Karl Marx and Friedrich Engels, *Manifesto of the Communist Party*, trans. Terrell Carver in *Marx: Later Political Writings*, ed. Carver (Cambridge: Cambridge University Press, 1996), p 1.
3. Marx and Engels, *Manifesto of the Communist Party*, p. 17.
4. Michel Foucault, *The Courage of Truth: Lectures at the Collège de France, 1983–1984*, trans. Graham Burchell (New York: Palgrave Macmillan, 2012), p. 186.
5. See Otto Friedrich, "France's Philosopher of Power," *Time*, November 16, 1981, p. 148.
6. Foucault, *Courage of Truth*, p. 186.
7. Edgell Rickword was a founding member and editor of the Communist Party of Great Britain's key literary journal, *Left Review*, a director of the CPGB's publishing house, Lawrence and Wishart, and was later to edit the Communist review, *Our Time*.
8. Sylvia Townsend Warner to Edgell Rickword, Letter of November 10, 1937. The Sylvia Townsend Warner Papers, The Dorset County Museum, Dorchester: QR2.
9. As is well known, Spender became an influential cold warrior. See James Smith, *British Writers and MI5 Surveillance, 1930–1960* (Cambridge: Cambridge University Press, 2013), pp. 75–9.
10. Perry Anderson, "Components of the National Culture," *New Left Review* 1/50 (July–August 1968), p. 11.
11. For an overview of Townsend Warner's and Ackland's activism, see Wendy Mulford, *This Narrow Place. Sylvia Townsend Warner and*

Valentines Ackland: Life, Letters and Politics, 1930–1951 (London: Pandora, 1988), pp. 70–103.

12. Versions of this interpretation are too numerous to begin to list here. For the genesis of this position in Orwell, see "Inside the Whale" (1940), in *Complete Works XII: A Patriot After All*, ed. Peter Davison (London: Secker & Warburg, 1998), pp. 99–111. To take one important example: as Andrew Thorpe points out, Henry Pelling is the historian with whom the paradigmatic Cold War anti-Communist line is most often associated. See Thorpe, "Comintern 'Control' of the Communist Party of Great Britain, 1920–1943," *English Historical Review* 113 (1998), pp. 637–8; and Pelling, *The British Communist Party: A Historical Profile* (New York: Macmillan, 1958).

13. Janet Montefiore, *Men and Women Writers of the 1930s: The Dangerous Flood of History* (London and New York: Routledge, 1996); Rod Mengham, "The Thirties: Politics, Authority, Perspective," in *The Cambridge History of Twentieth-Century English Literature*, ed. Laura Marcus and Peter Nicholls (Cambridge: Cambridge University Press, 2004), pp. 358–79; *Recharting the Thirties*, ed. Patrick Quinn (London: Associated University Presses, 1996); *Rewriting the Thirties: Modernism and After*, ed. Keith Williams and Steven Matthews (London and New York: Longman, 1997); and Michael Denning, *The Cultural Front: The Laboring of American Culture in the Twentieth Century*, rev. ed. (London and New York: Verso, 2010).

14. See, *inter alia*, Andrew Thorpe, *The British Communist Party and Moscow, 1920–1943* (Manchester: Manchester University Press, 2002), "Comintern 'Control' of the Communist Party of Great Britain, 1920–1943," pp. 637–62, "The Communist International and the British Communist Party" in *International Communism and the Communist International 1919–43*, ed. Tim Rees and Andrew Thorpe (Manchester: Manchester University Press), pp. 67–86; and Kevin Morgan, *Against Fascism and War: Ruptures and Continuities in British Communist Party Politics 1935–41* (Manchester: Manchester University Press, 1989).

15. E. P. Thompson, "The Peculiarities of the English," in *The Poverty of Theory and Other Essays* (London: Merlin, 1978), p. 74. As Thompson asserts in the course of this polemic against Perry Anderson and Tom Nairn, "it is, first of all, an elementary error to suppose that the political and industrial influence of the British Communist Party – or its intellectual influence – can be estimated from a count of party cards [...] this history is itself of great importance, most of all in the 1930s and 1940s, and not least in intellectual consequences" (p. 75).

16. See, respectively, Samuel Hynes, *The Auden Generation: Literature and Politics in England in the 1930s* (London and Boston: Faber and Faber, 1979; first pub. 1976); and Valentine Cunningham, *British Writers of the Thirties* (Oxford: Oxford University Press, 1988).
17. Judith Butler, "Merely Cultural," *Social Text* 52–3 (1997), pp. 265–77. One of the most prominent examples of the tendency Butler diagnoses is to be found in Eric Hobsbawm's assertion that "most collective identities are most like shirts than skin" in his "Sexual Politics and the Left," *New Left Review* 1/217 (1996), p. 1. Although Butler doesn't name names, it seems likely that this article was one of her main targets given the respective publication dates; her article was reprinted in the *New Left Review* the following year.
18. For a detailed political history of how this process continued in the postwar period and up to the 1990s, see Lucy Robinson, *Gay Men and the Left in Post-War Britain* (Manchester: University of Manchester Press, 2007).
19. Christopher Isherwood, *Christopher and His Kind* (Minneapolis: University of Minnesota Press, 2001; first pub. 1976), p. 334.
20. While not particularly concerned with homosexuality (some nods and winks about Auden's poetry notwithstanding), Neal Wood's *Communism and British Intellectuals* (London: Victor Gollancz, 1959) is a characteristic anti-Communist study of the supposed pathology of intellectuals' support of the Soviet Union.
21. Less damning than Banville's novel, the 2003 glossy BBC dramatization of the Cambridge spies' narrative does aim to portray the group relatively sympathetically, but still maintains a pathologizing attitude toward these "very British traitors." Four years later, the release of Auden's MI5 file prompted a round of wild speculation in the press about the Auden group's relationship to Guy Burgess. See Smith, *British Writers*, p. ix.
22. See Elisa Glick, *Materializing Queer Desire: Oscar Wilde to Andy Warhol* (Albany: SUNY Press, 2009), p. 9; and Kevin Floyd, *The Reification of Desire: Towards a Queer Marxism* (Minneapolis: University of Minnesota Press, 2009), p. 2.
23. Floyd, *Reification of Desire*, p. 5.
24. Michael Warner, "Introduction" to *Fear of a Queer Planet*, ed. Michael Warner (Minneapolis: University of Minnesota Press, 1993), p. xxiv.
25. See Raphael Samuel, *The Lost World of British Communism* (London: Verso, 2017); and Edward Upward, *The Spiral Ascent Trilogy* (London: Heinemann, 1977). See also Glyn Salton-Cox, "Literary Praxis Beyond

the Melodramas of Commitment: Edward Upward, Soviet Aesthetics, and Leftist Self-Fashioning," *Comparative Literature* 65/4 (2013), pp. 408–29.

26. Many of these developments have been charted in a recent special edition "Queer Studies and the Crises of Capitalism," *GLQ* 18/1 (2012), ed. Jordana Rosenberg et al. For book-length treatments see Floyd, *Reification of Desire*; Roderick Ferguson, *Aberrations in Black: Toward a Queer of Color Critique* (Minneapolis: University of Minnesota Press, 2003); José Esteban Muñoz, *Cruising Utopia: The Then and There of Queer Futurity* (New York and London: New York University Press, 2009); Eric O. Clark, *Virtuous Vice: Homoeroticism and the Public Sphere* (Durham, NC: Duke University Press, 2000); Matthew Tinkcom, *Working Like a Homosexual: Camp, Capital, Cinema* (Durham, NC: Duke University Press, 2002); Peter Drucker, *Warped: Gay Normality and Queer Anticapitalism* (Chicago: Haymarket, 2015); and Glick, *Materializing Queer Desire*. For a more adversarial study on the relationship between Marxism and queer theory see Rosemary Hennessy, *Profit and Pleasure: Sexual Identities in Late Capitalism* (London: Routledge, 2002); and for the genealogy of Communism and identity politics, Daniel Hurewitz, *Bohemian Los Angeles and the Making of Modern Politics* (Berkeley, Los Angeles, and London: University of California Press, 2007).

27. See Martin Esslin, "Brecht and the English Theater," *Tulane Drama Review* 11/2 (1966), pp. 63–70. Esslin's thesis of strong influence has been disputed: see Ronald Gray, *Brecht, the Dramatist* (Cambridge: Cambridge University Press Archive, 1976), p. 191.

28. Tyrus Miller, *Late Modernism: Politics, Fiction, and the Arts Between the World Wars* (Berkeley, Los Angeles and London: University of California Press, 1999); Leo Mellor, *Reading the Ruins: Modernism, Bombsites, and British Culture* (Cambridge: Cambridge University Press, 2011); Jessica Berman, *Modernist Commitments: Ethics, Politics, and Transnational Modernism* (New York: Columbia University Press, 2012); Gill Plain, *Literature of the 1940s: War, Postwar and 'Peace'* (Edinburgh: Edinburgh University Press, 2013); Jed Esty, *A Shrinking Island: Modernism and National Culture in England* (Princeton: Princeton University Press, 2004); Benjamin Kohlmann, *Committed Styles: Modernism, Politics, and Left-Wing Literature in the 1930s* (Oxford: Oxford University Press, 2014); Cathryn Setz, *Primordial Modernisms: Animals, Ideas, Transition 1927–1938* (Edinburgh: Edinburgh University Press, forthcoming); Marina

MacKay, *Modernism and World War II* (Cambridge: Cambridge University Press, 2007).

29. Ben Harker, "'Communism is English': Edgell Rickword, Jack Lindsay, and the Cultural Politics of the Popular Front," *Literature and History* 20/2 (2011), pp. 23–40.
30. "Peripheral Realisms Now," ed. Jed Esty and Coleen Lye, *MLQ* 73/3 (2012).
31. For an astute essay inverting realist and modernist studies in this fashion, see Paul K. Saint-Amour, "An Interlude: We Have Never Been Modernists," *English Literature in Transition, 1880–1920* 56/2 (2013), pp. 201–4.
32. There is a voluminous scholarly literature on this question impossible to adequately summarize here. Signal interventions are to be found in *Alternative Modernities*, ed. Dilip Parameshwar Gaonkar (Durham, NC: Duke University Press, 2011); for a more recent critique of this concept, see Naoki Yamamoto, "Dialectics without Synthesis: Tracking Japanese Documentary Theory," in *A Companion to Documentary Film History*, ed. Joshua Malitsky and Malin Wahlberg (Malden, MA: Wiley-Blackwell, forthcoming).
33. Fredric Jameson, "The Antimonies of the Realist-Modernist Debate," *MLQ* 73/3, p. 476.
34. Esty, *Shrinking Island*, p. 17.
35. Fredric Jameson, *The Antimonies of Realism* (London and New York, 2015), p. 26.
36. Esslin, "Brecht and the English Theater," pp. 63–70.
37. See the collection of Tretiakov's essays in the special edition "Soviet Factography," ed. Devin Fore, *October* 118 (2006).
38. For a discussion of the Lukács translations published in *International Literature* in the 1930s, as well as an overview of the publication, see Glyn Salton-Cox, "'Polemics Pertinent at the Time of Publication': Georg Lukács, *International Literature*, and the Popular Front," in Ben Harker, ed., "Communism and the Written Word," special edition of *Twentieth Century Communism* 12 (2017), pp. 143–69.
39. Muñoz, *Cruising Utopia*, p. 1.
40. Friedrich Engels, "Letter to Margaret Harkness," trans. H. Scott, *International Literature*, July 1933, p. 112.
41. V. I. Lenin, *What is to be Done?* in *Essential Works of Lenin*, ed. Henry M. Christman (New York: Dover, 1987), pp. 53–176.
42. For a discussion of the spontaneity/consciousness dialectic, see Katerina Clark, *The Soviet Novel: History as Ritual*, 2nd ed. (Bloomington: Indiana Press, 2000), pp. 15–24.

43. Judith (Jack) Halberstam, *Female Masculinity* (Durham, NC: Duke University Press, 1998), p. 99.
44. See, *inter alia*, Virginia Woolf, "The Leaning Tower," in *Collected Essays Vol.2* (London: The Hogarth Press, 1966), pp. 162–76.
45. W. H. Auden, epigraph to *The Orators* (1932), *Collected Poems*, ed. Edward Mendelson (New York: Random House, 2007), p. 54.
46. Cunningham, *British Writers*, pp. 148–50.
47. Christopher Hilliard, "Producers by Hand and by Brain: Working-Class Writers and Left-Wing Publishers in 1930s Britain," *The Journal of Modern History* 78 (2006), pp. 37–64.
48. Cunningham, *British Writers*, p. 150.
49. For a literary-historical account of these cross-class intimacies, see Frank Kermode, *History and Value* (Oxford: The Clarendon Press, 1988); for a social-historical study, Matt Houlbrook, *Queer London: Pleasures and Perils in the Sexual Metropolis 1918–1957* (Chicago: University of Chicago Press, 2005).
50. Christopher Isherwood to John Lehmann, Letter of July 18, 1936, The Beinecke Library, New Haven, Connecticut: GEN MSS 344.
51. For a biographical introduction, see Norman Page, *Auden and Isherwood: The Berlin Years* (New York: St. Martin's Press, 1998).
52. Michael Warner, *Publics and Counterpublics* (New York: Zone Books, 2005), pp. 67–117.
53. Perry Anderson, "A Culture in Counter-Flow II," *New Left Review* 1/183 (1990), p. 89.
54. See Morgan, *Against Fascism and War*, pp. 254–72.
55. Cooper has pursued this line of thinking across a number of different works. For her most recent, succinct statement, see her "Transformative State Publics," *New Political Science* 38/3 (2016), pp. 315–34.
56. Michael Sidnell, *Dances of Death: The Group Theatre of London in the Thirties* (London: Faber, 1984), p. 56.
57. W. H. Auden, *Selected Poems*, ed. Edward Mendelson (New York: Vintage, 2007), p. 43.
58. Auden, *Selected Poems*, p. 9.
59. See Lars H. Lih, *Lenin Rediscovered: What is to Be Done? in Context* (Leiden: Brill, 2006), pp. 456–9.
60. See Thorpe, "The Communist International and the British Communist Party," pp. 78–80; and James Eaden and David Renton, *The Communist Party of Great Britain Since 1920* (Basingstoke: Palgrave, 2002), pp. 15–19.
61. See Matthew Worley, *Class Against Class: The Communist Party in Britain Between the Wars* (London: I.B. Tauris, 2002), p. 314.

62. See Dave Cope, *Bibliography of the Communist Party of Great Britain* (London: Lawrence and Wishart, 2016), p. 123.
63. For a polemic against the compromises of the Popular Front, see Alun Howkins, "Class Against Class: The Political Culture of the Communist Party of Great Britain, 1930–5," in *Class, Culture, and Social Change: A New View of the 1930s*, ed. Frank Gloversmith (Brighton: Harvester, 1980), pp. 250–77; for an opposing view arguing that the Party retained a degree of its vanguardist ethos, see Morgan, *Against Fascism and War*.
64. "Queer Theory Without Antinormativity," special edition ed. Robyn Wiegman and Elizabeth A. Wilson, *differences* 26/1 (May 2015).
65. Dan Healey, "Homosexual Existence and Existing Socialism: New Light on the Repression of Male Homosexuality in Stalin's Russia," *GLQ* 8/3 (2002), pp. 359–62, and *Homosexual Desire in Revolutionary Russia: The Regulation of Sexual and Gender Dissent* (Chicago: University of Chicago Press, 2001), pp. 181–204.
66. Fyodor Gladkov, *Cement*, trans. A. S. Arthur and C. Ashleigh (Evanston: Northwestern University Press, 1994), p. 19.
67. Healey, "Homosexual Existence," p. 358.
68. Richard Hornsey, *The Spiv and the Architect: Unruly Life in Postwar London* (Minneapolis: University of Minnesota Press, 2010), p. 30.
69. Healey, "Homosexual Existence," p. 358.
70. As Healey puts it: "Despite the Party's prevailing suspicion of women who evaded their 'natural' reproductive role, some doctors allowed that masculinization imbued the lesbian with strength, public presence, and skillfulness, all politically admirable attributes. Male femininity, on the other hand, rendered men soft, frivolous, and obsessed with a cozy bourgeois domestic sphere. By the late 1930s a clear public ethic against play and pleasure prevailed, influencing even sympathetic doctors to erase the male homosexual's ironic femininity from their case histories." "The Disappearance of the Russian Queen, or How the Soviet Closet Was Born," in *Russian Masculinities in History and Culture*, ed. Barbara Evan Clements et al. (Basingstoke: Palgrave Macmillan, 2001), p. 162.
71. For a discussion of Gide's turn away from the Soviet Union, and the resulting homophobic reaction, see Patrick Pollard, "Gide in the U.S.S.R.: Some Observations on Comradeship," in *Gay Men and the Sexual History of the Political Left*, ed. Gert Hekma, Harry Oosterhuis, and James Steakley (New York and London: The Haword Press, 1995), pp. 179–98.

72. Lauren Berlant, *Cruel Optimism* (Durham, NC: Duke University Press, 2011), pp. 1–3.
73. See Healey, "Homosexual Existence," p. 350.
74. Dimitrov, *The Working Classes Against Fascism* (London: Martin Lawrence, 1935), p. 70 (emphasis in original). This stress on patriotism comes in the section of Dimitrov's speech entitled, "The Ideological Struggle Against Fascism." Dimitrov begins by upbraiding Communists for underestimating the "fascist capacity for ideological infection": despite its "stupidity" and "lunacy," fascist ideology has penetrated far deeper than many had expected (pp. 68–9). At the center of this mass appeal lies the fascist claim to speak for national tradition: "The fascists are rummaging through the entire *history* of every nation so as to be able to pose as their heirs and continuers of all that was exalted and heroic in its past" (p. 69). Dimitrov thus calls for the reclamation of the nation by Communists, who must counter this fascist ideology on its own grounds, by "enlighten[ing] the masses on the part of their own people, in a historically correct, a Leninist-Stalinist spirit" (p. 70). Dimitrov's speech reached readers in seven English-language editions in 1935 alone: three were published in New York, two in London, and one each in Moscow and Wellington. See Vilhém Kahan, *Bibliography of the Communist International 1919–1979* (London: Brill, 1990), pp. 174–5.
75. See Ben Harker, "'Communism is English'"; John Coombes, "British Intellectuals and the Popular Front," in *Class, Culture and Social Change*, ed. Frank Gloversmith, pp. 71, 72, 78; Kevin Morgan, *Against Fascism and War*, pp. 41–3; Margot Heinemann, "The People's Front and the Intellectuals," in *Britain, Fascism and the Popular Front*, ed. Jim Fyrth (London: Lawrence and Wishart), pp. 167–8, 177–80; Andy Croft, *Red Letter Days: British Fiction in the 1930s* (London: Lawrence and Wishart, 1990), pp. 206–9; and Mick Wallis, "Heirs to the Pageant: Mass Spectacle and the Popular Front," in *A Weapon in the Struggle: The Cultural History of the Communist Party in Britain*, ed. Andy Croft (London: Pluto Books, 1998), pp. 48–67. In the case of the US, in *The Cultural Front*, Denning deploys the Gramscian concept of the "national-popular" to elucidate the importance of the nation to Popular Front cultural politics (pp. 134–5); elsewhere, he has argued for the importance of this formation for the genesis of American studies as a discipline: see "'The Special American Conditions': Marxism and American Studies," *American Quarterly* 38/3 (1986), pp. 356–80.
76. Jack Lindsay, *England, My England: A Pageant of the English People*.

(London: Fore Publications, 1939), p. 64. See also his "May Day Traditions," *Left Review* 3/16 (May 1938), pp. 663–6, "Plea for Mass Declamation," *Left Review* 3/9 (October 1937), pp. 511–19, "William Shakespeare," *Left Review* 3/6 (July 1937), pp. 333–42, and "Requiem Mass for the Englishmen Fallen in the International Brigade" (1938), in *The Penguin Book of Spanish Civil War Verse*, ed. Valentine Cunningham (London: Penguin, 1990), pp. 179–83. See also Ralph Fox, *The Novel and the People* (New York: International Publishers, 1945), pp. 115–18.

77. Esty, *Shrinking Island*, pp. 10, 48, *inter alia*.
78. Dimitrov, *Working Classes Against Fascism*, p. 72.
79. Fox, *Novel and the People*, p. 148.
80. Paul Gilroy, *There Ain't No Black in the Union Jack* (Chicago: University of Chicago Press, 1991), pp. 54–5.
81. Glyn Salton-Cox, "Syncretic Utopia, Transnational Provincialism: Rex Warner's *The Wild Goose Chase*," in *Utopia, Modernism and Literature in the Twentieth Century*, ed. Nathan Waddell and Alice Reeve-Tucker (Basingstoke: Palgrave Macmillan, 2013), pp. 111–29.
82. Miranda Joseph, *Against the Romance of Community* (Minneapolis: University of Minnesota Press, 2002).
83. Fox, *Novel and the People*, p. 122.
84. John Sutherland, *Stephen Spender: A Literary Life* (Oxford: Oxford University Press, 2005), p. 205.
85. Ernest Hemingway, *For Whom the Bell Tolls* (London: Random House, 2004), p. 162.
86. *The Spanish Earth* drew tributes from a number of viewers, who saw it as a model of artistic propaganda. See, for instance, Graham Greene, "News Reels," *The Spectator*, September 29, 1939, reprinted in *Spanish Front: Writers on the Spanish Civil War*, ed. Valentine Cunningham (Oxford: Oxford University Press, 1986), p. 212.
87. Thomas Waugh, "'Men Cannot Act before the Camera in the Presence of Death': Joris Ivens' *The Spanish Earth*," in *Documenting the Documentary: Close Readings of Documentary Film and Video*, ed. Barry Keith Grant and Jeanette Sloniowski (Detroit: Wayne State University Press, 1998), p. 150.
88. "The Left-liberal humanitarian response to Guernica is part and parcel of the same group's response to the rise of the Right. Civilian bombing in general and Guernica in particular are often described in terms inseparable from this rise. Fear of machines, of non-humanity, of mass production, of obliteration of the individual, or maleness and male oppression, of death rather than life are pitted against traditional

ideas of women and children, family, vulnerability, democracy, home, dignity, individuality, culture, art, mutual aid, equality, compassion, suffering, martyrdom, and sacrifice. It is a complex web that results." Ian Patterson, *Guernica and Total War* (London: Profile Books, 2007), p. 70.
89. Sylvia Townsend Warner, *After the Death of Don Juan* (London: Virago, 1989), pp. 102–3.
90. Townsend Warner, *After the Death*, p. 103.
91. For discussions of metronormativity, see Scott Herring, *Another Country: Queer Anti-Urbanism* (New York and London: New York University Press, 2010); and Judith (Jack) Halberstam, *In a Queer Time and Place: Transgender Bodies, Subcultural Lives* (Durham, NC: Duke University Press, 2005), pp. 36–8.
92. See, *inter alia*, Janet Montefiore, *Men and Women Writers*, pp. 27–8, 51; and Daphne Patai, *The Orwell Mystique: A Study in Male Ideology* (Amherst: University of Massachusetts Press, 1984).
93. Nick Hubble, "Looking Back on the 1930s Without Being Anti-Communist: Cornford, Orwell, Spender, Sommerfield," special edition on Anti-Communism, ed. Benjamin Kohlmann and Matthew Taunton, *Literature and History* 24/2 (2015), p. 65; and Philip Bounds, *Orwell and Marxism: The Political and Cultural Thinking of George Orwell* (London: I. B. Tauris, 2009), p. 41.
94. See George Orwell, "My Country Right or Left" (1940), in *CW XII*, p. 271.
95. George Orwell, *Homage to Catalonia* in *Orwell in Spain*, ed. Peter Davison (London: Penguin, 2001), p. 167.
96. Orwell, *Homage to Catalonia*, p. 169.
97. See Keith Beattie, *Humphrey Jennings* (Oxford: Oxford University Press, 2013), p. 105. While some commentators have attacked the film's ambiguity, Beattie defends it on the grounds that "the central, productive function of ambiguity in *A Diary for Timothy* is linked to, and informed by, the practice of looking forward."
98. *A Diary for Timothy*, dir. Humphrey Jennings (London: The Crown Film Unit, 1945).
99. Lee Edelman, *No Future: Queer Theory and the Death Drive* (Durham, NC: Duke University Press, 2004).
100. Houlbrook, *Queer London*, p. 273.
101. David James Prickett, "Defining Identity by Homosexual Spaces: Locating the Male Homosexual in Weimar Berlin," *Women in German Yearbook* 21 (2005), p. 149.
102. Eve Kosofsky Sedgwick, "Paranoid Reading and Reparative Reading;

or, You're So Paranoid, You Probably Think This Introduction in About You," in *Novel Gazing: Queer Readings in Fiction*, ed. Sedgwick (Durham, NC: Duke University Press, 1998), pp. 1–40.
103. Leo Bersani, *Is The Rectum a Grave? And Other Essays* (Chicago: University of Chicago Press, 2010), and Edelman, *No Future*.
104. Judith (Jack) Halberstam, *The Queer Art of Failure* (Durham, NC: Duke University Press, 2011); Heather Love, *Feeling Backward: Loss and the Politics of Queer History* (Cambridge, MA: Harvard University Press, 2007); and Elizabeth Freeman, *Time Binds: Queer Temporalities, Queer Histories* (Durham, NC and London: Duke University Press, 2010).

Chapter 1

1. As David Thomas remarks, the phrase is "almost the obligatory starting point for discussions of Christopher Isherwood's fiction." "*Goodbye to Berlin*: Refocusing Isherwood's Camera," *Contemporary Literature* 13/1 (1972), p. 44.
2. See Samuel Hynes, *The Auden Generation: Literature and Politics in England in the 1930s* (London and Boston: Faber and Faber, 1979; first pub. 1976), p. 356, and Richard Johnstone, *The Will to Believe* (Oxford: Oxford University Press, 1982), p. 100. As Isherwood remarks of "I am a camera": "taken out of its context, it was to label Christopher himself as one of those eternal outsiders who watch the passing parade of life lukewarm-bloodedly, with wistful impotence." Christopher Isherwood, *Christopher and His Kind* (Minneapolis: University of Minnesota Press, 2001), p. 58.
3. See *Isherwood on Writing*, ed. James Berg (Minneapolis: University of Minnesota Press, 2007), p. 163; and *Christopher and His Kind*, pp. 333–6.
4. Maggie Clune, Gary Day, and Chris Maguire, in *Literature and Culture in Modern Britain, Volume Two: 1930–1955*, ed. Clive Bloom (New York: Longman, 1993), p. 53; also cited in Jamie Carr, *Queer Times: Christopher Isherwood's Modernity* (London: Routledge, 2006), p. 58.
5. Michael North, *Camera Works: Photography and the Twentieth-Century Word* (Oxford: Oxford University Press, 2005), p. 146.
6. Lara Feigel, "I am not a camera: camera consciousness in 1930s Britain and in the Spanish Civil War," *Textual Practice* 26/2 (2012), p. 220.

7. Carr, *Queer Times*, pp. 7, 58.
8. The Christopher Isherwood Papers, The Huntington Library, CIP: FAC 1357. Cited hereafter as CIP.
9. The Christopher Isherwood/John Lehmann Correspondence, The Beinecke Library, Yale University, New Haven, Connecticut: GEN MSS 344. Cited hereafter as CI/JL.
10. See, for instance, John Sutherland, *Stephen Spender: A Literary Life* (Oxford, Oxford University Press, 2005), p. 141.
11. Rolf Doser and Rainer Herrn record that Münzenberg was Hirschfeld's sister's "most prominent long-term tenant" during the period. See "Verloren 1933: Bibliothek und Archiv des Institutes für Sexualwissenschaft in Berlin," in *Jüdischer Buchbesitz als Raubgut*, ed. Regine Dehne (Frankfurt am Main: Vittorio Klostermann, 2006), p. 38; translation mine.
12. See Martin Esslin, "Brecht and the English Theater," *Tulane Drama Review* 11/2 (1966); and Ronald Gray, *Brecht, the Dramatist* (Cambridge: Cambridge University Press Archive, 1976), p. 191.
13. Joseph Boone, "Vacation Cruises; Or, The Homoerotics of Orientalism," *PMLA* 110/1 (1995), pp. 87–109.
14. See Katerina Clark, *Moscow, the Fourth Rome: Stalinism, Cosmopolitanism, and the Evolution of Soviet Culture* (Cambridge, MA: Harvard University Press, 2011), pp. 1–41.
15. See Sergei Tretiakov, "Hanns Eisler: Revolutionary Composer," *International Literature* (July 1934), pp. 113–18; "John Heartfield," *International Literature* (April 1932), pp. 103–6; and "Bert Brecht," *International Literature* (May 1937), pp. 60–70.
16. Tretiakov, "The Writer and the Socialist Village" (1931), trans. Devin Fore, *October* 118, pp. 63–70, "The New Leo Tolstoy" (1927), trans. Kristen Romberg, *October* 118, pp. 45–50, and "The Biography of the Object," *October* 118, pp. 57–62.
17. Clark, *Moscow, the Fourth Rome*, pp. 47–9.
18. Devin Fore, "Introduction," *October* 118, pp. 3–4. For more on factography, see *October* 118; Benjamin H. D. Buchloh, "From Faktura to Factography," *October* 30 (1984), pp. 82–119; and Clark, *Moscow, the Fourth Rome*, pp. 42–78.
19. Indeed, Tretiakov's lecture was, in the irritated words of Gottfried Benn, "attended by the entire literary world of Berlin." See "The New Literary Season," trans. E. B. Ashton, in *Primal Vision: Selected Writings* (New York: New Directions, 1971), p. 40.
20. Tretiakov, "The Writer and the Socialist Village," p. 65. Walter Benjamin responded enthusiastically three years later in his address

"The Author as Producer," and Brecht began to collaborate with Tretiakov, but responses from Siegfried Kracauer and Gottfried Benn were more critical. See Walter Benjamin, "The Author as Producer" (1934), in *The Work of Art in the Age of Its Technological Reproducibility, And Other Writings on Media* (Cambridge, MA: Harvard University Press, 2008), p. 82; Siegfried Kracauer, "On the Writer" (1931), in *The Weimar Republic Sourcebook*, ed. Martin Jay et al. (Los Angeles and London: University of California Press, 1994), pp. 307–9; and Gottfried Benn, "The New Literary Season." For details of Brecht and Tretiakov's collaboration – which included Tretiakov translating Brecht's *The Measures Taken* (1930) and Brecht unsuccessfully attempting to put on a production of Tretiakov's *Roar, China !* (1924) – see Clark, *Moscow, the Fourth Rome*, pp. 60–2.

21. Georg Lukács, "Reportage or Portrayal," trans. David Fernbach, in *Essays in Realism* (Cambridge, MA: The MIT Press, 1981), p. 51.
22. Georg Lukács, "Narration vs. Description," *International Literature* (July 1937), p. 94; emphasis in original.
23. Isherwood to Lehmann, CI/JL.
24. Christopher Isherwood, *The Berlin Stories* (1954; reprint, New York: New Directions, 2008), p. xiii. Page numbers cited parenthetically hereafter.
25. See, for instance, Samuel Hynes, *The Auden Generation: Literature and Politics in England in the 1930s* (London and Boston: Faber and Faber, 1979; first pub. 1976), p. 364.
26. Tretiakov, "The Writer and the Socialist Village," p. 68.
27. Tretiakov, "From the Photo-Series to Extended Photo-Observation," *October* 118, pp. 74, 77.
28. Tretiakov, "From the Photo-Series," p. 73.
29. Kevin Floyd, *The Reification of Desire: Towards a Queer Marxism* (Minneapolis: University of Minnesota Press, 2009), pp. 133–4.
30. Floyd, *Reification of Desire*, p. 74.
31. Dan Healey, *Homosexual Desire in Revolutionary Russia: The Regulation of Sexual and Gender Dissent* (Chicago: University of Chicago Press, 2001), pp. 181–204.
32. José Esteban Muñoz, *Cruising Utopia: The Then and There of Queer Futurity* (New York and London: New York University Press, 2009), p. 3.
33. Muñoz, *Cruising Utopia*, p. 35.
34. An ambitious social climber, Rastignac attains high office and great wealth as Balzac's *La Comédie Humaine* progresses. Following Marx's and Engel's championing of Balzac's realist method, Lukács reads

Rastignac as a paradigmatic example of typicality, arguing that "Rastignac's inner conflicts are those of the entire younger generation in the post-Napoleonic period." "The Intellectual Physiognomy in Characterization" (1936) in *Writer and Critic*, ed. and trans. Arthur Kahn (London: Merlin, 1970), p. 160.
35. Tretiakov, "The Writer and the Socialist Village," p. 68.
36. Edward Upward, "A Conversation with Edward Upward," *The Review* 11–12 (1964), p. 66.
37. Matt Houlbrook, *Queer London: Pleasures and Perils in the Sexual Metropolis 1918–1957* (Chicago: University of Chicago Press, 2005), pp. 167–95.
38. Frank Kermode, *History and Value* (Oxford: The Clarendon Press, 1988), pp. 22–83.
39. While Marx's view of the lumpenproletariat develops throughout his career, the group is always seen in entirely negative terms. See *The Communist Manifesto* where Marx and Engels call the lumpenproletariat "that passive dungheap of the lowest levels of the old society" (Karl Marx and Friedrich Engels, *Manifesto of the Communist Party*, trans. Terrell Carver in *Marx: Later Political Writings*, ed. Carver [Cambridge: Cambridge University Press, 1996], p. 11), and *The Eighteenth Brumaire of Louis Bonaparte*, which features several barrages of abuse directed against the Paris lumpenproletariat, the feckless followers of Louis Bonaparte (Marx, *The Eighteenth Brumaire of Louis Bonaparte*, in *Marx: Later Political Writings* [pp. 77–8, 111, 122, 125]). See also "The Class Struggle in France 1848–50," in *Surveys from Exile*, ed. David Fernbach (New York: Vintage, 1974), p. 53. For discussions of Marx's and Engels's conception of the lumpenproletariat, see Peter Stallybrass "Marx and Heterogeneity: Thinking the Lumpenproletariat," *Representations* 31 (1990), pp. 69–95; Hal Draper, "The Concept of the 'Lumpenproletariat' in Marx and Engels," *Economies et sociétés* 6/12 (1972), pp. 2285–2312; Robert Bussard, "The 'Dangerous Class' of Marx and Engels: The Rise of the Idea of the Lumpenproletariat," *History of European Ideas* 8/6 (1987), pp. 675–92; Peter Hayes, "Utopia and the Lumpenproletariat: Marx's Reasoning in 'The Eighteenth Brumaire of Louis Bonaparte'," *The Review of Politics* 50/3 (1988), pp. 445–65; and Michael Denning, "Wageless Life," *New Left Review* 66 (2010), pp. 79–97.
40. Otto Biha's 1930 attack in *Linkskurve*, for instance, berates Döblin's novel for portraying a fantastic vision of the (lumpen)proletarian "underworld" which "exists only in the mind of the poet." See Wulf Köpke, *The Critical Reception of Alfred Döblin's Major Novels*

(Rochester, NY and Woodbridge, Suffolk: Camden House, 2003), pp. 5–47 (extract from Biha's article cited in Köpke, p. 43). Ironically, however, we might see Döblin's novel as quite orthodox in a certain sense, for Biberkopf as the classic figure of the lumpenproletarian as seen in *The Communist Manifesto* – while susceptible to being swept up in revolutionary movements he is possessed of no genuine class consciousness of his own, equally able to be rather randomly involved with the Nazis as the Communists – and, indeed, Hirschfeld's organization at one point. See Alfred Döblin, *Berlin Alexanderplatz*, trans. Eugène Jolas (London: Continuum, 2004).

41. For a discussion of how both Hirschfeld and Radzuweit portrayed the queer lumpenproletariat, see David James Prickett, "Defining Identity by Homosexual Spaces: Locating the Male Homosexual in Weimar Berlin," *Women in German Yearbook* 21 (2005), pp. 139–48.
42. John Henry Mackay, *The Hustler: The Story of a Nameless Love from Friedrich Street*, trans. Hubert Kennedy (Boston: Alyson Publications, 1985), back cover.
43. Eve Rosenhaft, "Organizing the Lumpenproletariat: Cliques and Communists in Berlin during the Weimar Republic," in *The German Working Class 1880–1933: The Politics of Everyday Life*, ed. Richard J Evans (Totowa, NJ: Barnes and Noble Books, 1982), pp. 174–220.
44. Michel Foucault, *The Courage of Truth: Lectures at the Collège de France, 1983–1984*, trans. Graham Burchell (New York: Palgrave Macmillan, 2012), p. 186.
45. Orwell, *The Road to Wigan Pier* (1937), in *Orwell's England*, ed. Peter Davison (London: Penguin, 2001), p. 136. While *The Last of Mr. Norris* was published before Orwell's text, Orwell's vision is of course ideologically anterior.
46. Notebook Entry, 12/23/33, CIP: CI 2750.
47. Notebook Entry, 12/25/33, CIP: CI 2750.
48. Here Otto fulfills a similar role to that of George Heisler in Anna Seghers's classic antifascist novel of 1942: see Anna Seghers, *The Seventh Cross*, trans. James A. Galston (New York: Monthly Review Press, 1987).
49. W. H. Auden and Christopher Isherwood, *Journey to a War* (London: Faber, 1939), pp. 31, 122, *inter alia*; page numbers cited parenthetically hereafter. Boone, "Vacation Cruises."
50. Isherwood, "Diary of a Trip to Asia," unpublished MS, CIP: CI 1035.
51. For the classic discussion of the auratic art object, see Walter Benjamin, "The Work of Art in the Age of Mechanical Reproduction,"

trans. Harry Zohn, in *Illuminations*, ed. Hannah Arendt (New York: Shocken, 1968), pp. 217–52.
52. One exception is an unpublished Master's thesis by Timothy David Kaiser, which contends that Isherwood's "prose exhibits at a subconscious level all the typical manifestations of Orientalism." See Timothy David Kaiser, "Orientalism in Auden and Isherwood's Journey to a War," Master's thesis, Hong Kong University, 1997, p. 47 <http://hdl.handle.net/10722/40420>.
53. Tim Youngs, for instance, contents himself with asserting that "Auden and Isherwood take a critical view of their country and compatriots, empathizing with the Chinese." "Auden's Travel Writings," in *The Cambridge Companion to W. H. Auden*, ed. Stan Smith (Cambridge: Cambridge University Press, 2004), p. 77.
54. Having positioned his essay against Edward Said's *Orientalism*, Kerr seizes on a much-rehearsed play around the concept of orientation, arguing that Isherwood's prose fails to "orient itself," and thus that "China precipitates a kind of crisis of representation for the genre, mode and authority of Isherwood's writing, a crisis which that writing is too scrupulous not to admit, and from which it salvages its distinct tone of ironic comedy." Douglas Kerr, "*Journey to a War*: a 'test for men from Europe'," in *W. H. Auden: A Legacy*, ed. David Garrett Izzo (West Cornwall, CT: Locust Hill Press, 2002), pp. 277, 294. According to Stuart Christie, Kerr does not go far enough in recuperating Auden's contribution to *Journey to a War* from the structures of Orientalism: see Kerr, "Disorientations: Canon without Context in Auden's 'Sonnets from China'," *PMLA* 120/5 (2005), p. 1580.
55. Kerr, "*Journey to a War*: a test for men from Europe'," p. 280.
56. Marsha Bryant, *Auden and Documentary in the 1930s* (Charlottesville and London: University of Virginia Press, 1997), p. 169.
57. Maureen Moynagh, *Political Tourism and its Texts* (Toronto, Buffalo and London: University of Toronto Press, 2008), p. 85.
58. Indeed, Youngs cites this very passage of evidence of Auden and Isherwood's "distance" from the British and "empathy" with the Chinese. "Auden's Travel Writings," p. 77.
59. Boone, "Vacation Cruises," p. 91.
60. Boone, "Vacation Cruises," p. 89.
61. Boone, "Vacation Cruises," pp. 89–92; see also Joseph Massad, *Desiring Arabs* (Chicago: Chicago University Press, 2008), pp. 160–91.
62. Boone, "Vacation Cruises," p. 94.
63. The work of Jasbir Puar on global gay tourism is salient here: see "Global Circuits: Transnational Sexualities and Trinidad," *Signs* 26/4

(2001), pp. 1039–65; and "Circuits of Queer Mobility: Tourism, Travel and Globalization," *GLQ* 8/1–2 (2002), pp. 101–37.
64. Massad, *Desiring Arabs*, p. 191.
65. See David Bergman, "Isherwood and the Violet Quill," in *The Isherwood Century: Essays on the Life and Work of Christopher Isherwood*, ed. James J. Berg and Chris Freeman (Madison and London: University of Wisconsin Press, 2001), pp. 203–16; and Jamie Harker, *Middlebrow Queer: Christopher Isherwood in America* (Minneapolis: University of Minnesota Press, 2013).
66. See, for instance, Jonathan H. Fryer, "Sexuality in Isherwood," *Twentieth Century Literature* 22/3 (1976), p. 348. Auden's and Isherwood's move to the US on the eve of World War II was taken by many to be a defection or flight from the political strife of Europe. In addition to several snide brief notices in daily papers and denunciations in right-wing periodicals such as *Reynolds* and *Action*, the storm of criticism concerning Auden's and Isherwood's apparent desertion included Evelyn Waugh's depiction of the two writers as "Parsnip and Pimpernel" in *Put Out More Flags* (1942); a satirical poem by Anthony Powell, published in the *New Statesman* in February 1940; and – more distressing, as it came from a former ally on the left – an article by Cyril Connolly that Stephen Spender published in *Horizon*, also in February 1940. Connolly's article described Auden and Isherwood as "far-sighted and ambitious young men, with a strong sense of self-preservation, and an eye on the main chance, who have abandoned what they consider to be the sinking ship of European democracy, and by implication the aesthetic doctrine of social realism that has been prevailing there." For a discussion of these attacks, see Peter Parker, *Isherwood: A Life* (London: Macmillan), pp. 455–63; and Patrick Deer, *Culture in Camouflage: War, Empire and Modern British Literature* (Cambridge: Cambridge University Press, 2009), p. 88.
67. See Christopher Isherwood and Edward Upward, *The Mortmere Stories* (London: Enitharmon, 1994).
68. Christopher Isherwood to Edward Upward, 8/6/39, The Edward Upward Papers, The British Library, ADD 72688: 55. Cited as EUP hereafter.
69. Isherwood to Upward, 1947, EUP: ADD 72268: 31.
70. Upward to Isherwood, 1/30/31, CIP: CI 2415.
71. Upward to Isherwood, February 1930, CIP: CI 2401.
72. See Isherwood to Lehmann, 7/18/37, The Beinecke Library, New Haven, Connecticut: GEN MSS 344.

73. See Isherwood to Upward, 3/22/47 and 3/27/47, EUP: ADD 72688: 32, 33.
74. Upward to Isherwood, 2/24/70, CIP: CI 2532.
75. Isherwood to Upward, 12/29/73, EUP: ADD 72688.
76. Christopher Isherwood, *Christopher and His Kind* (Minneapolis: University of Minnesota Press, 2001), p. 1.
77. See, for instance, *Isherwood Century*, p. 277, and *Christopher and His Kind*, p. 48.
78. For a discussion of the emergence of this figure, see Houlbrook, *Queer London*, pp. 194–218.

Chapter 2

1. Gay Wachman, *Lesbian Empire: Radical Crosswriting in the Twenties* (New Brunswick, NJ and London: Rutgers University Press, 2001), pp. 71–102; Janet Montefiore, "Sylvia Townsend Warner and the Biographer's Moral Sense," in *Arguments of Heart and Mind: Selected Essays 1977–2000* (Manchester and New York: Manchester University Press, 2002), pp. 143–64, and *Men and Women Writers of the 1930s: The Dangerous Flood of History* (London and New York: Routledge, 1996), pp. 139–74; *Critical Essays on Sylvia Townsend Warner, English Novelist 1893–1978*, ed. Gill Davies et al. (Lewiston, Queenstown, and Lampeter: Edwin Mellen Press, 2006); Terry Castle, *The Apparitional Lesbian: Female Homosexuality and Modern Culture* (New York: Columbia University Press), pp. 74–91; Heather Love, *Feeling Backward: Loss and the Politics of Queer History* (Cambridge, MA: Harvard University Press), pp.129–45; Melanie Micir, "'Living in two tenses': The intimate Archives of Sylvia Townsend Warner," *Journal of Modern Literature* 36/1 (2012), pp. 191–31; and Maroula Jannou, "Sylvia Townsend Warner in the 1930s," in *A Weapon in the Struggle: The Cultural History of the Communist Party in Britain*, ed. Andy Croft (London: Pluto Books, 1998), pp. 89–105.
2. *The Diaries of Sylvia Townsend Warner*, ed. Claire Harman (London: Virago, 1995; first pub. 1994); Claire Harman, *Sylvia Townsend Warner, A Biography* (London: Chatto and Windus, 1989); *The Letters of Sylvia Townsend Warner*, ed. William Maxwell (New York: Viking, 1982). For a critique of these volumes' omissions, see Arnold Rattenbury, "'Literature, Lying and Sober Truth': Attitudes to the Work of Patrick Hamilton and Sylvia Townsend Warner," in *Writing and*

Radicalism, ed. John Lucas (London and New York: Longman, 1996), pp. 227–30. Rattenbury persuasively argues that Townsend Warner's "red loving heart" was cut out of Maxwell's *Letters*; this critique is confirmed by a series of letters between Maxwell and Rattenbury in Townsend Warner's archive. The Sylvia Townsend Warner Papers, the Dorset County Museum, STW: R(SL)/2/A/177-190. Cited as STW hereafter.

3. Sylvia Townsend Warner to Edgell Rickword, November 10, 1937. STW: QR2.
4. Maxwell (ed.), Preface to *The Letters of Sylvia Townsend Warner*, p. xiv.
5. See Wendy Mulford, *This Narrow Place. Sylvia Townsend Warner and Valentines Ackland: Life, Letters and Politics, 1930–1951* (London: Pandora, 1988), p. 70.
6. See Mulford, *This Narrow Place*, p. 78.
7. V. I. Lenin, *What is to be Done?* in *Essential Works of Lenin*, ed. Henry M. Christman (New York: Dover, 1987), p. 70; emphasis in original English-language text.
8. See Lenin, *What is to be Done?*, pp. 72–92; Katerina Clark, *The Soviet Novel: History as Ritual*, 2nd ed. (Bloomington: Indiana Press, 2000), pp. 15–19; see also Georg Lukács, *Lenin: A Study in the Unity of His Thought*, trans. Nicholas Jacobs (London, New Left Books, 1970), p. 22.
9. Lenin, *The State and Revolution*, in *Essential Works*, p. 288; emphasis in original English-language text.
10. Lukács, *Lenin*, pp. 9–10.
11. See Frantz Fanon, *The Wretched of the Earth*, trans. Richard Philcox (New York: Grove Press, 2001), pp. 63–96.
12. Clark, *The Soviet Novel*, p. 23.
13. Lenin, *State and Revolution*, p. 306.
14. Lukács, *Lenin*, p. 36.
15. V. I. Lenin, letter to Sylvia Pankhurst 8/28/19, in *Lenin on Britain*, 2nd ed. (London, Lawrence and Wishart, 1941), p. 246; emphasis in original.
16. In the course of his polemic against the organizational strategies of economistic determinism, Lenin writes: "The ideal leader, as the majority of the members of such circles pictures him, is something in the nature of a trade union secretary than a Socialist political leader. Any trade union secretary, an English one for instance, helps the workers to conduct the economic struggle, helps to expose factory abuses, explains the injustices of the laws and of measures which

hamper the freedom to strike and the freedom to picket (i.e. to warn all and sundry that a strike is proceeding at a certain factory), explains the partiality of arbitration court judges who belong to the bourgeois classes, etc., etc. In a word, every trade union secretary conducts and helps to conduct 'the economic struggle against the employers and the government.' It cannot be too strongly insisted that *this is not* enough to constitute Social-Democracy." Lenin, *What is to be Done?*, p. 113; see also *Lenin on Britain*, pp. 211–20.
17. Townsend Warner to Julius Lipton, 24/12/35, STW: S (LL)/32.
18. For Townsend Warner's and Ackland's scheme, see Mulford, *This Narrow Place*, p. 67; for a thorough discussion of the Left Book Club, see Kevin Morgan, *Against Fascism and War: Ruptures and Continuities in British Communist Party Politics 1935–41* (Manchester: Manchester University Press, 1989), pp. 254–72.
19. Townsend Warner to Julius Lipton, 12/5/36, STW: S (LL)/32.
20. Mulford, *This Narrow Place*, p. 67.
21. Townsend Warner diary entry, 28/2/35, STW: P(back)/56.
22. Townsend Warner to Julius Lipton, STW: 5/5/35.
23. For discussions of the ways in which Townsend Warner blends the local and the international, see David James, "Capturing the Scale of Fiction at Mid-Century," in *Regional Modernisms*, ed. Neal Alexander and James Moran (Edinburgh: Edinburgh University Press, 2013), pp. 104–23, and "Realism, Late Modernist Abstraction, and Sylvia Townsend Warner's Fictions of Impersonality," *Modernism/Modernity* 12/1 (2005), pp. 111–31. See also Mary Jacobs, "Sylvia Townsend Warner and the Politics of the English Pastoral, 1925–1934," in *Critical Essays*, pp. 62–82.
24. Townsend Warner, "Narrative 6," in *I'll Stand By You: Selected Letters of Sylvia Townsend Warner and Valentine Ackland*, ed. Susan Pinney (London: Pimlico, 1998), p. 123.
25. Ralph Fox, *The Novel and the People* (New York: International Publishers, 1945), pp. 121–9.
26. Eve Kosofksy Sedgwick, *Epistemology of the Closet* (Berkeley, Los Angeles and London: University of California Press, 2008), p. 1.
27. "False consciousness is an undeniable force throughout history. From age to age, serfs have revered their masters, young men have marched gaily off to be slaughtered on behalf of deities and nations, and wives have lovingly obeyed patriarchal husbands. Why should gay people be immune to similar mistakes about their interests?" Michael Warner, *The Trouble With Normal: Sex, Politics, and the Ethics of Queer Life* (Cambridge, MA: Harvard University Press, 2000), p. 105.

28. Lauren Berlant and Michael Warner, "Sex in Public," "Intimacy," special edition, ed. Berlant, *Critical Inquiry* 24 (1998), p. 565; Lauren Berlant, *Cruel Optimism* (Durham, NC: Duke University Press, 2011).
29. José Esteban Muñoz, *Cruising Utopia: The Then and There of Queer Futurity* (New York and London: New York University Press, 2009), p. 28; emphasis in original.
30. See Valerie Solanas, *The SCUM Manifesto* (London and New York: Verso, 2004); and Carl Wittman, *A Gay Manifesto* (San Francisco: Red Butterfly, 1970). With its infamous recommendation of small groups of highly-conscious revolutionary women, Solanas's text is more markedly vanguardist than Wittman's. An afterward to *A Gay Manifesto*, however, by the Red Butterfly group, is more explicitly vanguardist.
31. Muñoz, *Cruising Utopia*, p. 57.
32. Muñoz, *Cruising Utopia*, p. 78.
33. See Edward Upward, *The Spiral Ascent Trilogy* (London: Heinemann, 1977).
34. Townsend Warner to Ackland, 9/30/37, in *I'll Stand By You*, pp. 158–9. While still aiming to edit out some of the more patently Communist material, this collection of letters is much less anti-Communist than Maxwell's, no doubt partly because Townsend Warner's own commentary on the letters makes their political commitment very clear.
35. Townsend Warner to Edgell Rickword, 11/10/37, STW: QR2.
36. Wachman, *Lesbian Empire*, p. 32.
37. Wachman, *Lesbian Empire*, p. 31.
38. *The Diaries of Sylvia Townsend Warner*, p. 69. See also Harman, *Sylvia Townsend Warner*, p. 99.
39. Townsend Warner and Ackland, jointly composed poem, 1938, STW: H(R)/5/10.
40. Janet Montefiore, "Sylvia Townsend Warner and the Biographer's Moral Sense," p. 158.
41. See Deborah Cohler, *Citizen, Invert, Queer: Lesbianism and War in Early Twentieth Century Britain* (Minneapolis: University of Minnesota Press, 2010), pp. 1–31. Cohler underlines that public consciousness of lesbianism was very patchy prior to the 1928 obscenity prosecution of Radclyffe Hall's *The Well of Loneliness* in 1928, and indeed that even after this date female masculinity was not as closely identified with lesbianism as some work in gay and lesbian studies has assumed. Judith (Jack) Halberstam has influentially argued that the category of "lesbian" itself has usually functioned as a back projection of postwar queer identity onto a wide variety of different modes

of gender performance: see *Female Masculinity* (Durham, NC: Duke University Press, 1998), p. 46.
42. Dan Healey, "Homosexual Existence and Existing Socialism: New Light on the Repression of Male Homosexuality in Stalin's Russia," *GLQ* 8/3 (2002), p. 358.
43. Maroula Jannou, "Sylvia Townsend Warner in the 1930s," p. 94.
44. See Jodie Medd, *Lesbian Scandal and the Culture of Modernism* (Cambridge: Cambridge University Press, 2012), pp. 151–91; Laura Doan, *Fashioning Sapphism: The Origins of a Modern English Lesbian Culture* (New York: Columbia University Press, 2001), pp. 64–94; and Halberstam, *Female Masculinity*, pp. 91–5.
45. Healey, "Homosexual Existence," p. 358.
46. For a discussion of the *Great Soviet Encyclopedia* entry, see Dan Healey, *Homosexual Desire in Revolutionary Russia: The Regulation of Sexual and Gender Dissent* (Chicago: University of Chicago Press, 2001), pp. 170–1.
47. Halberstam, *Female Masculinity*, p. 109.
48. Ackland to Julius Lipton, undated letter (c.1935), STW: S (LL)/32; emphasis Ackland's.
49. Halberstam, *Female Masculinity*, p. 99.
50. Lukács, *Lenin*, p. 34.
51. Townsend Warner, Diary Entry, 2/3/1935, STW: P(back)/56.
52. Valentine Ackland, Diary Entries, 5/13/1935, 5/15/1935, STW: T(11)12-13.
53. Patrick Wright, *The Village that Died for England: The Strange Story of Tyneham* (London: Jonathan Cape, 1995), pp. 129–30.
54. This reading is adapted speculatively from Judith (Jack) Halberstam, *The Queer Art of Failure* (Durham, NC: Duke University Press, 2011).
55. Love, *Feeling Backward*, p. 132.
56. See Montefiore, *Men and Women Writers*, pp. 139–74.
57. Love, *Feeling Backward*, p. 131.
58. Love, *Feeling Backward*, pp. 133, 137.
59. Love, *Feeling Backward*, p. 140.
60. Castle, *The Apparitional Lesbian*, pp. 74–91.
61. Sylvia Townsend Warner, *Summer Will Show* (New York: New York Review Books, 2009), p. 224. Page numbers cited parenthetically hereafter.
62. See Clara Zetkin, "Recollections of Lenin" (1925), in V. I. Lenin, *On the Emancipation of Women* (Chippendale, Australia: Resistance Books, 2003), pp. 94–116.
63. One possible contemporary source for this passage might be an article

published in *International Literature* that deals with Marx's "struggle against romanticism." See M. Lifshitz, "Marx and Engels on Esthetics," *International Literature* 1933 2, pp. 78–80.
64. Karl Marx, *The Eighteenth Brumaire of Louis Bonaparte*, in *Marx: Later Political Writings*, ed. Terrell Carver (Cambridge: Cambridge University Press, 1996), p. 78.
65. Marx, *Eighteenth Brumaire*, pp. 77–8.
66. See Daniel Cottom, *International Bohemia: Scenes of Nineteenth-Century Life* (Philadelphia: University of Pennsylvania Press, 2013).
67. Wachman puts the dilemma well: "She [Sophia] cannot escape responsibility for her class position within British imperialism simply because she falls in love and learns her communism in Paris." *Lesbian Empire*, p. 179.
68. Love, *Feeling Backward*, p. 145.
69. STW: uncatalogued. The first two chapters of *The Historical Novel* appeared as "Walter Scott and the Historical Novel," *International Literature*, April 1938, pp. 61–77, and "The Historical Novel Part II," *International Literature*, December 1938, pp. 73–84.
70. See Mulford, *This Narrow Place*, p. 122.
71. Maxwell (ed.), *The Letters of Sylvia Townsend Warner*, p. 39.
72. Friedrich Engels, Letter to Margaret Harkness, April 1888, *International Literature*, July 1934, p. 112.
73. Edward Upward, "A Conversation with Edward Upward," *The Review* 11–12 (1964), p. 66; Maxwell (ed.), *The Letters of Sylvia Townsend Warner*, p. 40.
74. Lukács, "Healthy Art or Sick Art," trans. Arthur Kahn, in *Writer and Critic*, ed. and trans. Arthur Kahn (London: Merlin, 1970), pp. 103–9.
75. Lukács, "The Intellectual Physiognomy of Literary Characters," *International Literature*, August 1936, p. 66.
76. Lukács, "Intellectual Physiognomy," p. 67.
77. Lukács, "Intellectual Physiognomy," p. 78.
78. Halberstam, *Female Masculinity*, p. 217.

Chapter 3

1. Burdekin, *Swastika Night* (New York: The Feminist Press at CUNY, 1985), p. 6. Page numbers cited parenthetically hereafter.
2. Another characteristic 1937 dystopia, Rex Warner's *The Wild Goose Chase*, features an identification of queer sexuality and fascistic governance, a nightmarish vision also to be found in Ruthven Todd's *Over*

The Mountain (1939). Drawing on the figure of the "homosexual storm trooper," Storm Jameson's novel of fascist victory in England, *In the Second Year* (1936), pursues a similar line of attack in a less fantastic register, as does Winifred Holtby's and Norman Ginsbury's 1939 play on the same theme, *Take Back Your Freedom*, which garnered praise from Orwell. Daphne Patai disputes Orwell's reading on the grounds of its (undeniable) misogyny, but the play does have unmistakably homophobic resonances that are not merely Orwell's projections. See *The Orwell Mystique: A Study in Male Ideology* (Amherst: University of Massachusetts Press, 1984), p. 251.

3. Katharine Burdekin, *Swastika Night*; *Proud Man* (New York: The Feminist Press at CUNY, 1993), and *The End of This Day's Business* (New York: The Feminist Press at CUNY, 1989).
4. As Patai puts it her introduction to the 1985 reprinting of *Swastika Night*, Burdekin's novel offers "a resounding critique of the dangers of male supremacy" which "set[s] Burdekin's novel apart from the many other antifascist dystopias produced in the 1930s and 40s" (pp. iv, xiv), a claim that echoes Andy Croft's argument in "Worlds Without End Foisted Upon the Future – Some Antecedents of *Nineteen Eighty-Four*," in *Inside the Myth: Orwell: Views from the Left*, ed. Christopher Norris (London: Lawrence and Wishart, 1984), p. 209. See also Patai, "Orwell's Despair, Burdekin's Hope: Gender and Power in Dystopia," *Women's Studies International Forum* 7/2 (1984), pp. 85–98, *The Orwell Mystique*, pp. 256–63, "Forward" and "Afterword" to *Proud Man*, "Afterword" to *The End of This Day's Business*, "Imagining Reality: The Utopian Fiction of Katharine Burdekin," in *Rediscovering Forgotten Radicals: British Women Writers 1889–1939*, ed. Angela Ingram and Daphne Patai (Chapel Hill: University of North Carolina Press, 1993), pp. 226–43; Kenneth Payne, "Grania, 'a mad woman ... Doomed to attempt the impossible': Imagining Utopia in Katherine [sic] Burdekin's *The End of This Day's Business*," *Lamar Journal of the Humanities*, 30/2 (2005), pp. 33–42; and Loretta Stec, "Dystopian Modernism vs. Utopian Feminism: Burdekin, Woolf, and West Respond to the Rise of Fascism," in *Virginia Woolf and Fascism: Resisting the Dictator's Seduction*, ed. Merry M. Pawlowski (Basingstoke: Palgrave, 2001), pp. 178–93.
5. Elizabeth English, *Lesbian Modernism* (Edinburgh: Edinburgh University Press, 2015), p. 35; emphasis in original.
6. English, *Lesbian Modernism*, p. 49.
7. While English does remark in passing that for Burdekin "male same-

sex desire is often presented as a natural extension of male dominance in its worship of masculinity and denigration of women," she does not probe this problem further, merely noting (of course rightly) that for Burdekin inversion is "by no means synonymous with homosexuality" (*Lesbian Modernism*, p. 51).
8. English, *Lesbian Modernism*, p. 51.
9. Dan Healey, *Homosexual Desire in Revolutionary Russia: The Regulation of Sexual and Gender Dissent* (Chicago: University of Chicago Press, 2001), p. 182.
10. For accounts of the Röhm affair, see Laurie Marhoefer, *Sex and the Weimar Republic: German Homosexual Emancipation and the Rise of the Nazis* (Toronto: University of Toronto Press, 2015), pp. 150–74; and Andrew Wackerfuss, *Stormtrooper Families* (New York and York: Harrington Park Press, 2015), pp. 175–84. See also Healey, *Homosexual Desire*, p. 183; Harry Oosterhuis, "Male Bonding and Homosexuality in German Nationalism," in *Homosexuality and Male Bonding in Pre-Nazi Germany: The Youth Movement, The Gay Movement, and Male Bonding Before Hitler's Rise*, ed. Harry Oosterhuis (New York and London, The Haworth Press, 1991), pp. 251, 261, n. 30; Manfred Herzer, "Communists, Social Democrats, and the Homosexual Movement in the Weimar Republic," in *Gay Men and the Sexual History of the Political Left*, ed. Gert Hekma et al. (New York: Harrington Press, 1995), p. 206.
11. Healey, *Homosexual Desire*, p. 185. The book was entitled *Braunbuch über Reichstagbrand und Hitler-Terror* (Basel: Universum-Bücherei, 1933).
12. Harry Whyte, "Can a Homosexual Be a Member of the Communist Party?" (1934), reprinted in Evgeniy Fiks, *Moscow* (Brooklyn: Ugly Duckling Presse, 2012), no pagination.
13. Healey, *Homosexual Desire*, pp. 188–90.
14. See James W. Jones "'Gegenwartsbewältung': The Male Homosexual Character in Selected Works about the Fascist Experience," in *Der Zweite Weltkrieg and die Exilanten: Eine Literarische Antwort*, ed. Helmut F. Pfanner (Bonn and Berlin: Bouvier Verlag, 1991), pp. 303–11.
15. See Andrew Hewitt, *Political Inversions: Homosexuality, Fascism, and the Modernist Imaginary* (Stanford, CA: Stanford University Press, 1996), pp. 79–129; Oosterhuis, "Male Bonding"; and Judith (Jack) Halberstam, *The Queer Art of Failure* (Durham, NC: Duke University Press, 2011), pp. 155–7.
16. George S. Mosse, *Nationalism and Sexuality: Respectability and*

Abnormal Sexuality in Modern Europe (New York: Howard Fertig, 1985), p. 42. See also Marhoefer, *Sex and the Weimar Republic*, pp. 151–4.

17. See Healey, *Homosexual Desire*, p. 329, n. 11; Harry Oosterhuis, "The 'Jews' of the Antifascist Left," *Journal of Homosexuality* 29/2–3 (1995), pp. 237–45, and "Medicine, Male Bonding and Homosexuality in Nazi Germany," *Journal of Contemporary History* 2 (1997), pp. 187–205.
18. Halberstam, *Queer Art*, pp. 147–72.
19. Geoffrey J. Giles, "Same-Sex Incidents in Himmler's SS and Police," *Journal of the History of Sexuality* 11/1–2 (January–April 2002), p. 259.
20. Wackerfuss, *Stormtrooper Families*, p. 174.
21. Halberstam, *Queer Art*, p. 155.
22. See William Ostrem, "The Dog Beneath the Schoolboy's Skin," in *The Isherwood Century: Essays on the Life and Work of Christopher Isherwood*, ed. James J. Berg and Chris Freeman (Madison and London: University of Wisconsin Press, 2001), pp. 162–71.
23. Spurlin, *Lost Intimacies: Rethinking Homosexuality Under National Socialism* (New York: Peter Lang, 2009), p. 73.
24. Andrew Hewitt, "Sleeping with the Enemy: Genet and the Fantasy of Homo-Fascism," in *Gender and Fascism in Modern France*, ed. Melanie Hawthorne and Richard J. Goslan (Hanover and London: University Press of New England), p. 119. See also Susan Sontag, "Fascinating Fascism" (1974) in *Under the Sign of Saturn* (London: Writers and Readers Publishing Cooperative Society, 1983), pp. 73–108. For a critique of Sontag's essay, see David Forgacs, "Days of Sodom: The Fascism-Perversion Equation in Films of the 1960s and 1970s," in *Italian Fascism: History Memory and Representation*, ed. R. J. B. Bosworth and Patrizia Dogliani (Basingstoke: Macmillan, 1999), pp. 217–36.
25. Laura Frost's study of the erotics of fascism in literary modernism is an important reference point here, but she does not address the anti-homosexual discourse of Popular Front antifascism in any detail. See Frost, *Sex Drives: Fantasies of Fascism in Literary Modernism* (Ithaca: Cornell University Press, 2002).
26. Ralph Fox, *The Novel and the People* (New York: International Publishers, 1945), p. 122. Dimitrov, by contrast, is characterized not only by his steadfast Communism, but also his sanity and love for his wife, who died during the trial (p. 125).
27. George [sic] Dimitrov, "Revolutionary Literature in the Struggle

Against Fascism" (Speech at an Antifascist Meeting at the Moscow Writers' House), *International Literature*, April 1935, p. 55.
28. Ben Harker, "'Communism is English': Edgell Rickword, Jack Lindsay, and the Cultural Politics of the Popular Front," *Literature and History* 20/2 (2011); and Glyn Salton-Cox, "Syncretic Utopia, Transnational Provincialism: Rex Warner's *The Wild Goose Chase*," in *Utopia, Modernism and Literature in the Twentieth Century*, ed. Nathan Waddell and Alice Reeve-Tucker (Basingstoke: Palgrave Macmillan, 2013).
29. Rex Warner, *The Wild Goose Chase* (London: Merlin, 1990), p. 90.
30. Warner, *Wild Goose Chase*, p. 93.
31. Warner, *Wild Goose Chase*, p. 94.
32. See James Jones, "Male Homosexual Character," pp. 303–4.
33. Vera Brittain, "Introduction" to Winifred Holtby and Norman Ginsbury, *Take Back Your Freedom* (London: Jonathan Cape, 1939), p. 7.
34. Richard Lawrence, "Dick" to Arnold Clayton, not only recalls the male member, but also T. E. Lawrence (an important queer icon between the wars), and D. H. Lawrence.
35. *Take Back Your Freedom*, p. 86.
36. *Take Back Your Freedom*, p. 90.
37. Spurlin, *Lost Intimacies*, p. 69. The passage Spurlin is discussing can be found in Theodor Adorno, *Minima Moralia: Reflections from Damaged Life*, trans. E. F. N. Jephcott (London and New York: Verso, 2005), Section 24 "Tough baby," pp. 49–50. In this passage Adorno sets up the equation "totalitarianism and homosexuality belong together" not only in relation to the hard-boiled American film star, but also with the observation that "in Oxford two sorts of student are distinguished, the tough guys and the intellectuals" (p. 50). Hewitt argues suggestively that, "the symptomatic [. . .] reading of homosexuality in the Frankfurt School's classic analyses of fascism and late capitalism itself constitutes a pathological compensation for the steering crisis in their own overarching theory" (*Political Inversions*, p. 41).
38. Holtby, *Take Back Your Freedom*, p. 43.
39. Holtby, *Take Back Your Freedom*, p. 7.
40. Spurlin, *Lost Intimacies*, p. 73.
41. Adorno, *Minima Moralia*, pp. 49–50.
42. Jed Esty, *A Shrinking Island: Modernism and National Culture in England* (Princeton: Princeton University Press, 2004), pp. 10–11, *inter alia*.
43. Sedgwick scathingly describes this critique as "a currently respectable

homophobic feminist-theory fantasy." *Tendencies* (Durham, NC: Duke University Press, 1993), p. 49; also cited in Hewitt, *Political Inversions*, p. 2. For an extended critique of the feminist identification of fascism and phallic masculinity, see Spurlin, *Lost Intimacies*, pp. 65–84.

44. "Publisher's Note" to *Swastika Night*, 2nd ed. (London: Victor Gollancz, 1940); no pagination; emphasis in original.
45. Katharine Burdekin, *No Compromise* (c. 1934–6), p. 62. Unpublished MS, the Katharine Burdekin Papers, NYC. Page numbers cited parenthetically hereafter.
46. For a characteristic leftist homophobic depiction of the bourgeois homosexual aesthete see Mike Gold, "Wilder: Prophet of the Genteel Christ" (1930), in *Mike Gold: A Literary Anthology* (New York: International Publishers, 1972), pp. 197–202.
47. Burdekin, *Proud Man*, pp.17–18, 88–9, *inter alia*.

Chapter 4

1. *The Lion and The Unicorn: Socialism and the English Genius* (1941), in *Complete Works XIII: A Patriot After All* (London: Secker and Warburg, 2001), p. 401. References drawn from the *Complete Works* are cited hereafter *CW*; novels from *Complete Novels* (London: Penguin, 2000) as *CN*.
2. See *CW XX*, p. 226, and *CW XVII*, p. 114.
3. Stefan Collini, *Absent Minds: Intellectuals in Britain* (Oxford: Oxford University Press, 2005), p. 360.
4. Feminist critiques of Orwell have noted Orwell's opposition to birth control, but have not dwelt extensively on its implications. See Daphne Patai, *The Orwell Mystique: A Study in Male Ideology* (Amherst: University of Massachusetts Press, 1984), pp. 90–1, and Deidre Beddoes, "Hindrances and Help-Meets," in *Inside the Myth: Orwell: Views from the Left*, ed. Christopher Norris (London: Lawrence and Wishart, 1984), p. 150. John Rodden glibly defends Orwell's philoprogenitivism from these critiques: see *The Politics of Literary Reputation: The Making and Claiming of 'St. George' Orwell* (New York and Oxford: Oxford University Press, 1989), pp. 220–1.
5. *The English People*, *CW XVII*, p. 223.
6. Michel Foucault, *Security, Territory, Population: Lectures at the Collège de France, 1977–78*, trans. Graham Burchall (Basingstoke: Palgrave Macmillan, 2007).

7. See, for instance, Arthur Koestler, "Obituary: George Orwell," *The Observer*, January 29, 1950, in *George Orwell: The Critical Heritage*, ed. Jeffrey Meyers (London: Routledge, 1975), p. 296; and V. S. Pritchett, "Obituary: George Orwell," *New Statesman and Nation*, January 28, 1950, in Myers, *Critical Heritage*, p. 294. See also George Woodcock's 1966 study, *The Crystal Spirit: A Study of George Orwell* (London: Jonathan Cape, 1966); Alex Zwerdling, *Orwell and the Left* (New Haven and London: Yale University Press, 1974); Lionel Trilling, "George Orwell and the Politics of Truth" (1952), in *The Moral Obligation to Be Intelligent: Selected Essays*, ed. Leon Wieseltier (Northwestern University Press, 2008), pp. 259–74; Christopher Hitchens, *Why Orwell Matters* (New York: Pluto, 2002), and *Orwell's Victory* (London: Penguin, 2003). These are merely some salient examples: for an extended discussion of the huge body of hagiographic work on Orwell see Scott Lucas's critiques, *The Betrayal of Dissent: Orwell, Hitchens, and the New American Century* (London: Pluto Press, 2004), and *Orwell* (London: Haus Publishing, 2003); and the less critical (at points itself hagiographic) but detailed work of John Rodden on Orwell's reception, including *Politics of Literary Reputation*, *The Unexamined Orwell* (Austin: University of Texas Press, 2012), and *Every Intellectual's Big Brother: George Orwell's Literary Siblings* (Austin: University of Texas Press, 2006).
8. Kristen Bluemel, *George Orwell and the Radical Eccentrics: Intermodernism in Literary London* (London: Palgrave Macmillan, 2004). Bluemel sets out with the stated intention of "demythologizing" Orwell, but her study's use of him as a "charismatic figurehead" (p. 2) actually has precisely the opposite effect.
9. See Christopher Hitchens's attacks on Raymond Williams in *Why Orwell Matters*, pp. 35–78, and *Unacknowledged Legislation: Writers in the Public Sphere* (London: Verso, 2003), p. 38. For a critique of Hitchens's polemics, see Lucas, *The Betrayal of Dissent*, pp. 50–2. See also John Newsinger, *Orwell's Politics* (London: Macmillan, 1999), pp. 123–4.
10. Christopher Norris, "Language, Truth and Ideology: Orwell and the Post-war Left," in *Inside the Myth*, p. 242; Alex Woloch, *Or Orwell: Orwell and Democratic Socialism* (Cambridge, MA: Harvard University Press, 2016). For a critique of Woloch's study, see Glyn Salton-Cox, "Or Not So Well," *The Los Angeles Review of Books*, September 19, 2016 <https://lareviewofbooks.org/article/or-not-so-well/>.
11. Daphne Patai, *The Orwell Mystique*. For pushback against Patai,

see Erika Gottlieb, "Review of *The Orwell Mystique*," *Dalhoisie Review* 64/4 (1984–1985), pp. 807–11; and Arthur Eckstein, "Orwell, Masculinity, and Feminist Criticism," *The Intercollegiate Review* 21/1 (1965), pp. 46–54. Patai later disowned her polemic, part of her new purge of "academic feminism" and "postmodern rhetoric": see her "Third Thoughts about Orwell" in *Orwell: Into the Twenty-First Century*, ed. Thomas Cushman and John Rodden (London: Routledge, 2016; first pub. 2004), pp. 200–14.

12. See, for instance, Janet Montefiore, *Men and Women Writers of the 1930s: The Dangerous Flood of History* (London and New York: Routledge, 1996), pp. 27–8, 51.
13. See Raymond Williams, *Orwell* (London: Fontana, 1991), p. 64, and "Orwell" in *Politics and Letters: Interviews with the New Left Review* (London: New Left Books, 1979), p. 385.
14. Ben Clark captures some of this dynamic – albeit at times in somewhat star-struck tones – in his *Orwell in Context: Communities, Myths, Values* (London: Palgrave Macmillan, 2007), particularly p. 173.
15. *The Lion and The Unicorn*, CW XII, pp. 408, 415.
16. The phrase is taken from the title of Hitchens's polemic. For postwar homophobia, see Alan Sinfield, *Literature, Politics and Culture in Postwar Britain* (London: Continuum, 2004); Richard Hornsey, *The Spiv and the Architect: Unruly Life in Postwar London* (Minneapolis: University of Minnesota Press, 2010); and Matt Houlbrook, *Queer London: Pleasures and Perils in the Sexual Metropolis 1918–1957* (Chicago: University of Chicago Press, 2005). For the sexist pronatalism of wartime and postwar gender politics, see, *inter alia*, Denise Riley, "Some Peculiarities of Social Policy Concerning Women in Wartime and Postwar Britain," *Behind The Lines: Gender and the Two World Wars*, ed. Margaret Randolph Higonnet et al. (New Haven: Yale University Press, 1987), pp. 260–71.
17. Owen Hatherley, *The Ministry of Nostalgia* (London: Verso, 2017), p. 122.
18. Hornsey, *Spiv and the Architect*, p.16.
19. George Orwell, *The Road to Wigan Pier* (1937), in *Orwell's England*, ed. Peter Davison (London: Penguin, 2001), p. 136.
20. This striking convergence is probed at length by Philip Bounds in *Orwell and Marxism: The Political and Cultural Thinking of George Orwell* (London: I B Tauris, 2009).
21. There is a huge secondary literature on Orwell, the state, and *Nineteen Eighty-Four* which is impossible to adequately summarize here. To my mind, Stuart Hall's analysis of Orwell's contradictory relation to the

state remains the most lucid overview: see his "Conjuring Leviathan: Orwell on the State," in *Inside the Myth*, pp. 217–41.
22. *CN*, pp. 580, 589, 707.
23. Terry Eagleton, *Exiles and Émigrés: Studies in Modern Literature* (Chatto and Windus: London, 1970); Rita Felski, "Nothing to Share: Identity, Shame, and the Lower Middle Class," in "Rereading Class," ed. Cora Kaplan, special issue, *PMLA* 115/1 (2000), pp. 33–45.
24. *CW XVI*, p. 356. Unmentioned in the index, Orwell also uses the adjective "Freudian" in his famous essay "My Country Right or Left" (1940) to describe his own conversion to patriotism: see *CW XII*, p. 271.
25. Loraine Saunders, *The Unsung Artistry of George Orwell* (Aldershot: Ashgate, 2008), p. 4; Christopher Hitchens, *Orwell's Victory*, p. 164.
26. Even Felski ignores this aspect in writing that Gordon's "conversion" to lower-middle-class values at the novel's close is "largely unmotivated and singularly unconvincing" ("Nothing to Share," p. 36). Less surprisingly perhaps, Eagleton is also silent on the issue of birth control in the novel.
27. See *Orwell's England*, ed. Peter Davison (London: Penguin, 2001), pp. 185–202; see also, *inter alia*, Review of *The Natural Order: Essays on the Return to Husbandry*, ed. H. J. Massingham, *Manchester Evening News*, January 25, 1945, in *CW XVII*, pp. 27–9.
28. Orwell, *Road to Wigan Pier*, p. 115.
29. Nick Hubble, "Looking Back on the 1930s Without Being Anti-Communist: Cornford, Orwell, Spender, Sommerfield," special edition on Anti-Communism, ed. Benjamin Kohlmann and Matthew Taunton, *Literature and History* 24/2 (2015), p. 65.
30. See also *Coming Up For Air* (1939), *CN*, pp. 515; Letter to Geoffrey Gorer, September 15, 1937, *CW XI*, p. 81; Review of *The Problem of the Distressed Areas* by Wal Hannington, *Grey Children* by James Hanley, and *The Fight for the Charter* by Neil Stewart, *Time and Tide*, November 27, 1937, *CW XI*, p. 99; Review of *Workers' Front* by Fenner Brockway, *New English Weekly*, February 17, 1938, *CW XI*, pp. 123–4; Letter to the Editor, *New English Weekly*, May 26, 1938, *CW XI*, p. 153; Letter to Yvonne Davet, August 18, 1938, *CW XI*, p. 189; Review of *The Communist International* by Franz Borkenau, *New English Weekly*, September 22, 1938, *CW XI*, p. 203; "Political Reflections on the Crisis," *The Adelphi*, December 1938, *CW XI*, pp. 242–3; Letter to Jack Common, December 26, 1938, *CW XI*, p. 260; Letter to Herbert Read, January 4, 1939, in *CW XI*, p. 313; "Caesarean Section in Spain," *The Highway*, March 1939, *CW XI*, p. 332.

31. *Orwell's England*, p. 216.
32. For a discussion of *Left Review*, see Christopher Hilliard, "Producers by Hand and by Brain: Working-Class Writers and Left-Wing Publishers in 1930s Britain," *The Journal of Modern History* 78 (2006); Peter Marks, "Art and Politics in the 1930s: *The European Quarterly* (1934–5), *Left Review* (1934–8), and *Poetry of the People* (1938–40)," in *The Oxford Critical History of Modernist Magazines, Vol. I*, ed. Peter Brooker and Andrew Thacker (Oxford, Oxford University Press, 2009), pp. 623–46, and "Illusion and Reality: The Spectre of Socialist Realism in Thirties Literature," in *Rewriting the Thirties*, pp. 23–36. For an overview of the English-language edition of *International Literature* see Glyn Salton-Cox, "'Polemics Pertinent at the Time of Publication': Georg Lukács, *International Literature*, and the Popular Front," in Ben Harker, ed., "Communism and the Written Word," special edition of *Twentieth Century Communism* 12 (2017), pp. 143–69.
33. Orwell, *Road to Wigan Pier*, pp. 171–2.
34. Bounds, *Orwell and Marxism*. See also Ben Harker, "'Communism is English': Edgell Rickword, Jack Lindsay, and the Cultural Politics of the Popular Front," *Literature and History* 20/2 (2011); and John Connor, "Jack Lindsay, Socialist Humanism and the Communist Historical Novel," *The Review of English Studies* 66/274 (2014), pp. 324–63.
35. Glyn Salton-Cox, "Syncretic Utopia, Transnational Provincialism: Rex Warner's *The Wild Goose Chase*," in *Utopia, Modernism and Literature in the Twentieth Century*, ed. Nathan Waddell and Alice Reeve-Tucker (Basingstoke: Palgrave Macmillan, 2013).
36. George Orwell, *Homage to Catalonia* in *Orwell in Spain*, ed. Peter Davison (London: Penguin, 2001), p. 167.
37. Orwell, *Homage to Catalonia*, p. 169.
38. See Benedict Anderson, *Imagined Communities: Reflections on the Origin and Spread of Nationalism*, 2nd ed. (London: Verso, 2006), pp. 195–6.
39. Patrick Wright, *On Living in an Old Country* (London: Verso, 1985), pp. 81–7; Angus Calder, *The Myth of the Blitz* (London: Jonathan Cape, 1991), pp. 180–208.
40. Hall, "Conjuring Leviathan," p. 218.
41. Collini, *Absent Minds*, p. 395.
42. For a discussion of Winteringham's advocacy of a "People's War," see Tom Buchanan, *The Impact of the Spanish Civil War on Britain: War, Loss and Memory* (Eastbourne: Sussex University Press, 2007), pp. 181–2.

43. See list, *CW XII*, p. 189.
44. See Houlbrook, *Queer London*, p. 95.
45. *The Lion and the Unicorn*, *CW XII*, p. 407; Collini, *Absent Minds*, p. 360.
46. "Don't Let Colonel Blimp," *CW XII*, p. 364.
47. See James Burnham, *The Managerial Revolution: What is Happening in the World* (New York: John Day, 1941). For Orwell's critiques, see, *inter alia*, "As I Please," *Tribune*, January 14, 1944, *CW XVI*, pp. 60–4; "Review of *The Machiavellians* by James Burnham," *Manchester Evening News*, January 20, 1944, *CWXVI*, pp. 72–4; and "Second Thoughts on James Burnham" (1946), *CW XVIII*, pp. 268–84. For a useful overview of Orwell's often contradictory relationship with Burnham, see William Steinhoff, *George Orwell and the Origins of 1984* (Ann Arbor: University of Michigan Press, 175), pp. 43–54.
48. *Proud City* (1945), dir. Ralph Keene (London: Greenpark Productions, 1945). For a discussion of Abercrombie as "master planner" and his role in the film, see John R. Gold and Steven V. Ward, "Of Plans and Planners: Documentary Film and the Challenge of the Urban Future," in *The Cinematic City*, ed. David Clark (London: Routledge, 2005), p. 7.
49. Hornsey, *Spiv and the Architect*, p. 14.
50. See Hall, "Conjuring Leviathan," pp. 223–4.
51. See Croft, "Worlds Without End Foisted Upon the Future – Some Antecedents of *Nineteen Eighty-Four*," in *Inside the Myth*, pp. 183–216; and Daphne Patai, "Orwell's Despair, Burdekin's Hope: Gender and Power in Dystopia," *Women's Studies International Forum* 7/2 (1984), pp. 85–96 and *The Orwell Mystique*, pp. 256–63.
52. Judith (Jack) Halberstam, *Female Masculinity* (Durham, NC: Duke University Press, 1998), p. 99.
53. See, *inter alia*, Montefiore, *Men and Woman Writers*, pp. 50–1. Montefiore draws on Raynor Heppanstall's account of Orwell's "crush" on him which apparently manifested itself in violent abuse.
54. Robert Graves, *Goodbye to All That* (London: Cassell, 1957), p. 221.
55. Laura Frost, *Sex Drives: Fantasies of Fascism in Literary Modernism* (Ithaca: Cornell University Press, 2002), p. 28.

Coda

1. W. H. Auden, "September 1, 1939," in *W. H. Auden: Selected Poems*, p. 95.
2. Auden, "September 1, 1939," p. 96.
3. For a discussion of these attacks, see Chapter 1, note 66.
4. W. H. Auden, 1939 Journal, The W. H. Auden Papers, The British Library, ADD MS 89035: 1939. Auden lays out a fourteen-point plan for a future socialist democracy, in which "state must own all land and real estate" and tenants would pay their rent as taxation, but agriculture would not be collectivized. Auden also insists that the "right to discharge an employee must be taken out of the hands of the management"; he also makes further suggestions such as the installation of voting machines in every household, and a radio station devoted to politics that would broadcast all parliamentary debates.
5. Richard Bozorth, *Auden's Games of Knowledge: Poetry and the Meanings of Homosexuality* (New York: Columbia University Press, 2001), p. 16.
6. Auden, 1939 Journal, ADD MS 89035: 1939.
7. Auden, "September 1, 1939," p. 96.
8. Bozorth, *Auden's Games*, p. 24.
9. Matt Houlbrook, *Queer London: Pleasures and Perils in the Sexual Metropolis 1918–1957* (Chicago: University of Chicago Press, 2005), p. 256.
10. See Peter Wildeblood, *Against the Law* (New York: Julian Messner, 1959); for a critique of the memoir, see Alan Sinfield, *Literature, Politics and Culture in Postwar Britain* (London: Continuum, 2004), pp. 64–5. Sinfield argues that Wildeblood's condemnation of male femininity is "thoroughly self-oppressed."
11. Daniel Hurewitz, *Bohemian Los Angeles and the Making of Modern Politics* (Berkeley, Los Angeles, and London: University of California Press, 2007), particularly pp. 231–68.
12. See Elizabeth Freeman, *Time Binds: Queer Temporalities, Queer Histories* (Durham, NC and London: Duke University Press, 2010).
13. This reading has been resisted by Melanie Micir, who contends instead that Townsend Warner's late work is deeply invested in queer futurity through her practice of the intimate archive. See Micir, "'Living in two tenses': The intimate Archives of Sylvia Townsend Warner," *Journal of Modern Literature* 36/1 (2012).

14. See Claire Harman, *Sylvia Townsend Warner, A Biography* (London: Chatto and Windus, 1989), p. 273.
15. See the interview "A Conversation with Sylvia Townsend Warner," *PN Review* 23 8/3 (1981), p. 35, where she continues to praise Georgi Dimitrov.
16. The concept is Benjamin's; for an influential account, see Wendy Brown, "Resisting Melancholia," *boundary 2*, 26/3 (1999), pp. 19–27; see also Enzo Traverso, *Left-Wing Melancholia: Marxism, History, and Memory* (New York: Columbia University Press, 2016). For an application of the concept to the work of Edward Upward, see Joseph Elkanah Rosenberg, "Edward Upward's Remains," in *Edward Upward and Left-Wing Literary Culture in Britain*, ed. Benjamin Kohlmann (London and New York: Routledge, 2013), pp. 173–88.
17. Sylvia Townsend Warner, "A Love Match," in *Selected Stories of Sylvia Townsend Warner*, ed. Susanna Pinney and William Maxwell (London: Viking, 1988), p. 9. Page numbers cited parenthetically hereafter.
18. Townsend Warner to David Garnett, 10/23/67 in *Sylvia and David: The Townsend Warner/Garner Letters*, ed. Richard Garnett (London: Sinclair-Stevenson, 1994), p. 127; also cited in Micir, "'Living in Two Tenses'," p. 126.
19. Sinfield, *Literature, Politics and Culture*, p. 66.
20. Sinfield, *Literature, Politics and Culture*, p. 69.
21. See *Letters Between Forster and Isherwood on Homosexuality and Literature*, ed. Richard E. Zeikowitz (Basingstoke: Palgrave Macmillan, 2008), particularly pp. 74–5 and 15–152.
22. Jonathan H. Fryer, "Sexuality in Isherwood," *Twentieth Century Literature* 22/3 (1976), p. 348.
23. Isherwood, *A Single Man* (1964) in *Where Joy Resides: An Isherwood Reader*, ed. Don Bachardy and James P. White (London: Methuen, 1989), p. 415.
24. Jamie Harker charts this relationship throughout *Middlebrow Queer: Christopher Isherwood in America* (Minneapolis: University of Minnesota Press, 2013).
25. Interview with Clifford Solway, *The Tamarack Review*, Spring 1966 (originally filmed for the Canadian Broadcasting Network, May 30, 1965), p. 25; emphasis in original.
26. Christopher Isherwood, *Christopher and His Kind* (Minneapolis: University of Minnesota Press, 2001), p. 212.
27. Isherwood, *Christopher and His Kind*, p. 339.
28. The phrase most prominently appears as the title of Shulamith

Firestone's 1970 polemic *The Dialectic of Sex: The Case for Feminist Revolution* (London: Farrar, Straus and Giroux, 2003).
29. John Lehmann, *I Am My Brother: Autobiography II* (London: Longman, 1960), p. 313.
30. Sinfield, *Literature, Politics and Culture*, p. 67.
31. Isherwood to Lehmann, 7/18/36, The Beinecke Library, New Haven, Connecticut: GEN MSS 344.
32. John Lehmann, *In the Purely Pagan Sense* (London: Gay Modern Classics, 1989), p. 191. Page numbers cited parenthetically hereafter.
33. Bond was always rather queer given his genesis in Somerset Maugham's Ashenden, who is not explicitly homosexual but an intriguing, glamorous epicure with a distinct eye for male beauty. See Somerset Maugham, *Ashenden* (London: Vintage, 2000; first pub. 1928), particularly Ashenden's transfixed gaze upon a Mexican fellow agent's "feline elegance" that he feels with "a secret, shameful fascination" (p. 103).
34. Michel Foucault, *History of Sexuality Vol. 1: An Introduction*, trans. Graham Burchill (New York: Vintage, 1990), p. 39.
35. Leo Bersani, *Is The Rectum a Grave? And Other Essays* (Chicago: University of Chicago Press, 2010).
36. Karl Marx, *The Poverty of Philosophy* in *Karl Marx: Selected Writings*, ed. David McLellan (Oxford: Oxford University Press, 2000), p. 227.

Index

Ackland, Valentine
  book-lending scheme, 83
  commitment, 25, 85, 89–90
  Country Dealings, 78
  CPGB, 91–2, 178
  female masculinity, 14, 90, 93–4, 169; *see also* Halberstam, Jack
  journalism, 78
  Pollitt, 82; *see also* Pollitt, Harry
  rurality, 13, 37, 106
  Spanish Civil War, 33
  unpublished diaries, 94–5
  vanguardism, 14, 79, 180
Adorno, Theodor, 12
  homo-fascism, 120, 124, 128, 217n
Anderson, Perry, 4, 19
antihumanism, 13, 45, 50, 51, 55, 58, 67, 71, 75, 184
Auden, W. H.
  anti-Communist attacks, 7
  Bloomsbury, 14–16, 183
  Brecht, 9
  collaboration with Isherwood, 20, 46, 64–72, 73; *see also* Isherwood, Christopher
  fascism, 119
  fellow traveler, 4–5, 178
  Journey to a War, 64–72
  Look, Stranger!, 21
  move to the US, 173, 177, 207n
  The Orators, 16
  respectable homosexuality, 41, 76, 174–6
  "September 1, 1939," 174–6
  unpublished diaries, 174, n224
  Weimar Berlin, 18

Balzac, Honoré de, 11, 50, 57, 59, 108, 109, 203–4n
Beauman, Ned, 44
Benjamin, Walter, 96, 202–3n
Berlant, Lauren, 8, 26–7, 86–7, 139
Bersani, Leo, 43, 188
Beveridge Report, 143, 165
Bloomsbury Group, 14–15, 24–6
Bluemel, Kristen, 141
Blüher, Hans, 118
Boone, Joseph, 70
Bounds, Philip, 38, 152, 154
Brand, Adolf, 118
Brecht, Bertolt, 9, 20, 46, 47, 48
Britten, Benjamin, 20
Burdekin, Katharine, 113–39
  celibacy, 138
  Communism, 4, 133, 135
  heterosexuality, 129–33
  homo-fascism, 36, 125–9
  homophobia, 20, 31–2, 126, 131, 132
  nationalism, 31, 31–2, 129–32
  No Compromise, 32, 115–16, 132–9
  Popular Front, 26, 135, 139; *see also* Popular Front
  post-gender, 138
  Swastika Night, 20, 113, 115, 125–32
  transformative normalcy, 129–32
Burnham, James, 163
Butler, Judith, 6, 141

Carpenter, Edward, 60, 115, 116
Carr, Jamie, 45
Castle, Terry, 91, 96–8
cell, 15, 21–3, 63, 88, 103, 176–7
Clark, Katerina, 47, 48, 81

Collini, Stefan, 140, 159, 160
Communist International (Comintern), 6, 16, 27, 28, 31, 46
Communist Party of Great Britain (CPGB)
  influence, 6, 22
  Orwell, 144, 154
  patriotism, 154
  publications, 81–2, 191n
  Spender, 4, 33, 77
  Townsend Warner and Ackland, 3–4, 5, 77–8, 82–3, 85, 90–2
  Upward, 74
Connolly, Cyril, 156, 207n
Cooper, Davina, 8, 20
coteries, 14–15, 16–17
counterpublics, 15, 18–21, 75, 89, 106, 183; see also Warner, Michael
Cripps, Stafford, 19
Croft, Andy, 114, 169
Cunningham, Valentine, 16–17

Denning, Michael, 5, 37
Dimitrov, Georgi, 28, 29, 85, 120–1, 130, 153, 198n
Döblin, Alfred, 61, 64, 204–5n
Doone, Rupert, 20
Dos Passos, John, 45

Eagleton, Terry, 145
Edelman, Lee, 43, 40, 152
Engels, Friedrich, 99, 100
  Britain, 81
  The Communist Manifesto, 1
  lumpenproletariat, 103, 204n
  On the Origin of the Family, Private Property, and the State, 1
  realism, 109
  typicality, 13, 108
English, Elizabeth, 115, 138
Esslin, Martin, 46
Esty, Jed, 10, 11
  redemptive Anglocentrisms, 9, 29, 130

factography, 12, 48–9, 50, 55, 56, 184; see also Tretiakov, Sergei
Fanon, Frantz, 81
Feigel, Lara, 45
Felski, Rita, 145
Floyd, Kevin, 7–8, 12, 54–5, 57
Forster, E. M., 14, 16, 39, 40
  Isherwood, 73, 183, 186
  Maurice, 110, 183

Foucault, Michel
  The Courage of Truth, 2–3, 22, 31, 61–2
  The History of Sexuality, Vol. 1, 187
  Security, Territory, Population, 141
Fox, Ralph, *The Novel and the People*, 29–30, 74, 85, 121
Freeman, Elizabeth, 43, 178
Freudianism, 145, 147
Frost, Laura, 172

Gibarti, Louis, 46
Gide, André, 26, 74, 110
Gilroy, Paul, 30
Ginsbury, Norman, 123
Gladkov, Fyodor, *Cement*, 23–4, 74
Gollancz, Victor, 19
Greene, Graham, 114
Group Theatre, 20–1

Halberstam, Jack, 14, 43, 93, 94, 110, 118–20, 169, 211–12n
Hall, Stuart, 157, 167
Hamilton, Patrick, 11, 114
Harker, Ben, 9
Harman, Claire, 76, 84, 96
Healey, Dan, 23, 24, 26, 55, 91, 92, 117
Heartfield, John, 47, 85, 121
Hemingway, Ernest, 33–4, 35
Hewitt, Andrew, 118, 119, 120, 128
Hill, Christopher, 29
Hilliard, Christopher, 17
Hirschfeld, Magnus, 18, 41, 46, 61, 64, 93, 118
Hobsbawm, Eric, 193n
Holtby, Winifred, 113, 152
  Take Back Your Freedom, 123–5, 161
Home Guard, 28, 159, 160
Hornsey, Richard, 24, 143, 166, 176
Houlbrook, Matt, 41, 59, 176
Hubble, Nick, 38, 152, 154
humanism, 12, 49, 50, 54, 55, 67, 112, 117, 121
Hurewitz, Daniel, 176
Huxley, Aldous, 150
Hyndman, Tony, 32–3
Hynes, Samuel, 8

International Literature, 12, 48, 49, 107, 108, 109, 121, 153

Index

Isherwood, Christopher, 44–76
  The Berlin Stories, 12–13, 44–5, 50–64
  Bloomsbury, 14, 16
  Brecht, 9
  camera-I, 44–5, 50–6
  Christopher and His Kind, 42, 46, 47, 73–5, 177, 184–5
  class-crossing queer intimacies, 17–18, 59–64
  collaboration with Auden, 9, 20, 65–72; *see also* Auden, W. H.
  Communism, 4, 5, 7, 45–6
  Journey to a War, 47, 65–72
  Lehmann, 17–18, 75; *see also* Lehmann, John
  Lukács, 13, 56–9; *see also* Lukács, Georg
  lumpenproletariat, 61–2
  move to the US, 207n
  Münzenberg, 46; *see also* Münzenberg, Willi
  Orientalism, 68–72
  realism, 11, 56–9
  respectable homosexuality, 41–2, 183–6
  A Single Man, 73, 183–4
  Tretiakov, 12–13, 46–7, 50–9, 75; *see also* Tretiakov, Sergei
  Upward, 8, 73–4
  Weimar Berlin, 18, 45–64, 115

Jameson, Fredric, 11, 12, 141
Jameson, Storm, 113
Jannou, Marolua, 92
Jennings, Humphrey, 39
Joseph, Miranda, 30
Joyce, James, 47, 48, 59, 123

Kant, Immanuel, 54, 106
Kermode, Frank, 60
Kohlmann, Benjamin, 9–10
Kollontai, Alexandra, 167

Lawrence, D. H., 116, 146, 153–4, 156, 184
Lawrence and Wishart, 78, 191n
Left Book Club (LBC), 19–20, 27, 83, 132
Left Review, 5, 78, 85, 95, 153, 178
Lehmann, John
  Evil Was Abroad, 17–18
  In the Purely Pagan Sense, 42, 186–90

Isherwood, 46, 50, 74, 75; *see also* Isherwood, Christopher
  as publisher, 16, 17, 186
  respectable homosexuality, 41, 76, 177, 178, 183, 186
Lenin, V. I.
  consciousness and spontaneity dialectic, 80, 102
  "glass of water" conversation with Clara Zetkin, 99
  Lenin on Britain, 81–2
  queer theory, 86–8
  The State and Revolution, 80
  Townsend Warner, 82, 86, 93; *see also* Townsend Warner, Sylvia
  vanguardism, 13–14, 79, 80–2, 94
  What is to be Done?, 13, 82, 86
Lindsay, Jack, 29, 122, 154, 156
Lipton, Julius, 78, 85, 91, 93
Lipton, Queenie, 78, 85, 93
Love, Heather, 43, 87, 96–7, 106
Lukács, Georg
  Brecht, 12, 46
  "Healthy Art or Sick Art," 109
  The Historical Novel, 84
  History and Class Consciousness, 54
  "The Intellectual Physiognomy of Literary Characters," 109
  International Literature, 195n
  Isherwood, 47, 50, 56–9
  Lenin: A Study in the Unity of his Thought, 81, 87, 94
  "Narration vs. Description" ("Narrate or Describe"), 49
  realism, 10, 13, 47, 49, 56–9, 80, 109
  reification, 54–5
  "Reportage or Portrayal," 49
  totality, 54
  Townsend Warner, 81, 84; *see also* Townsend Warner, Sylvia
  Tretiakov, 12, 46–7, 49–50, 59
  typicality, 56–8, 80, 106–11
lumpenproletariat, 25, 55, 61–3, 66, 72, 103–5, 204n

Mackay, John Henry, 61, 64, 110
Marx, Karl
  on aesthetics, 109, 173
  Britain, 81
  The Communist Manifesto, 1, 61
  immiseration thesis, 162
  lumpenproletariat, 61, 103–4, 204n
  The Poverty of Philosophy, 190

Medley, Robert, 20
modernism, 9–11, 48, 59, 109, 111
Montefiore, Janet, 5, 91, 95
Mulford, Wendy, 77, 84
Muñoz, José Esteban, 13, 43, 56, 87–8, 94, 111
Münzenberg, Willi, 46, 58

New Writing, 17, 186
Norris, Christopher, 141

Orwell, George, 140–73
  anti-Communism, 5, 143, 169, 173
  Burnham, 163; *see also* Burnham, James
  A Clergyman's Daughter, 38, 145–8
  Cold War
  de-blimping, 142, 156–63
  The English People, 140, 144, 163–7
  family, 26, 62, 142: England as, 140, 158
  Gemeinschaft, 140, 144, 165, 167
  Homage to Catalonia, 38, 154–5
  homophobia, 37, 114, 142, 143, 148–9, 165, 172–3
  Keep the Aspidistra Flying, 140, 145–6, 149–52
  The Lion and the Unicorn, 38, 132, 140, 156–63
  misogyny, 37, 141–2, 165
  nationalism, 125, 140, 157–9, 164
  Nineteen Eighty-Four, 8, 24, 39, 144, 167–73
  nostalgia, 62, 168
  "People's War," 28, 41, 156–63
  Popular Front, 38–9, 41, 125, 139, 152–6
  proles, 38, 140, 170
  realism, 11
  reproductive anxieties, 38, 40, 140, 142–3, 145–52, 165
  "revolutionary patriotism," 38
  The Road to Wigan Pier, 62, 144, 150, 153, 168, 170
  Spanish Civil War, 39
  state, 144, 163, 165–7, 169, 171
  transformative normalcy, 38, 152, 169

Patai, Daphne, 114–15, 141–2, 196
Patterson, Ian, 35
Pollitt, Harry, 33, 82, 85
Popular Front, 6–7, 9, 15, 19, 20, 22, 26–39, 41, 42, 85, 89, 111–12, 113, 116, 120–3, 125, 126, 130, 132, 133, 134, 135, 139, 143, 152–6, 160, 161, 165, 167, 169, 173
Priestly, J. B., 143

Radek, Karl, 47
Radzuweit, Friedrich, 61, 118
realism, 10–12, 47, 49, 58–9, 80, 107–9
Rickword, Edgell, 3, 89, 91, 191n
Röhm, Ernst, 31, 116–19, 121, 173
Rosenhaft, Eve, 61
Rubin, Andrew, 164

Samuel, Raphael, 8
Second Sino-Japanese War, 47, 72
Sedgwick, Eve Kosofsky, 42, 86, 97, 119, 175
Sinfield, Alan, 182–3, 186, 188
socialist realism, 6, 8, 10, 45
Solanas, Valerie, 88, 138
Sontag, Susan, 119, 120, 131
Soviet Union, 4, 6, 26, 27, 55, 91, 95, 116, 117, 118, 120, 167
Spanish Civil War, 5, 27, 32–7, 38–9, 159
The Spanish Earth (dir. Joris Evens), 34
Spender, Stephen, 3–4, 20, 32, 77, 89, 177
spontaneity/consciousness dialectic, 79, 80–1, 86
Stalin, Joseph, 27, 117, 178
Strachey, John, 19
Strachey, Lytton, 14, 172
Sutherland, John, 32

Thompson, E. P., 6, 29
Townsend Warner, Sylvia, 77–112
  Ackland, 78, 89–91, 94; *see also* Ackland, Valentine
  After the Death of Don Juan, 34–6
  book-lending scheme, 83
  commitment, 5, 25, 33, 95
  CPGB, 82, 85, 91–2
  Leninism, 82, 86, 93
  "A Love Match," 177–82
  Lukács, 13; *see also* Lukács, Georg
  realism, 11, 106–9
  respectability, 42, 178–82
  rurality, 37, 84
  Spender, 3–4, 89; *see also* Spender, Stephen

Summer Will Show, 95–106, 108–9, 152
  typicality, 13, 80, 106–9
  vanguardism, 14, 37, 76, 84, 86, 95–106
Tressell, Robert, 143
Tretiakov, Sergei, 12, 13, 46, 47–56, 58, 59, 75, 106, 184

Upward, Edward, 8, 10, 11, 59, 88, 105, 108, 114
  correspondence with Isherwood, 47, 73–4

van der Lubbe, Marinus, 31, 117, 120–1, 135
vanguardism, 8, 13, 14, 25, 26, 37, 76, 79, 80–8, 94, 180, 190
Vertov, Dziga, 45

Wachman, Gay, 89–90, 213n
Warner, Michael, 7–8, 15, 18–19, 86, 87

Warner, Rex, 29, 113, 152
  The Wild Goose Chase, 122–3
Waugh, Evelyn, 207n
Waugh, Thomas, 34
Weimar Berlin, 7, 15, 18, 19, 41, 44, 45, 47, 57, 88, 183, 184
The Well of Loneliness obscenity trial, 16, 91, 92, 110, 211n
Wilde, Oscar, 32, 141
Wildeblood, Peter, 176
Williams, Raymond, 29, 96, 142
Winteringham, Tom, 36, 91
Wittman, Carl, 88
Wolfenden Report, 24, 41, 176, 182, 183
Woloch, Alex, 141
Woolf, Virginia, 14, 15, 16, 17, 66, 183, 186
Worsley, T. C., 4, 5
Wright, Basil, 39
Wright, Patrick, 39, 95, 156

Zola, Émile, 109

EU representative:
Easy Access System Europe
Mustamäe tee 50, 10621 Tallinn, Estonia
Gpsr.requests@easproject.com